BEING F

C000050190

Expressivism—the sophisticated conten͞
nitivist research program of Ayer, Stevenson, and Hare—is no longer
the province of metaethicists alone. Its comprehensive view about the
nature of both normative language and normative thought has recently been applied to many topics elsewhere in philosophy—including
logic, probability, mental and linguistic content, knowledge, epistemic
modals, belief, the *a priori*, and even quantifiers.

Yet the semantic commitments of expressivism are still poorly understood and have not been very far developed. As argued within,
expressivists have not yet even managed to solve the 'negation problem'—to explain why atomic normative sentences are inconsistent with
their negations. As a result, it is far from clear that expressivism even
could be true, let alone whether it is.

Being For seeks to evaluate the semantic commitments of expressivism,
by showing how an expressivist semantics would work, what it can do,
and what kind of assumptions would be required in order for it to
do it. Building on a highly general understanding of the basic ideas
of expressivism, it argues that expressivists can solve the negation
problem—but only in one kind of way. It shows how this insight
paves the way for an explanatorily powerful, constructive expressivist
semantics, which solves many of what have been taken to be the deepest
problems for expressivism. But it also argues that no account with these
advantages can be generalized to deal with constructions like tense,
modals, or binary quantifiers. Expressivism, the book argues, is coherent
and interesting, but false.

Mark Schroeder is Associate Professor of Philosophy at the University
of Southern California.

Being For

*Evaluating the Semantic Program
of Expressivism*

MARK SCHROEDER

CLARENDON PRESS · OXFORD

OXFORD

UNIVERSITY PRESS

Great Clarendon Street, Oxford OX2 6DP

Oxford University Press is a department of the University of Oxford.
It furthers the University's objective of excellence in research, scholarship,
and education by publishing worldwide in

Oxford New York

Auckland Cape Town Dar es Salaam Hong Kong Karachi
Kuala Lumpur Madrid Melbourne Mexico City Nairobi
New Delhi Shanghai Taipei Toronto

With offices in

Argentina Austria Brazil Chile Czech Republic France Greece
Guatemala Hungary Italy Japan Poland Portugal Singapore
South Korea Switzerland Thailand Turkey Ukraine Vietnam

Oxford is a registered trade mark of Oxford University Press
in the UK and in certain other countries

Published in the United States
by Oxford University Press Inc., New York

British Library Cataloguing in Publication Data

Data available

Library of Congress Cataloging in Publication Data

Data available

Typeset by Laserwords Private Limited, Chennai, India
Printed in Great Britain
on acid-free paper by
MPG Books Group, Bodmin and King's Lynn

ISBN 978-0-19-953465-4 (Hbk.)
978-0-19-958800-8 (Pbk.)

1 3 5 7 9 10 8 6 4 2

FOR Maria Nelson

Contents

Preface

> The obvious and crucial challenge was . . . as a first step, to develop
> a working assertability-conditional semantics for a toy model of
> some small fragment of empirical language. But that challenge
> was shirked. Anti-realists preferred to polish their formulations of
> the grand programme rather than getting down to the hard and
> perhaps disappointing task of trying to carry it out in practice.
> [. . .] Anti-realists have simply failed to develop natural language
> semantics in that form, or even to provide serious evidence that
> they could so develop it if they wanted to. They proceed as if
> Imre Lakatos had never developed the concept of a degenerating
> research programme.[1]

The project in metaethics is to understand central questions in metaphysics, epistemology, the philosophy of language, and the philosophy
of mind, insofar as they relate to the normative. The interest is in the
narrowly moral, of course, but also in the broad family of issues that re-
semble it—questions about what is correct, rational, appropriate, fitting,
and so on. Sometimes metaethics proceeds by narrowly applying lessons
or ideas from elsewhere in philosophy—the cut-and-paste that is the
bread and butter of philosophical endeavor. But it is at its most exciting
when it challenges us to rethink major issues elsewhere in philosophy.
When it does so, metaethics forces us to ask what is really at issue when
we do metaphysics, stretches our imaginations about what is possible in
the philosophy of language, reinvents the issues in epistemology, and
leads us to ask new and exciting questions in the philosophy of mind.

No view in metaethics has done more to stretch our imaginations than
metaethical expressivism. The heir to the noncognitivist views of the
middle of the twentieth century, expressivism promises tidy solutions
to the traditional problems of metaethics, at the cost of pushing us to
globally rethink everything that we thought we knew about semantics,
thought, and logic, as well as raising very hard questions and pushing
the boundaries everywhere in the core areas of philosophy. And all while
remaining completely neutral as to the questions of normative ethics.

[1] Williamson (2006: 180–1).

This book is about the ways in which expressivism pushes us to rethink important issues in semantics. The project is very simple: to start with a very minimal conception of the key idea of expressivism, and then to draw out further commitments of the view in the philosophy of language, by seeing what is necessary in order to solve a series of very simple problems. What I try to do is to carry out the semantic program of expressivism, something that I think no proponents of expressivism have gotten very far at doing. I claim that I get much farther than they have gotten, and to show how to solve a number of open problems for expressivism along the way. I also claim that my attempt to carry out the semantic program of expressivism proves for the first time that expressivism is a coherent semantic hypothesis, which could possibly be true of an elementary normative language with ordinary logical properties and the expressive power of the predicate calculus.

I don't do this in order to *defend* expressivism, but rather in order to illustrate its costs. The problems that I show how expressivists can solve respect only some of the very simplest constructions in natural languages, and only some of their very simplest semantic properties. But solving these problems, I claim to show, requires accepting very large costs. Once we see what an expressivist semantics needs to look like in order to solve even some of its simplest problems, I think that it is very easy to see that expressivism is a very unpromising hypothesis about the semantics of natural languages. In fact, I can show—and do, in Chapter 12—that there are constructions in natural languages that *cannot* be treated in the very way that I argue expressivists need to treat other constructions.

If I've set things up properly, the argument of this book therefore constitutes a Master Argument that expressivism is false. For if I've set things up properly, then all that I am doing in this book is drawing out commitments of expressivism—the only way of developing an expressivist semantics that actually solves the open problems facing expressivism, rather than simply hypothesizing that they have a solution. If the only semantic view that can do these things is one that is not true of natural languages, then expressivism cannot be true of natural languages, either.

My strategy is unlike those of a number of philosophers working on expressivism at the moment, many of whom start with a con-cern for philosophical taxonomy.[2] Their idea is often to try to say

---

[2] Compare Ridge (2006), Chrisman (2006), Barker (2002), Boisvert (forthcoming), Eriksson (2006).

what expressivism is by trying to formulate a thesis that every extant expressivist would assent to, or by investigating how the word 'express' is used in ordinary English. But I am unimpressed by the attempt to do conceptual analysis of how philosophers have used the word 'expressivism'—the project seems completely uninteresting to me. And I see no reason why the right way to interpret expressivists' use of 'express' must be in accordance with anyone's antecedent linguistic intuitions, so long as it plays an important role in their theory.

What I am interested in, is whether there is some important idea that expressivists or anyone like them have put to work, and what the merits of that idea might be. The way to evaluate some view, I think, is not to do a survey of the people who have held it and see what they believe, or to consult our own linguistic intuitions about how to use their words. That may be excellent sociology, but I don't think that it is good philosophy. To evaluate a view philosophically, we need to isolate the core, central ideas of the view one by one, and then to see what commitments they lead to. That is what I try to do in this book with expressivism. You may use the words 'expressivism' or 'noncognitivism' differently than I do, but that is not the point. The point is whether I've isolated a view that is powerful and important, and whether I've successfully evaluated some of its key commitments in the philosophy of language.

In a way, I think that the problems that I tackle in this book on behalf of expressivism should have been tackled long before, and in the very way that I tackle them. As philosophers have recognized that normative issues come up across all areas of philosophy, they have applied expressivism to problems across all areas of philosophy. Expressivism has been defended about mental and linguistic content, in epistemology, about logic, about knowledge, about the distinction between belief and other mental states, and more. Every philosophical issue in which normativity might be discovered is ripe for a journal article in which it is treated with expressivism. The fact that expressivism can be so readily applied all across philosophy suggests that it has a very high degree of credibility in the field—that it is a highly respectable option in philosophy.

But despite my capacity for sympathy with the expressivist project, this is something that I find very hard to understand. For expressivism is a hypothesis about the semantics of natural languages like English. But expressivists have not yet demonstrated that they can give a satisfactory account of the meaning of the word 'not'. Forget conditionals; moreover, forget tense, and modals, and all of the other important constructions in natural languages that expressivists are committed to being able to understand, but have not even gotten as far as thinking about, while linguists and philosophers of language have made great strides in understanding their semantics in ways that are incompatible with expressivism. Even forget quantifiers, which had not even been discussed in the literature on expressivism until Horgan and Timmons (2006). Expressivists have not yet given a remotely satisfactory treatment of the meaning of 'not'—for no expressivist view has yet explained why atomic normative sentences are inconsistent with their negations. This is not the kind of thing that respectable semantic theories are supposed to have difficulty explaining. We are a considerable ways from catching up with Frege, if we are still having trouble with it.

This is, I think, a compelling reason for anyone sympathetic to expressivism to be concerned with the kind of project I pursue in this book. But not all metaethicists are sympathetic to expressivism. 'So what?' some metaethicists will say. 'That is a merely technical problem.' (This is supposed to be pejorative.) 'Even if those problems can be solved, expressivism would still fail for *deep* reasons.' These philosophers may think that they don't need to dirty their hands with the kinds of details that concern me in this book, in order to pursue metaethical inquiry in a responsible way.

I don't think anything could be further from the truth. Every allegation that expressivism fails for 'deep' reasons turns on some allegation about what follows from expressivism. These claims about what follows from expressivism are couched in English—a natural language about which a fully developed version of expressivism constitutes a semantic theory. There is no way of evaluating whether expressivism accepts these commitments that is independent of evaluating what predictions expressivism makes about the truth or assertability of such sentences. Claims to be able to *just see* that expressivism has certain commitments, or to be able to tell what expressivists *really think*, amount either to brute posturing, or else simply to insistence on the question-begging assumption that the expressivist's semantic theory is *wrong*.

Of course, the expressivist's semantic theory *may* be wrong. In fact, that's what I'll ultimately be arguing in this book. But there is no responsible way to tell that simply by rational intuition. The only way to tell whether expressivism is wrong—and correspondingly the only way to tell whether it is right—is to do the dirty work of constructing its semantic theory in as much detail as we can, in order to see what kinds of predictions it makes—and hence what expressivists are, and are not, committed to. That is why both expressivists and their opponents should be interested in the kind of task that I pursue in this book. In the end, it is the only responsible way of evaluating expressivism.

So I think that the project of understanding how to construct an expressivist semantics is particularly pressing, both if expressivist views in any area of philosophy are to be taken at all seriously, and if we are to understand them well enough to see why they are false. In this book, I claim to show how to construct an expressivist semantics, but only in a limited kind of way. I also claim that my way of doing it is the most promising way, and will argue that its limits are the limits of expressivism itself. If that turns out to be wrong, and someone else can improve on my efforts, then hurrah—bully for expressivism. Improving on my efforts is exactly the kind of thing that expressivists need to do, if their view is to be a respectable option in metaethics proper, let alone as a view about content, knowledge, or belief.

A final note: the exposition and argument in this book are strictly cumulative. I have worked hard at making it as easy to follow as possible, so long as you work your way through from start to finish. Everything that you need to understand the material in later chapters is present in the earlier chapters, and though it may seem highly technical if you flip straight to the later chapters, at each point everything that I do is fully explained and motivated, with careful attention to *why* I am doing it. And the less straightforward proofs and discussions are reserved for appendices.

Many metaethicists will not be used to the level of detail at which I argue, being more familiar with the broad sweeping strokes of the Big Picture that are more common in the metaethical literature. But as I hope the following volume illustrates, the fruit of theorizing is always in the details. Exploring details is, as Tim Williamson (2006) has noted, what provides discipline to our thought. It also leads to new questions we never would have known before that we could have asked. Openness to exploring details and accepting their verdict is what makes for the difference between a discipline and a subject. Details are far from everything, of course—it is important to appreciate the significance of the Big Picture in order to know *which* details are worth working on, and I will spend a fair bit of time in this volume arguing for just why the details I explore are so worth exploring. But grandstanding on the Big Picture without accountability to the details is, I think in the end, no more than so much posturing. If we are responsible investigators, we must get down to the details eventually, and as I think this book will also illustrate, sometimes they can surprise us.

My outlook on philosophical methodology is illustrated by the cover illustration, which is from Rembrandt's *Philosopher in Meditation*. The title, on a painting which depicts two figures, not one, always makes me feel compelled to ask, 'which one is the philosopher?' In at least a couple of different respects, the two figures depicted represent to me opposing vices in philosophical work. One basks in the aura of external illumination, but builds nothing of his own, while the other cultivates his own flame in what is otherwise the dark. The expansive space around the left-hand figure reminds me of the Big Picture, while the furtive character on the right is surely concerned with small details. In both respects, I find the painting advising me, the path upward lies between, and brings these approaches together. I hope this conception of how to make progress in philosophy is visible in the pages that follow.

* * * * *

The bulk of the ideas in this book were developed in late April 2006, while I was giving my graduate seminar on expressivism at the University of Maryland, with refinements and adjustments in the following months, particularly in October of 2006, when I developed the approach to truth-conditions for descriptive sentences outlined in Chapter 10, and in May and June of 2007, including significant improvements in the treatment of attitude ascriptions and truth. I am especially indebted, in my early thinking about expressivism, to conversations with Mike McGlone and Be Birchall while in graduate school at Princeton, and my enthusiasm for the development of the views in the later chapters was fueled largely by discussions with Barry Lam about the existence of a state of *disbelief* or *doubt* that rationally conflicts with belief but is weaker than belief in the negation.

Among those from whom I have received helpful feedback or sugges-tions, or from conversations with whom I have benefited significantly, the following quickly come to mind: Be Birchall, Jamie Dreier, Billy Dunaway, Matti Eklund, Steve Finlay, Jeff Horty, Jeff King, Matt King, Sari Kisilevsky, Barry Lam, David Manley, Mike McGlone, Paul Pietroski, Jacob Ross, Scott Soames, Jeff Speaks, Mark van Roojen, an anonymous referee for *Noûs*, and the participants in my grad-uate seminars at the University of Maryland and the University of

Southern California in the spring and fall of 2006. The material presented here also draws on both 'Expression for Expressivists', *Philosophy and Phenomenological Research* 6(1): 86–116, and on 'How Expressivists Can and Should Solve Their Problem with Negation', forthcoming in *Noûs*.

More people read and commented on a complete draft in the fall of 2006 than I had assumed would ever read the book when I first sat down to write it, and for that response, which I've tried to learn from, I'm enormously grateful to Jamie Dreier, Steve Finlay, Jeff King, and Mark van Roojen. As Jamie and Mark were a large proportion of my intended audience, I feel the project has already been a success. In addition to his helpful comments, Billy Dunaway was the one who saved me from a glaring error in one of that early draft's key arguments, and his help in combing the final manuscript for further errors has been both fruitful and priceless. Scott Soames and Jeff King each attended my seminar on expressivism at the University of Southern California in the fall of 2006, and their questions and comments have been extraordinarily helpful to me in trying to nail down my central points, and further conversations with Jeff about tense and philosophical methodology were both enjoyable and stimulating. And two anonymous referees for Oxford University Press were both generous with helpful comments.

The two people who have been most valuable to me in pursuing this project have been Jamie Dreier and Jeff Horty. I invited Jamie to give a talk at Maryland in February of 2005, partly with the idea that if he gave his paper on expressivist negation, that would give me an opportunity to think further about the topic. I was right—during his talk my ideas about how to solve the problem came together, although I didn't yet understand why the solution worked, or how general the result was, until I had a chance to think more about it a year later. Throughout the process of my thinking about these issues, Jamie has been a fantastic intellectual colleague, and he also read and provided enormously useful feedback on a complete draft of the manuscript. I couldn't be more intellectually indebted.

Before I arrived at Maryland three years ago, Chris Morris advised me that one thing he had learned over the years was that there are always pleasant surprises about which colleagues one will have productive interactions with, as well as surprises about with whom one's discussions turn out to be less productive or stimulating. Jeff Horty was a pleasant surprise of the first order. Over my two years at Maryland, our conversations, mostly about reasons, default logic, undercutting defeat, deontic logic, and the semantics of 'ought', were the highlight of my professional interactions. When I turned to Jeff, needing someone to bounce these ideas off, he took days of his time to go through everything with me, from the ground up. Those discussions were instrumental to me in being able to formulate in the right way what I wanted to prove in order to account for the logical features of sentences in biforcated attitude semantics (in Chapter 8).

I think it will be apparent throughout how indebted I am to Allan Gibbard. Nothing I could say here in thanks could speak as forcefully to how much of my understanding of the issues in this area I owe to studying his work, or to the example he has been to me as a philosopher, as does the content of the chapters that follow. He, along with Jamie Dreier and Mark van Roojen, is the audience I originally sat down to write for.

Finally, the book is dedicated with love to Maria Nelson, among whose many virtues is that she makes me happy: HOORAY!(her).

PART I

THE SEMANTIC PROGRAM
OF EXPRESSIVISM

1

Introduction

1.1 EXPRESSIVISM, WHAT

Noncognitivist views in metaethics were originally views about moral *language*. Moral language, they said, is much different from ordinary descriptive language. Moral sentences aren't *true or false*, they don't purport to *represent reality*, they aren't used to make *assertions* about *matters of fact*, they don't *correspond to the world*, and they don't express *beliefs*. Noncognitivist views told us what moral sentences do instead of these things. So the emotivisms of Ayer (1936) and Stevenson (1944,1963) and the prescriptivism of Hare (1952) were first and foremost views about moral language. But the currently dominant noncognitivist view, *expressivism*, purports to be instead primarily a view about moral *thought*. According to expressivism, as I understand it, the only differences between moral language and descriptive language derive from the difference between moral thought and descriptive thought.

Expressivists say that the way to understand moral language is to understand that moral sentences are related to noncognitive, desire-like states of mind in the same way that ordinary descriptive sentences are related to ordinary beliefs—they *express* them. This leads expressivists to deny the view of earlier noncognitivists that moral language plays a different role or operates differently from ordinary descriptive language, and insist that the real difference between the moral and the descriptive is not at the level of language at all, but at the level of thought. This simple but fundamental idea is at the heart of the attractions of expressivism.

There are a variety of reasons why expressivism has been thought to be the most viable kind of noncognitivist view. For example, expressivism is most directly related, of all noncognitivist views, to motivational arguments for noncognitivism. These motivational arguments contend that moral thoughts motivate, but ordinary beliefs don't motivate, so moral thoughts must not be ordinary beliefs.

A second advantage of expressivism over other noncognitivist views is that the other noncognitivist views, being views primarily about moral language, do not directly yield any obvious story about the nature of moral thought. Such views typically tell us the meaning of moral terms by telling us what speech acts they are used to perform. But there is no obvious or direct general connection between speech acts and states of mind. For example, though you may promise by saying, 'I promise', or marry by saying 'I do', there is no particular state of mind associated with being bound by a promise, or—unfortunately—with being married. In 1950 this may not have seemed to be a pressing question, but since then it has been a serious one. Not only do we have moral sentences in our language, we also think moral thoughts—for example, some of us think that murder is wrong. So moral thought is something of which noncognitivists owe us an account, just as much as moral language is. Expressivism is a noncognitivist view out of which this account drops directly, and its accounts of moral language and moral thought are directly connected. It gives an account of moral language *by* giving an account of moral thought.

Yet a third advantage of expressivism over other noncognitivist views is that expressivism turns out, as I'll explain in section 2.1, to differ minimally from ordinary speaker subjectivism in exactly the way required in order to deal with the deepest and most obvious objections to that view. Prior to the twentieth century, the motivational, disagreement, and naturalistic arguments that have since been offered in favor of noncognitivist views had already all been offered in favor of speaker subjectivism. But expressivism has mostly come to replace speaker subjectivism, on the grounds that it avoids the most devastating objections to speaker subjectivism. Since expressivism differs from speaker subjectivism in precisely the way required in order to get out of these objections, that licenses thinking that it has a better claim than other noncognitivist views to be seen as the proper heir to subjectivism.

But the biggest reason why expressivism has been seen as the most promising kind of noncognitivist view derives from the simple obser-vation that moral language *does* seem to work very much like ordinary descriptive language. One of the simplest examples of this is that we seem to be able to say of moral sentences that they are true, or that they are false. Yet noncognitivism used to be *defined* as the view that moral sentences cannot be true or false. Another simple example is that moral terms can be used to ask questions: I can ask, 'is murder wrong?' and if you say, 'murder is wrong', then you have answered my question.

We also disagree with each other, if you say, 'murder is wrong' but I say, 'murder is not wrong'. And when we formulate moral arguments, we evaluate these for validity in exactly the same way as we evaluate descriptive arguments for validity.

In fact, and this cannot be emphasized enough, *every* natural-language construction that admits of descriptive predicates admits of moral predicates, and seems to function in precisely the same way: tense; conditionals; every kind of modal—alethic, epistemic, or deontic; qualifiers like 'yesterday'; generics and habituals; complement-taking verbs like 'proved that' and 'wonders whether'; infinitive-taking verbs of every class, including 'expects to', 'wants to', and 'compels to'; binary quantifiers like 'many' and 'most'; and more. It is crucially important to understand that the embedding problem for noncognitivism is not simply a problem about the validity of *modus ponens*, or even simply about logic. *Every* construction in natural languages seems to work equally well no matter whether normative or descriptive language is involved, and to yield complex sentences with the same semantic properties.

So any view on which moral language works in some way that is deeply different from descriptive language seems extraordinarily unlikely to be true—at least if it is a hypothesis about the language that we actually speak. We get almost nowhere, for example, by simply substituting Ayer's paraphrases: we do not even understand 'boo murder?', let alone is it clear why this question would be answered by 'boo murder!'. We do not even understand 'not boo murder!', let alone is it clear why it is inconsistent with 'boo murder!'. And we do not even understand 'if boo murder, then boo defenestration!', let alone is it remotely clear how it, together with 'boo murder!', should yield a logically valid argument for 'boo defenestration!'. Yet 'murder is wrong' has precisely these relationships with 'is murder wrong?', 'murder is not wrong', and 'if murder is wrong, then defenestration is wrong'. It is not clear where Ayer could even start, in responding to these questions, beyond taking back how accurate of a paraphrase he meant 'boo murder!' to be for 'murder is wrong'.

Expressivism, on the other hand, unlike other noncognitivist views, says that moral language works in exactly the same way as ordinary descriptive language works. So expressivism seems to be ideally situated to be able to explain why moral and descriptive predicates operate linguistically in all of the same ways. They do so because of how language works, according to the expressivist, and what is distinctive about the moral domain derives entirely from what is distinctive about moral *thought*.

1.2 CURRENT INTEREST IN EXPRESSIVISM

After being the dominant view in metaethics in the middle of the twentieth century, noncognitivism became relatively unpopular during the 1970s and 1980s as philosophers discovered the defensibility of other views, and worried about the intractability of the embedding problem for noncognitivism—the problem of explaining how moral sentences function when embedded as parts of complex sentences, as in the examples of the last section. But then something changed. Simon Blackburn and Allan Gibbard developed expressivist views which focused considerable energy on explaining how expressivists could account for the meanings of complex sentences formed by means of 'not', 'and', 'or', and 'if. . . then', and on explaining why such sentences have the expected logical properties. After viewing Blackburn and Gibbard's efforts, many philosophers took the view that the embedding problem was not such a deep problem after all, and noncognitivism gained renewed respectability in the form of expressivism.

In fact, Blackburn and Gibbard's efforts have gone so far toward making expressivism a respectable view that expressivism is now being widely applied across the 'core areas' of philosophy. As philosophers discover normative dimensions of the subjects of inquiry of epistemology, the philosophy of language, and the philosophy of mind, the standard questions of metaethics come to apply in those areas, and the standard views in metaethics are naturally brought to bear. So Hartry Field (2000), for example, has defended expressivism about the *a priori* and evaluative concepts in epistemology more generally. Matthew Chrisman (2007) has defended expressivism specifically about *knowledge*, and David Velleman and Nishi Shah (2005) now advocate expressivism about what it is for a mental state to be a *belief*, in contrast to something you merely accept. Expressivism is also a respectable view about the *content* of both sentences and mental states, and has even been defended about logic (Brandom 2001).

It is natural that philosophers would apply expressivism to all of these topics—the topics seem to involve normative issues, metaethics is the study of the metaphysics, epistemology, philosophy of language, and philosophy of mind with respect to normative issues, and expressivism is considered to be one of the main options in metaethics. But it is also, in many ways, remarkably premature. For despite the fact that Blackburn and Gibbard are often said in the literature to have 'solved' the embedding problem for expressivism, the 'Frege-Geach Problem', in fact remarkably little progress has actually been made.

1.3 OUTSTANDING PROBLEMS

Even some of the most straightforward questions for expressivists remain without satisfactory answers. For example, as we'll explore further in Chapter 2, there is no clear expressivist view about what *expression* is. In 1990, Gibbard offered an account of the expression relation, but he retracted this account in his 2003 book, in favor of asserting his confidence that there must be some acceptable account of expression that will suit the expressivists' purposes. But as I'll explain in Chapter 2, it should not be at all obvious that there is any account of expression that will suit the expressivists' purposes. The simplest and most straightforward explanation of the cases that Gibbard thinks require us to have *some* account of the expression relation appeals to a sense of 'expression' that is incompatible with expressivism.

To take another simple example, no expressivist to date has given a satisfactory explanation of why the sentences 'murder is wrong' and 'murder is not wrong' are inconsistent, let alone of why they are logically inconsistent.[1] Every existing expressivist treatment of this problem takes as brute the hypothesis that there is an infinite hierarchy of distinct, logically unrelated attitude-kinds, which nevertheless are mysteriously hypothesized to bear primitive relations of consistency and inconsistency, or 'agreement' and 'disagreement' in Gibbard's (2003) terms, with one another. Gibbard thinks that everyone, cognitivists included, needs to explain a similar kind of thing. But as we'll see in Chapter 3, though he is right that there is *something* that everyone needs to explain, the kind of disagreement that Gibbard needs to appeal to is

---

[1] I will argue this more completely in Chapter 3. Here, and in the rest of this book, I will pretend simply in order to fix examples that 'murder is wrong', 'stealing is wrong', and 'stealing is better than murder' are atomic sentences, and that 'wrong' is a basic normative predicate. In the views of some expressivists, 'wrong' is really to be analyzed in terms of some further normative predicate, which itself is to be given an expressivist treatment. The *negation problem* that I mention here and discuss in Chapter 3 is a problem for the *basic* predicates given any expressivist view.

more puzzling and different in kind from the kind of disagreement that everyone else needs to explain.

Third, even if we granted Gibbard his explanation of the inconsistency of 'murder is wrong' and 'murder is not wrong', he has never even attempted to explain why they are *logically* inconsistent. Though Gibbard has done much to try to explain why it is possible to *reason* with normative language, he has never even claimed to establish that normative sentences can be subject to logic, strictly construed. On the sense in which Gibbard rules that 'grass is green' and 'grass is not green' are inconsistent, he also rules that 'Lake Winnebago is filled with water' and 'Lake Winnebago is not filled with H_2O' are inconsistent. But the inconsistency of these latter two sentences is metaphysical inconsistency—in order to know that they are inconsistent, we have to know which interpretation has been assigned to 'water' and to 'H_2O'. But any account of logical inconsistency should be indifferent to the assignment of interpretations to the non-logical terms. Horgan and Timmons (2006) claim to have an expressivist account of logic, but their 'logic' works only for a language in which normative and descriptive sentences are syntactically marked.

Fourth, just as no expressivist view has given an adequate account of logical inconsistency, none has explained how to move past the kinds of sentences constructed by 'truth-conditional' connectives. There is no genuinely explanatory expressivist account of how to understand the meaning of normative predicates, distinct from a story about what attitudes are expressed by complete normative sentences, and until very recently, no one has even attempted to explain how to interpret ordinary quantifiers in an expressivist language.[2] Expressivism purports to be a hypothesis about the workings of natural languages, but natural languages include many constructions far more complex than the unary Fregean quantifiers of the predicate calculus. But expressivists have for the most part not yet even explained how to make sense of these elementary constructions, thinking it an achievement to account for disjunction.

Fifth, and in my view most strikingly, no expressivist view still defended, and none offered in the last twenty years, offers an actual

---

[2] Horgan and Timmons (2006) have an 'expressivist language' which includes constructions that behave like quantifiers, but for the reasons mentioned in the next paragraph and discussed in Chapter 3, I think their account stipulates more than it explains. One major complication in their treatment of quantifiers is that officially, their expressivist language has no normative predicates—only an 'ought' operator. So it remains unclear how to extend it.

account of the mental state expressed by any logically complex sentence. It is not that existing expressivist accounts don't tell us *anything* about the mental states expressed by complex sentences; it is just that all that they tell us about them amounts to a characterization of the properties that these mental states *need* to have, if expressivism is to work. So, for example, Blackburn (1988) told us that the mental state expressed by 'murder is wrong or stealing is wrong' is the one that it is inconsistent to be in, if you are also in the mental states expressed by 'murder is not wrong' and by 'stealing is not wrong'. Obviously, any story about what mental state was expressed by 'murder is wrong or stealing is wrong' that did not predict it as having this property would be incorrect. But Blackburn's account doesn't say *what* mental state is expressed by the disjunction, or explain why it has this property. It is like listing the criteria that an expressivist account must explain, and then stipulating that the account has explained them.

Similarly, Gibbard's (1990, 2003) view only characterizes the states expressed by complex sentences in terms of the properties that we want to explain. As we'll see in more detail in Chapter 3, Gibbard's view essentially tells us that the state expressed by 'murder is wrong and stealing is wrong' is the weakest mental state that is inconsistent with all of the mental states that are inconsistent with the states expressed by each of its conjuncts. Again, this is a minimal criterion of adequacy for an account of the state expressed by the conjunction. If you think that murder is wrong and stealing is wrong, then it had better turn out that what you think is inconsistent with everything that is inconsistent with thinking that murder is wrong, and likewise for the other conjunct. But this does not really tell us anything about what this state of mind is like! All it does is to tell us what properties it must have. It is like giving a list of the criteria that an expressivist account of this mental state must satisfy, in lieu of actually giving an account of that state and showing that it satisfies those criteria. If Gibbard is allowed to stipulate that there are mental states satisfying these criteria, then he can show that they satisfy other criteria. But he has no constructive story about what these mental states are, and no explanation of why they satisfy these criteria. And no one else does, either: *all* extant expressivist accounts look like this.[3]

<hr />

[3] See also Horgan and Timmons (2006) and Björnsson (2001). Actually, I should qualify. Early expressivist accounts, such as the 'higher-order attitudes' account in Blackburn (1984), do give a constructive account of the mental states expressed by complex sentences. But 'higher-order attitudes' accounts are plagued with fatal problems,

It is particularly striking that expressivists have offered no constructive account of the mental states expressed by complex sentences, given that their view purports to be one on which we understand the meanings of sentences *by* understanding what mental states they express. So a satisfactorily complete expressivist view, one might hope, would have to be able to give a *constructive* account of the mental states expressed by complex sentences. After all, this is something that any ordinary account of belief can do. The belief that is expressed by 'grass is green and snow is white' is the belief in the conjunctive proposition that grass is green and snow is white. Any ordinary account of belief, moreover, can explain the properties of this conjunctive belief in terms of the properties of believing in general and the properties of this belief's content. This is something no extant expressivist view is able to do.

These are just the simplest and most pressing outstanding problems for expressivism as it exists today. And this is just a summary; I will explain them in more detail as we go along. They constitute explanatory burdens that expressivists need to discharge, before rational investigators should actually place credence on expressivism, as opposed merely to noticing that it *would* be a powerful view *if* it could be made to work.

1.4 LICENSE FOR OPTIMISM

In lieu of offering answers to these questions, expressivists often instead offer us grounds for *licensed optimism* that they will be able to answer the questions, even though they have not done so, thus far. For example, in *Thinking How to Live*, Gibbard (2003: 75–9) backs down off of the details of his account of what *expression* is from his earlier book, and instead offers an argument that there *must* be an account to which expressivists can appeal. This strategy doesn't tell us what *expression* is; it doesn't help to actually carry out the expressivists' semantic agenda. It just tries to provide grounds for licensed optimism that it should be *possible* to carry out the expressivists' agenda.

Similarly, expressivists have argued that there are grounds for licensed optimism that expressivists should be able to give a satisfactory account of *negation* that can explain why 'murder is wrong' and 'murder is not wrong' are inconsistent sentences. After all, according to Hare (1952)

and I know of no one who still accepts one. See van Roojen (1996) for the best discussion of their problems.

and Smart (1984), 'open the door' and 'don't open the door' are contradictory commands. So first point: there seems to be no general problem understanding commands as subject to negations, despite the fact that commands are not ordinary assertions of fact. And second point: negated commands appear to have the same sorts of semantic properties as negated indicative sentences—they are inconsistent, in some appropriate sense, with their unnegated counterparts. So, Hare and Smart suggested, we should all agree that an account of how this works can be given for commands. And if it can be given for commands, they held, then it is reasonable to suppose that some such account can be given for normative sentences, too. Gibbard (2003) offers a similar argument focusing on negative plans.

Similarly, it is possible to give conjunctive commands, such as 'shut the door and open the window'. And these commands behave like conjunctions—for example, this one is inconsistent with each of 'don't shut the door' and 'don't open the window'. So, expressivists have argued, it must be possible to make sense of conjunctions when it comes to commands, and that gives us license for optimism that it should be possible to make sense of conjunctions of normative sentences, too. Pushing this line further, we might notice that quantifiers function in commands as well: 'shut every door' makes perfect sense, and is inconsistent with 'don't shut *this* door', for any choice of 'this door'. Again, the expressivist idea would be that this suggests license for optimism—if quantifiers can work with commands, then they aren't the special province of ordinary descriptive indicative sentences, and hence perhaps we should be optimistic that an expressivist account of quantified normative sentences can be made to work, even though none has been, yet.

It is important to see that expressivists are right, to at least some extent, about these grounds for optimism. Negations, conjunctions, disjunctions, and quantifiers all seem to work on commands. But it is also important to see that the grounds for optimism provided by cases like these do not extend very far. For example, it is tricky to form conjunctions between imperative and indicative sentences using 'and' that actually function like conjunctions. 'Offer' sentences like 'shut the door and I'll give you a reward' are perfectly fine, of course, but they don't work like conjunctions, because someone who says this is not committed to 'I'll give you a reward'. This is evidence that 'offer' sentences like this one are really conditionals rather than conjunctions. Use of 'but' allows us to do slightly better: sentences like 'it's freezing in here but leave the door open' appear to allow indicative-imperative conjunctions, but for some reason the contrast appears to be necessary, since 'it's freezing in here and leave the door open' doesn't seem okay. And imperative-indicative conjunctions seem to be more controversial. However, even if those were all fine, there do not appear to be conditionals in English with imperative antecedents and imperative consequents, or with imperative antecedents and indicative consequents.

Normative and descriptive sentences can be combined indiscriminately by all of the logical connectives, but looking at imperatives does not make it obvious that imperatives and indicatives can be so combined, or that the resulting sentences should have all of the expected logical properties. So even if there are grounds for optimism that expressivists at least *should* be able to deal with sentences like 'murder is not wrong', 'murder is wrong and stealing is wrong', and 'everything is wrong', it is far from clear that there are good grounds for optimism that expressivists should be able to deal with sentences like 'murder is wrong and grass is green' and 'if murder is wrong, then grass is green'. I am not, here, arguing that they can't; I am simply pointing out that the grounds for optimism extend only so far.

And finally, consideration of imperatives, so far as I can tell, provides no grounds at all to be optimistic that expressivism ought to be able to be made to work for past-tense sentences, many modal constructions, generics, and so on. But these constructions all make perfect sense when applied to normative sentences. The moral of this, I think, is that we probably *should* be optimistic that expressivists can do better than they have done so far, but that it is not at all clear why we should be optimistic about expressivists being able to account for the full range of constructions that they are committed to being able to explain. But more to the point, the moral is that expressivists can't settle for giving us arguments that they ought to be able to construct a view. They need to actually go out and construct a view.

1.5 THE PROJECT IN THIS BOOK

That is what this book is about. It is about seeing what choices expressivists need to make in order to actually construct a positive semantic view that solves some of these problems, rather than settling for indirect arguments that there must be a workable view.[4] In particular, I am going to show how to develop an expressivist view that solves each of the outstanding problems for expressivism catalogued in section 1.3. In Chapter 2, I am going to show how to understand the *expression* relation, which involves setting out a conception of the underlying semantic program to which expressivism is committed. In Chapter 3, I'll explain why expressivists have an important and unsolved problem about negation, and I'll show, in Chapter 4, how to solve it, for the first time giving an expressivist explanation of why 'murder is wrong' and 'murder is not wrong' are inconsistent. The solution that I offer will explain more, by appealing to far weaker assumptions, than any previous account. I will also offer a general argument that any genuinely compositional expressivist account of sentential negation will have to look like mine.

Then I am going to show how to do expressivist logic. In Chapter 5, I will illustrate how my solution to the negation problem generalizes nicely to a treatment of the other 'truth-functional' connectives. I will give formally adequate accounts of logical inconsistency, logical entailment, and logical validity for a language with normative atomic sentences and the expressive power of propositional logic, and I'll again offer a general argument that only an account that has the structural features of the one that I am offering will be able to do these things. In Chapter 6 our toy language will start to look a little more realistic and the treatment will be more rigorous. If the account of Chapter 5 is on the right track, then one might hope that it can be expanded to deal with predicates and quantifiers. So I'll show how to give a formally adequate account of logical inconsistency for a language with normative predicates given an expressivist interpretation, this time with the expressive power of the predicate calculus.

The account offered in Chapters 4 through 6 tells us how to treat a language with only normative predicates. It works exactly in parallel to the way in which expressivists would construct a semantics for a purely descriptive language. So everything would be great, if we spoke one normative language and one descriptive language. But we don't—we speak a language with both normative and descriptive predicates, and logical connectives that can take both normative and descriptive sentences as arguments—in fact, which can take both

---

[4] I don't mean to imply that expressivists have *only* settled for indirect arguments for licensed optimism; only that this is the usual fallback position when holes appear in their positive accounts.

normative and descriptive arguments at the same time. At the beginning of Chapter 7, I will argue that there is only one way to bring these two accounts together in a way that would be consistent with expressivism, and that this turns on an expressivist analysis of *belief* in terms of a further noncognitive attitude.

One possible conclusion, at this point, is that this amounts to a *reductio* of expressivism. I'm vaguely sympathetic to this conclusion. Moreover, such a conclusion would match our grounds for optimism about what expressivists should be able to accomplish. Here is what I mean by this: as I noted, it is clear that negation, conjunction, and quantifiers can all operate on imperatives, with the usual logical properties. But I also noted that it is very unclear that binary connectives can combine imperatives and indicatives indiscriminately. So if the semantics of Chapter 6 allows for a purely expressivist language with the expressive power of the predicate calculus, but the project crashes when we try to allow for a language in which there are complex sentences with both normative and descriptive parts, then that would match our grounds for optimism. Nevertheless, what I'll do in the later chapters of the book is to explore how an expressivist account *could* try to generalize on the semantics of Chapter 6. In Chapter 7, I'll motivate an analysis of belief in terms of a noncognitive attitude, and explain some of its merits.

Then, in Chapter 8, I'll show how to generalize the semantic account of Chapter 6 in order to yield a semantic framework that can allow for both normative and descriptive predicates. Again, we will see how to provide a general account of logical inconsistency, entailment, and validity, although things will work out somewhat less neatly for this view. In the process of doing so, I will show how to develop a formal semantics for expressivism that is able to give a uniform treatment of normative and descriptive predicates, despite the fact that descriptive sentences express ordinary descriptive beliefs and normative sentences do not, and which offers a *constructive* account of which mental state is expressed by arbitrarily complex sentences.

There is an important feature which makes this not an entirely happy view for expressivists to take. The feature is that it turns out that complex descriptive sentences do not, in general, turn out to express beliefs with the corresponding complex descriptive contents. This is a problem not only because it violates expressivists' usual claim that a sentence like 'every bachelor is unmarried' expresses the belief that every bachelor is unmarried. It is a *big* problem, because it makes it very puzzling how an expressivist semantics can assign truth-conditions to ordinary descriptive sentences, *at all*. In Chapter 9, I explore one not entirely happy way for expressivists to solve this problem; in Chapter 10, I explore a second not entirely happy way of solving the problem. Each approach has some interest, and each is formally adequate, given a certain list of assumptions with at least some initial plausibility—though it is far from clear whether the required assumptions on either list are true. I offer them as alternative avenues for further inquiry by expressivists.

In Chapter 11, I'll consider how one would try to generalize the resulting view, in order to apply it in the service of nondescriptivist projects in domains other than the normative, and offer (not entirely satisfactory) toy theories of conditionals and of truth, in order to illustrate the idea's fruitfulness. Then in Chapter 12, I'll sum up the progress that we've made, and contrast this with the strength of the assumptions we had to make in order to get that far, and with the breadth and scope of the problems that remain.

The lesson, I take to be very simple: to even account for a language with the expressive powers of the predicate calculus, expressivists need to take on an extraordinary range of quite radical commitments. But natural languages have much richer expressive power than the predicate calculus. If it is this hard to do predicate logic, how much harder will it be to successfully capture the full range of attitude verbs, modals, tense, and other constructions? Expressivists have not offered detailed enough proposals about any of these further questions that it is yet safe to evaluate them conclusively. But I'll argue in Chapter 12 that the prospects are bleak, and specifically that there are constructions in natural languages—binary quantifiers like 'most'—that cannot be captured at all in a framework that satisfies the small number of central assumptions needed in order to solve the negation problem and incorporate normative and descriptive terms into the same language. So if the arguments in this book are right, about the scope of expressivism's radical commitments in the philosophy of language, and even philosophy of mind, then we would do well to rethink the importance of the advantages that it gleans for us.

But before we can get to my arguments against expressivism, we must start by trying to make the most of it. I'll start, in Chapter 2, by explaining how to think about expressivism in a very minimal way. From there, we'll quickly see how many commitments it acquires.

2

Expression

2.1 A MINIMAL CONCEPTION OF EXPRESSIVISM

Expressivists and their critics often write as if we all know what they mean by 'express', and we all have views about it:

> That words express judgments will, of course, be accepted by almost everyone.
> If moral judgements cannot express beliefs, what do they express?[1]

But this turns out, surprisingly, to be controversial. In fact, it is far from clear what expressivists mean by 'express', and not at all clear whether the rest of us have views about expression at all, once we understand what it is supposed to be. This is far from clear, because we can see exactly what makes expressivism appealing without endorsing any view about what expression is.

To see this, we need only to take a look at why it is that expressivism is supposed to be an improvement over its relative, *speaker subjectivism*. Speaker subjectivism holds that 'murder is wrong' is true relative to a context of utterance just in case 'I disapprove of murder' is. And this leads to two obvious and famous problems. The first is the modal problem. It follows from this view that 'If I didn't disapprove of murder, then murder wouldn't be wrong' is true just in case 'If I didn't disapprove of murder, then I wouldn't disapprove of murder' is. But the latter is indexically valid, so the former must be so, as well. Yet surely the former is not a theorem

---

[1] The first quotation is from Gibbard (1990: 84); the second is from Alexander Miller's metaethics textbook (2003: 6). In addition, arguments about expressivism often turn on what is meant by 'express'. This is particularly obvious in Cuneo (2006), who offers a creative argument against expressivism whose key assumption is that expressing an attitude is an illocutionary act type. Though he defends the other assumptions in his argument in detail, in defense of this one he says only that it is one of the 'platitudes about illocutionary acts that all philosophers ought to accept' (2006: 67).

in the mouth of any speaker! That is the modal problem for speaker subjectivism.[2]

The other problem is the *disagreement problem*. On a naïve understanding, the disagreement problem is that if Phil says, 'murder is wrong' and Sally says, 'murder is not wrong', they are not really in disagreement, on this view. But that is only the *shallow* disagreement problem. Speaker subjectivists can take advantage of a move made by Stevenson (1937) and insist that 'murder is wrong' and 'murder is not wrong' are not like 'I'm in Seattle' and 'I'm in New York'; rather, they can say, they are more like 'I'm for the Mariners' and 'I'm for the Yankees'. Two people who say the latter, at least sincerely, *are* in a *kind* of disagreement—disagreement in attitude. So that constitutes some kind of answer to the shallow disagreement problem. The real disagreement problem, however, remains untouched. The *deep* disagreement problem is that this only explains why Sally can disagree with Phil by saying, 'murder is not wrong'. It does not allow that she can disagree with him by saying that what he said was false. On the contrary! It follows from the view that what Phil said was true, provided that he really does disapprove of murder. But on the face of it, participants in moral discussions can say that what each other says is false, if they disagree with it. And that is the disagreement problem for speaker subjectivism.

The beauty of expressivism lies in the improvement that it can yield over speaker subjectivism when it comes to these problems. What expressivists observe is that the same problems would arise if we conflated 'grass is green' with 'I believe that grass is green'. If we conflated those, then we would think that 'If I didn't believe that grass was green, then grass wouldn't be green' is true just in case 'If I didn't believe that grass was green, then I wouldn't believe that grass was green' is. But that's the modal problem! And similarly, if we conflated them, then we would think that Phil and Sally couldn't disagree about the color of grass, so long as they really had different beliefs. So the central hypothesis of expressivism is that speaker subjectivism is on the right track, but has otherwise made exactly the same mistake as our conflation of 'grass is green' with 'I believe that grass is green'. The correct view,

---

[2] Actually, I've been slightly sloppy here. I've defined 'speaker subjectivism' so that *actually-rigidified speaker subjectivism* is a version of speaker subjectivism that doesn't face this problem. For problems with actually-rigidified speaker subjectivism, see Schroeder (forthcoming b) and Soames (2002: 39–50).

according to expressivism, is that 'murder is wrong' *stands to* disapproval of murder in the *same way as* 'grass is green' stands to the belief that grass is green. Notice that the beauty of this solution is that it requires taking no view at all about what this relationship is. Whatever this relationship turns out to be, the expressivist will say, it must be adequate to explain why there is no modal or disagreement problem for 'grass is green'. For we all agree that there is no problem there. So obviously, she will go on, it must be sufficient to explain why there is no modal or disagreement problem for 'murder is wrong'. To see that much, it seems, we don't even need to know what the relationship turns out to be! Whatever it is, we'll call it 'expression', and be content to know that everyone needs an account of expression—cognitivists and expressivists alike. After all, everyone needs to distinguish 'grass is green' from 'I believe that grass is green'.

This is the fundamental idea of expressivism, and it gives us a model for how expressivists are going to treat any number of important problems. What they will do is to appeal to the central way in which normative and descriptive language are the *same*. Then, they will inform us that everyone needs to understand why descriptive language works in that way. And finally, they will tell us that their account is going to take advantage of the same explanatory resources that everyone needs. This procedure is the *Basic Expressivist Maneuver*, and there is something incredibly elegant about it. But as we'll be seeing, it is based on an idea that is only half-right. It is right that by insisting that what is going on with normative language is the *same* as what is going on with descriptive language, expressivists can give a uniform treatment of normative and descriptive language in a relatively wide variety of cases and for a relatively wide variety of purposes. But it is *not* right that expressivists can simply help themselves to whatever makes things work for ordinary descriptive language. On the contrary, insisting on their analogy is going to force expressivists into very strong commitments about how ordinary descriptive language works.

In the remainder of this chapter, I am going to draw out two instances of this lesson. First, I am going to explain the embedding problem as it was originally formulated by Geach and Searle, who believed that noncognitivists could not explain why normative sentences have the same meaning in embedded contexts. There is a simple move that all expressivists make in response to this objection that claims to be able to offer the *same kind* of explanation of this as ordinary descriptivist semanticists would. It is a second instance of the Basic Expressivist

Maneuver. I'll explain why this move quickly commits expressivists to some very strong views about the way that ordinary descriptive sentences acquire their semantic content. And then, once this teaches us a little bit more about what we need to know about the kinds of work to which expressivists put the *expression* relation, I'll return to ask just what that is, and again we will see that not just any old account will suit the expressivists' purposes. I'll close the chapter by explaining the account of the expression relation that looks best suited to the expressivists' purposes, and consequently how I think it is most promising to think of the expressivists' semantic program.

2.2 THE ORIGINAL EMBEDDING PROBLEM

Originally, noncognitivists told us that the way to see what a moral sentence means is to see what speech act it is used to perform. But obviously when you embed moral sentences in complex sentences, they are no longer used to perform the same speech act.[3] So given the most obvious interpretations of what the speech act theories were committed to, this seemed to lead to the conclusion that moral sentences must mean something *different* when embedded. Geach's original case of a *modus ponens* argument involving moral terms was not offered as a challenge to noncognitivists to explain why it is a rational inference:

P1 Lying is wrong.
P2 If lying is wrong, then getting your little brother to lie is wrong.
C Getting your little brother to lie is wrong.

It was offered as conclusive evidence that moral terms *do* mean the same thing when embedded. Only if they mean the same thing, Geach pointed out, could we say that the argument is *logically* valid.

Other important examples cited by Geach (1960, 1965) and Searle (1962) were the cases of questions and negated sentences. If someone asks, 'is murder wrong?', then someone who says, 'murder is wrong' has answered her question. This, again, was not supposed to be a

---

[3] This is, I should point out, only obvious given certain assumptions about *which* speech act is being performed. Davis (2003, 2005) has a view on which each clause in a sentence is used to perform a distinct speech act, and the same speech act wherever it appears. See also Barker (2004).

challenge for noncognitivists, to explain why people who say these two things can count as having a conversation—the point was, rather, that this looks like conclusive evidence that their words mean the same thing, despite the fact that they are engaging in two different speech acts. And finally, someone who says, 'murder is wrong' *disagrees* with someone who says, 'murder is not wrong'. Again, the challenge was not to explain why there might be something *like* disagreement going on; this was instead supposed to be excellent evidence that the terms *meant* the same thing, despite the fact that different speech acts were involved. Noncognitivism, the proponents of the original embedding problem contended, is committed to something false—it is committed to holding that moral terms *mean* something different in embedded contexts than when unembedded.

Beginning with Hare (1970), noncognitivists have offered the same general kind of answer to this objection, and every expressivist attempt to answer the embedding problem starts with this same simple idea. Their answer is that normative sentences have the same meaning when embedded as when unembedded because the meaning of the complex sentence is a *function* of the meaning of its parts. Compare the ordinary truth-conditional semanticist's explanation of why 'grass is green' means the same thing when embedded in 'grass is not green' as when unembedded.[4] *Prima facie*, expressivists suggest, there ought to be a problem. After all, 'grass is not green' does not have the same truth-conditions as 'grass is green'. So if meaning is truth-conditions, then how could 'grass is green' mean the same thing when appearing with a 'not' as when appearing without it? The answer is that what we say is that the truth-conditions of 'grass is not green' are a function of the truth-conditions of 'grass is green'—a function that is given by the meaning of 'not'. Similarly, expressivists claim, 'murder is not wrong' expresses some mental state *distinct* from that expressed by 'murder is wrong'. But which mental state this is, is a function of the mental state expressed by 'murder is wrong', and the function is given by the meaning of 'not'.

The idea, here, is that the problem is not that expressivists *can't* say why the meaning of normative sentences is the same when embedded

---

[4] Don't get distracted by the fact that the sequence of letters, 'murder is wrong' does not appear anywhere in 'murder is not wrong', into thinking that 'murder is wrong' is not really embedded in 'murder is not wrong'. It's simply a feature of the syntax of English sentential negation that the 'not' appears in the middle of the sentence it governs, rather than at the beginning.

as unembedded; it is simply that they haven't done so, yet. And to do so, the idea goes, simply requires giving a compositional semantics for the meanings of complex sentences, treating them as a function of the meanings of their parts. So expressivists are committed to a compositional semantics for complex normative sentences.

There are two points that I want to raise here, to come back to later. The first is that there is still something glib about this response to the embedding problem. Truth-conditional semanticists say that the truth-conditions of a complex sentence are a function of the truth-conditions of its parts because its parts *really do* have truth-conditions, even when embedded—the same ones as they have when unembedded. They can say this, because they think that the truth-conditions of a sentence are a semantic property of the sentence, not a kind of speech act performed by someone who utters that sentence. But ordinary noncognitivists, and all of the explicit expressivist views on the table, seem to suggest that expression is a kind of speech act. If expressing disapproval of murder is the speech act performed by ordinary utterances of 'murder is wrong', then it seems extremely unlikely that this speech act is performed when someone says 'murder is not wrong'. And so it would seem to follow that *strictly speaking*, the parts of complex normative sentences don't *actually* express the noncognitive attitudes that are taken as arguments in the compositional determination of the attitude expressed by the whole. So the situation is not exactly parallel to that for truth-conditional semantics. This is what I call the *composition problem*.

The other important thing to note is that this answer in no way makes the embedding problem go away. Geach and Searle originally treated questions and answers, disagreement, and valid arguments as *evidence* that normative terms mean the same thing when embedded as when unembedded. But we can do just as well to treat them as *constraints* on an adequate account of *just which* attitude is expressed by the complex sentences. Not just any old function assigning 'murder is not wrong' a mental state that it expresses as a function of the mental state expressed by 'murder is wrong' will do. To be adequate, the function must assign these mental states in such a way that someone who says 'murder is wrong' and someone who says 'murder is not wrong' are in disagreement—indeed, that what they say are logically inconsistent. Similarly, not just any mental state can be assigned to conditional sentences by a compositional function—it has to be one which makes *modus ponens* out to be a logically valid rule of inference. It is not enough just to do compositional semantics; expressivists need a compositional semantics which correctly predicts why complex sentences have the properties that they do. This is the *real* embedding problem, and it is the problem on which expressivists' work on embedding has focused since 1970.

2.3 SEMANTIC COMMITMENTS

It takes no more knowledge about expressivism in order to see that what started as a view about normative language has already acquired strong commitments about ordinary descriptive language. In order to give their compositional semantics for normative sentences, expressivists must treat the sentential connectives, 'not', 'and', 'or', and 'if . . . then' as operating on mental states. The response to the original embedding problem was precisely to say just this—complex normative sentences express attitudes that are a function of the attitudes that would be expressed by their parts. That's great for complex sentences like 'murder is wrong and stealing is wrong'—both of its parts express noncognitive attitudes. But 'murder is wrong and grass is green' has one part expressing a noncognitive attitude and one part expressing a belief. And 'grass is green and snow is white' has two parts, each of which express beliefs. Yet all three sentences contain the word 'and'!

If there are not going to be four or more senses of 'and', of 'or', and of 'if . . . then', then expressivists are going to need to give a univocal treatment of the sentential connectives. Moreover, there are compelling arguments that any satisfactory account will *have* to give a univocal treatment of the sentential connectives. Any account that does not will require syntactic markers to distinguish between normative and descriptive sentences, simply in order to evaluate whether a sentence is well formed, and natural languages have no such markers. Moreover, any account that does not treat the sentential connectives in a uniform way will have only a poor claim to being able to account for *logic*. The inconsistency between 'P' and '∼P' should be guaranteed by the meaning of '∼', not by the joint fact that if we first interpret 'P' as normative and '∼' as normative-sentence-negation, they are inconsistent, together with the fact that if we interpret 'P' as descriptive and '∼' as descriptive-sentence-negation, they are inconsistent, and if we interpret it in any other way it is not well formed. So if we hope to get very far at all, the pressure to have a uniform account of the sentential connectives is very high.

But since they treat the sentential connectives in the purely normative case as contributing functions from the mental states expressed by the parts to the mental state expressed by the whole, it seems that they will have to say the same thing about the sentential connectives in the purely descriptive case. So it follows that the meaning of 'and' in 'grass is green and snow is white' is a function from the mental states expressed by 'grass is green' and by 'snow is white' to the mental state expressed by the whole.

Now I want to make a very simple observation. The observation is that since 'grass is green and snow is white' is an ordinary descriptive sentence, it should have an ordinary propositional content. It is not hard to say what this content should be. It should be the proposition that grass is green and snow is white. Now an ordinary compositional semantics would explain this in the following way: it would say that 'grass is green' has as its content the proposition that grass is green, that 'snow is white' has as its content the proposition that snow is white, and that 'and' gives a function from the propositional contents of the parts to a conjunctive propositional content of the whole. But expressivists cannot accept this explanation! They are committed to believing, as we have seen, that 'and' contributes, instead, a function from pairs of mental states to mental states. Since 'grass is green and snow is white' gets its meaning from that of 'and', therefore, they must hold that if it has a propositional content, it must get that content *from* the mental state that it expresses. Fortunately, they will be able to explain why this can happen, however, because they will say that, provided things turn out correctly, 'grass is green and snow is white' expresses the belief that grass is green and snow is white, and that *belief* has the propositional content that grass is green and snow is white. So, expressivists will say, the conjunctive sentence must get its content from the belief that it expresses.

This is a nontrivial commitment about how to understand compositional semantics for ordinary descriptive language, and a nontrivial commitment about the relationship between linguistic content and mental content, for ordinary descriptive language and thought. In order to give their answer to the original embedding problem—the only kind of answer that any expressivist has ever tried to give to that problem—expressivists have quickly become committed to a very strong account of the relationship between linguistic and mental content, at least for the case of complex descriptive sentences. Call this commitment of expressivism *mentalism* about complex descriptive sentences.

Mentalism is the view that descriptive language gets its content from the contents of corresponding mental states—beliefs.

Must expressivists also believe that atomic descriptive sentences receive their contents from the beliefs that they express? Must they also be mentalists about atomic descriptive sentences? The answer to that, I think, depends on what we say about what the *expression* relation is. The meanings of complex descriptive sentences are a function of the mental states *expressed* by their parts—that is what sentential connectives do. They map from the states expressed by the parts to the state expressed by the whole. So atomic descriptive sentences must express mental states in the *same sense* as complex ones do—whatever sense that is. So let's turn to take a look at what expressivists mean by 'expression', in order to try to evaluate that. Doing so will also allow us to see whether they can make use of whatever explanation anyone else can give of the difference between 'grass is green' and 'I believe that grass is green'.

2.4 EXPRESSION—EARLY PASSES

It turns out to be easy to see that despite the elegance of their initial response to the modal and disagreement problems for Cognitivist Speaker Subjectivism, expressivists cannot really, as it turns out, make use of just any explanation that might be given of the *expression* relation—the relation between 'grass is green' and 'I believe that grass is green'. For on the most natural account of the connection between these two, the first sentence has the *same content* as the belief that the second mentions. On this view of *expression*, a sentence expresses a mental state when they have the same content. The same-content account of expression is adequate for all of the cognitivist's purposes. If everyone has to agree that there is some adequate account of expression, this account is all that 'everyone' has to agree to.

But this account is clearly inadequate for the expressivists' purposes.[5] First, it does not appear to apply to the connection between 'murder is wrong' and disapproval of murder at all, because expressivists do not believe that either the sentence or the mental state has an ordinary propositional content. We can also see a more precise version of the point

---

[5] This is pointed out incidentally by Jackson and Pettit (1998: 244–5), although Jackson and Pettit don't acknowledge that expressivists might therefore mean something different by 'express'.

by drawing on the commitment of expressivism to mentalism diagnosed in the last section. In the last section, I argued that expressivists are committed to holding that the sentence 'grass is green and snow is white' gets its content *from* the belief that it expresses. But in order for that to happen, it must *first* express a belief, and only *then* acquire a content. But the same-content account says that a sentence expresses a belief *by* having the same content as that belief. So the same-content account is not compatible with expressivism's commitment to mentalism—they require different orders of explanation of why a complex sentence with the propositional content that *p* expresses the belief that *p*. Expressivists need to explain its having that content by appeal to its expressing that belief, but the same-content account explains its expressing that belief by appeal to its having that content.

This is bad! Expressivism started with the idea that it could take advantage of whatever everyone else had to say about the difference between 'grass is green' and 'I believe that grass is green'. But it turns out that they cannot! Expressivists owe us a story not only about the relationship between 'murder is wrong' and 'I disapprove of murder', but of that between 'grass is green' and 'I believe that grass is green' as well. And it is not at all obvious, without actually seeing how to construct such an account, that expressivists will be able to construct an account that works as well as the same-content account. To see how well they are going to be able to do, we are going to have to consider some further ideas about what the relationship between 'grass is green' and the belief that grass is green could be.

One next idea, suggested by some of the emotivists including, I think, Ayer, is that expression is a *causal* relation. The idea is that 'grass is green' is typically *caused*, in normal, sincere, cases, by the belief that grass is green.[6] So perhaps it expresses that belief in just those cases. But it is easy to see that this idea is hopeless for expressivism. Expressivism says that the *meaning* of a sentence—descriptive as well as normative—is given by the mental state that it expresses. But then it straightforwardly turns

---

[6] One of the uses of moral language that Ayer (1936: 103) distinguishes, is to make 'ejaculations'. Ejaculations are plausibly some kind of causal notion. Simon Blackburn also certainly suggests a causal reading when he characterizes expressivism as holding that when we 'assert values', 'we *voice* our states of mind' (1998: 50) (italics in the original), although Blackburn denies ever having been sympathetic to the causal account. Blackburn suggests a quite different view 19 pages later when he says that '[s]aying that something is good when we do not really value it is either deceiving others about our state, or is the result of self-deception' (1998: 69).

out that liars do not mean the same thing by their utterances as those who speak truthfully. And that result is a disaster—liars had better turn out to mean the same thing as the rest of us, because they are accountable for what they *say*. The problem with a causal account of the expression relation, no matter how modified or qualified, is that causation requires the expressed mental state to actually *exist*. But insincerity requires there to be sentences that express mental states that do *not* actually exist. In order to utter a sentence insincerely but with the same meaning as a sincere utterance, it has to be possible for you to express a mental state that you are not actually in. And that places an important constraint on any adequate account of the *expression* relation—it must be possible to bear it to a mental state that the speaker is not actually in.

Realizing that the expression relation must be in this sense *intentional*, Allan Gibbard suggested in *Wise Choices, Apt Feelings* (1990) that expression is a matter of the speaker's *intentions*. According to the Gricean account advocated by Gibbard in that book, you express a mental state when you try to convey to your audience (in the right kind of way) that you are in it. Gibbard's account has neither the obvious disadvantages of the same-content account nor the problem with insincerity of the causal account. But it has two problems of its own.[7]

The first problem with Gibbard's account is one that is shared with the causal account. The problem arises from the fact that on both accounts, the expression relation is a matter of what is going on in the speaker's head at the time. The problem is that it is difficult to gel such accounts with a compositional expressivist semantics: this is the composition problem that I introduced in section 2.2. According to the compositional expressivist semantics, the mental state expressed by a complex sentence is a function of the mental states expressed by its parts. But the causal account then requires that in order for the part, 'murder is wrong', to express the attitude of disapproval of murder in the complex sentence, 'if murder is wrong, then defenestration is wrong', it must be caused by the speaker's disapproval of murder. But clearly, sincere speakers can utter the conditional sentence without disapproving of murder. Similarly, Gibbard's Gricean account requires that in order for the part to express disapproval of murder, the speaker who utters the conditional must be trying, at least in part, to convey to her listener that she disapproves of murder. But this seems clearly not to be the case.

---

[7] I raised a third problem for Gibbard's account in 'Expression for Expressivists'.

The causal and informational accounts of *expression* are inconsistent with saying that the attitude expressed by a complex sentence is *strictly speaking* a function of the attitudes expressed by its parts. This is the composition problem that I brought up in section 2.2. The obvious way for expressivists to respond is to say that, strictly speaking, the attitude expressed by the whole is a function of the attitudes that *would* be expressed by the parts, *were* the speaker to assert them. The solution is to go counterfactual. This, I think, is the best that expressivists will be able to do, so long as they offer accounts of expression on which it is a kind of speech act at the level of whole sentences.

But there are obvious problems with the counterfactual approach. Perhaps the closest possible world in which Jane would assert, 'being friendly is wrong' is one in which either 'being friendly' meant something other than it does, or 'wrong' did. But still, when Jane says, 'if being friendly is wrong, then being friendly to strangers is wrong', the embedded sentence 'being friendly is wrong' means that being friendly is wrong, and not something else—whatever attitude she would have expressed in the closest possible world in which she would actually assert such a thing. Moreover, it wouldn't help to constrain the counterfactual to worlds in which Jane uses 'being friendly' and 'wrong' with the same meaning as in her present conditional sentences, because the point of the problem is precisely to explain why she means what she does, when she utters the conditional sentence.[8] So one might reasonably hope for a better expressivist solution to the composition problem.

The other important problem with Gibbard's approach was brought out by Mark van Roojen (1996). Van Roojen pointed out that if what a sentence expresses is up to the speaker's intentions, then even given linguistic constraints, it will still turn out that sentences can be used to express too many mental states. Suppose, for example, someone says, 'I believe that Moriarty has arrived', with the intention of getting her audience to infer that she believes that Moriarty has arrived, so that they will be able to use this belief, together with their knowledge that the speaker is an authority on Moriarty's whereabouts, to infer that Moriarty has arrived. On the original Gibbardian account, these sentences look like they will turn out to express the belief that Moriarty

[8] Notice that the problem here has nothing essentially to do with counterfactuals. Any way of trying to make the mental state expressed by a complex sentence a function of the mental states expressed by unembedded counterparts of its parts must restrict itself to unembedded counterparts of its parts *with the same meaning*. But all the expressivist has told us so far about what gives a sentence meaning, is what attitude it expresses.

has arrived. But since sentences get their contents from the mental states that they express, it then turns out that this sentence will have the propositional content that Moriarty has arrived, rather than the content that the speaker believes that Moriarty has arrived.[9] And this is a problem, because then it will be seen that these sentences turn out to be inconsistent with the wrong things. Speakers should not have so much control over what mental states their sentences express.

In *Thinking How to Live*, Gibbard offered a reply to this latter objection.[10] He backed down from his 1990 account of expression, pointing out that any account of expression that allowed 'I believe that Moriarty has arrived' to count as expressing the belief that Moriarty has arrived, rather than the belief that one believes that Moriarty has arrived, would be an inadequate account of expression. He then rested on confidence that everyone needs some adequate account of expression, so there must be some account that will avoid this problem. But Gibbard is wrong. It is true that everyone owes an account of expression that does not result in this conflation. But the same-content account is sufficient to avoid that conflation. The same-content account is all that cognitivists need. But expressivists need more. They need a *different* account of expression, because the same-content account, which easily avoids these other problems, is inconsistent with their commitments. And that is something that expressivists have still not provided.

2.5 ASSERTABILITY EXPRESSIVISM

An expressivist account of *expression* therefore needs to have several important properties. It must avoid collapsing into the same-content account. It must allow sentences to express mental states that their utterers are not actually in. It should ideally allow us to say why embedded sentences really do express the mental states that they need to in order for those states to be taken as arguments in the function determining the mental state expressed by the complex sentences in which they figure. And it should provide a good explanation of why

[9] According to Ayer, these *would* count as expressions of the belief that Moriarty has arrived: 'Thus I may simultaneously express boredom and say that I am bored, and in that case my utterance of the words, "I am bored", is one of the circumstances which make it true to say that I am expressing or evincing boredom' (1936: 109).

[10] Actually, I offered an alternative reply on Gibbard's behalf in Schroeder (2008), but there I also argued that this led to a further problem for Gibbard's account of expression.

'I believe that Moriarty has arrived' cannot be used with its ordinary English meaning to express the belief that Moriarty has arrived.

An account of the *expression* relation that satisfies these criteria may not be an account of any ordinary-language sense of 'expression'. But as I argued in section 2.1, there is no reason why we should think that expressivists are wedded to *expression* being something of which we have any pre-theoretical understanding. All that they are wedded to is the thesis that it is the relationship that 'murder is wrong' bears to disapproval of murder *and* which 'grass is green' bears to the belief that grass is green. Exactly what this relationship looks like may bear some surprises.

The minimal way to solve this problem, I think, is to appeal to *assertability* conditions on sentences. Allowing for insincerity requires us to have an account of expression on which it is possible to express mental states that you are not actually in. The way that Gibbard treats this is to say that expressing a mental state is really bearing some relation to the *proposition* that you are in that mental state. So far, I think, this is on the right track. That is how we typically treat intentional relations. But then Gibbard's account goes on to interpret what the relationship to this proposition is, and it is Gibbard's interpretation which gets his account into trouble. According to Gibbard's interpretation, expressing a mental state is something that a *speaker* does, and which is subject to the speaker's *intentions*. It is these two features that make it subject to the problems that we raised in the last section.[11]

But a more minimal account of the expression relation could resist these moves. It is right, according to the minimal view, that a sentence expresses a mental state by being associated with the proposition that the speaker is in that mental state. But on the minimal view, this is not due to something that the speaker does or intends. Being associated with this proposition is merely a semantic property of the sentence.

Why think that sentences are associated with propositions to the effect that the speaker is in a certain mental state? These conditions, according to the view that I am suggesting, are the *assertability conditions* of the sentence. Linguistic rules governing sentences say when it is permissible, at least as far as the semantic rules of the language go, to assert them.

---

[11] Gibbard also claims that the intentions of the speaker which matter are intentions to provide the information to her audience that she is in the requisite state of mind. This is the feature of Gibbard's view that was the basis of a third objection to his account that I posed in 'Expression for Expressivists'.

These are the *semantic correctness conditions* of the sentence. According to a common view, semantic correctness conditions are *truth*-conditions. According to this view, an utterance is semantically correct just in case it is true. But it is natural to resist this view. Imagine that Allison has been out of touch since late October 2004, and believes that John Kerry was elected president of the United States. If you ask her who is president of the United States, she will say, 'John Kerry is president of the United States'. Now what Allison says is false, and it is clear that in saying something false, she is making some kind of mistake. But it is natural to think that her mistake is not really linguistic—rather, it is a mistake about US politics.

Assertability semantics explains this in the following way: Allison has violated the truth-conditions of 'John Kerry is president of the United States', but she has not violated its semantic correctness conditions. She is following the semantic rules of the language perfectly, and following the rules of keeping up with electoral politics only imperfectly. On this view, semantic correctness conditions are not truth-conditions, but *assertability* conditions. The semantic correctness conditions of a sentence are the conditions under which it is semantically appropriate to assert it.

So what are these conditions, under which it is appropriate to assert a sentence? According to assertability semantics, they are always the presence of some mental state of the speaker. It is permissible to assert 'grass is green' only if you believe that grass is green. It is permissible to assert 'snow is white' only if you believe that snow is white. It is permissible to assert 'grass is green and snow is white' only if you believe that grass is green and snow is white. And so on.

Everyone agrees, after all, according to the assertability semanticist, that there is a 'norm of assertion'. Some think that the norm of assertion is to assert S only if you believe p, where S means that p. Some think that it is to assert S only if you justifiably believe p. And others say that it is to assert S only if you know p. Those who discuss the 'norm of assertion' typically take for granted that sentences have propositional contents, and then ask under what conditions it is permissible to assert a sentence with a given propositional content. There is one over-arching rule, on their views, which governs this: the 'norm of assertion'.[12]

Assertability expressivists explain the same data from the inside out. Each sentence, on this view, is associated with a condition under which

---

[12] See, for example, Williamson (2000).

it is permissible (as far as semantics goes) to assert it. For example, the sentence, 'grass is green' is semantically associated with the condition that the speaker believes that grass is green. As a shorthand, we can say that the sentence 'expresses' this belief. This belief has the content that grass is green. And so the sentence comes to count as having this content derivatively. So it is permissible to assert 'grass is green' only if you believe that grass is green, but not because the sentence has the content that grass is green—rather, it has that content because those are the conditions under which it is permissible to assert it.

Assertability semantics gives an account of the expression relation that satisfies all of our criteria. It does not collapse into the same-content relation, because according to assertability semantics, descriptive sentences acquire their contents from the beliefs which they express, rather than conversely. It also allows for insincerity—insincere utterances are cases in which a speaker breaks the semantic rules governing the language, and asserts something that she is not allowed to assert. It gives us an account on which expression is not a matter of what the speaker does, so there is no puzzle about why 'murder is wrong' expresses the same attitude even when embedded in 'if murder is wrong, then defenestration is wrong'. So it allows the attitudes expressed by complex sentences to be literally a function of the attitudes expressed by their parts, solving the composition problem. And it leaves the mental state expressed by a sentence outside of the control of individual speakers at individual times, so it allows for an easy explanation of why it is not possible to use 'I believe that Moriarty has arrived' to express the belief that Moriarty has arrived while using English in its conventional usage. This is because the semantic rules of English guarantee that it is permissible to assert 'I believe that Moriarty has arrived' only if you believe that you believe that Moriarty has arrived, rather than only if you believe that Moriarty has arrived.[13]

So I think that we should think of expressivism as committed to an underlying semantic program that looks something very much like assertability semantics. The central ideas of assertability semantics are: (1) that the role of semantics is to assign an assertability condition to each sentence of the language, understood as the condition under which it is semantically permissible for a speaker to assert it. (2) These assertability conditions typically or always say that the speaker needs

---

[13] Non-semantic facts may predict that it will be okay to assert these two sentences in similar circumstances, of course.

to be in a certain mental state. (3) Descriptive sentences inherit their propositional contents (truth-conditions) from the belief that it is their assertability condition to be in. And (4) the assertability conditions of complex sentences are a function of the assertability conditions of their parts, where this function is given by the meaning of the sentential connectives that are used to form the complex sentence.

Assertability semantics, so conceived, is not obviously wrong. In fact, it has several nice features, including that it helpfully explains why Allison is not making a linguistic mistake when she says, 'John Kerry is president of the United States'. Moreover, it is the kind of semantic program that is going to be necessary in order to make sense of expressivists' commitments to provide a compositional semantics for normative and descriptive sentences, without yielding the wrong results about cases of insincerity, funny counterfactuals, or speaker intentions. I think that it is an improvement for expressivists to adopt this picture as a model of their foundational semantic commitments, and will assume that it is how we are to make sense of talk about 'expression' in coming chapters.

But it is clearly a strong view about the semantics of ordinary descriptive language. It forms the basis for my model of how to think about expressivism: the central idea of expressivists that the same thing is going on for normative language as for ordinary descriptive language allows them to construct a picture on which, for at least some important central range of phenomena, we can make sense of how normative language works in an expressivist framework. But this does not come by applying what we know about ordinary descriptive language; rather, it comes at the cost of forcing us to new and strong views about the workings of ordinary descriptive language.

The following diagrams show the contrast between the standard conception of semantics, and the expressivist conception, ignoring complications arising due to context-dependence, and focusing on the case of ordinary descriptive sentences. In the first diagram, each atomic sentence is assigned by the semantics to a propositional content—'grass is green' is assigned to the proposition, *grass is green*, and 'snow is white' is assigned to the proposition, *snow is white*. Then 'and' makes a semantic contribution which generates a mapping from these two propositions to the proposition, *grass is green & snow is white*, as shown in the highlighted box. As a result, this proposition is assigned by the semantics to the sentence, 'grass is green and snow is white'. So on this view, the primary semantic values of sentences are always propositions, and are here indicated by the solid arrows, and connectives like 'and' operate at this level of semantic content. Then, as an extra-semantic matter, according to this picture, it turns out that each proposition is associated with a belief—the belief that has that proposition as its content. In the picture these are represented by the dashed arrows. And finally, as an extra-semantic matter, each sentence gets associated, derivatively, with the belief that has the same content as the semantics assigns to the sentence. This is the 'same-content' expression relation, and is represented by the dotted arrows.

The standard semantic picture

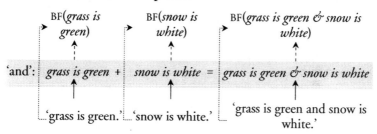

On the picture to which expressivists are committed, in contrast, the order of explanation is inverted, and everything turns out to be semantic. The primary job of the semantics is to assign to each atomic sentence a mental state—the state that you have to be in, in order for it to be permissible for you to assert that sentence. So 'grass is green' gets assigned *directly* to the belief that grass is green (which I write as 'BF(*grass is green*)'), and similarly for 'snow is white'. Then sentential connectives like 'and' operate at *this* level of semantic content, semantically contributing a mapping from the mental states associated with the atomic sentences to the mental state associated with the conjunction, as shown in the shaded box. These primary semantic values of the sentences are the states that are *expressed* by the sentences, in the minimal sense advocated by the interpretation of expressivism as assertability semantics, and are represented by the solid arrows. Then, since in the case of descriptive sentences, each mental state assigned by the semantics is a belief with a propositional content, each is associated with that proposition, as represented by the dashed arrows. And so finally, each descriptive sentence is derivatively associated with a propositional content, as represented by the dotted arrow. So even on the expressivist view, descriptive sentences have ordinary descriptive propositions assigned as semantic values—but they are not the *primary* semantic values of sentences—only derivative ones, and importantly, the sentential connectives are not understood to operate at this level of semantic content.[14]

The expressivist semantic picture

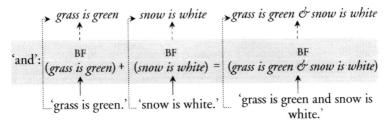

2.6 WHERE NEXT?

In the following chapters, I am going to consider how expressivists are to put this semantic program into effect. The original embedding problem, I said, was the problem of explaining how normative terms could have the same meaning in embedded contexts as in unembedded contexts. A compositional expressivist semantics construed under the program of assertability semantics gives expressivists the tools that they need to explain in a satisfactory way how normative terms could have the same meaning when embedded as when unembedded. But it does *not* yet do anything to explain why complex sentences have the properties that they are supposed to have.

Yet a compositional expressivist semantics will only be adequate if it can be explained why complex sentences constructed under this compositional semantics have the properties that we expect them to have: why, for example, 'murder is not wrong' is inconsistent with 'murder is wrong'. This is the *real* embedding problem which has

---

[14] This picture thus has two salient features. First, it understands sentential connectives to operate at the level of mental states rather than at the level of propositional contents. And second, it understands propositional contents to be inherited from mental states, rather than conversely. The first of these features will be in the foreground in Part II of this volume; the second will be important in Part III.

received so much attention.[15] The inconsistency of atomic normative sentences with their negations looks like it would have to be one of the easiest such things to explain. Surely negation is one of the simplest complex-sentence-forming constructions, and atomic sentences would surely have to be the easiest case. Yet as we will see in Chapter 3, there is no satisfactory expressivist explanation of why 'murder is wrong' and 'murder is not wrong' are inconsistent, let alone of why they are logically inconsistent. In Chapter 4, I'll give an expressivist solution to this *negation problem*, and then show in chapter 5 how to extend it to a general account of logical inconsistency. Later chapters will build on this approach, and argue that the fact that it is able to do so many things that no other expressivist account has been able to do is no coincidence—any expressivist account that can do these things, I'll be arguing, will have to look very much like the one that I will be constructing.

[15] For example, from Hare (1970), Blackburn (1973, 1984, 1988), Schueler (1988), Gibbard (1990, 2003), Zangwill (1992), Hale (1993), Stoljar (1993), Price (1994), van Roojen (1996), Dreier (1996, 2006), Unwin (1999, 2001), Sinnott-Armstrong (2000), and Ridge (2006).

PART II

EXPRESSIVISTS' PROBLEMS WITH LOGIC

3

The negation problem

3.1 EXPRESSIVIST INCONSISTENCY

An ordinary descriptivist account of why 'grass is green' and 'grass is not green' are inconsistent would point out that 'grass is green' can be true only if grass is green, and that 'grass is not green' can be true only if grass is not green, but that grass cannot be both green and not green: the inconsistency of their contents guarantees the inconsistency of the sentences. An explanation of why they are *logically* inconsistent would point out that given their structure, this feature would hold no matter what interpretation we assigned to 'grass' and no matter what interpretation we assigned to 'green'. So their inconsistency is guaranteed by the logic of 'not'.

Expressivists cannot appeal to such an explanation, because they don't want to tell us what it would be for murder to be wrong. The only resource that expressivists have to appeal to, in order to explain the inconsistency of 'murder is wrong' and 'murder is not wrong', is the mental states that are expressed by each.[1] So an expressivist account of their inconsistency is going to have to work by appealing to some 'inconsistent' feature of the attitudes that each expresses. And this is, in fact, the shape of all expressivist attempts to explain inconsistency, entailment, and validity. All try to account for inconsistency of sentences in terms of inconsistency of the states of mind expressed, entailment among sentences in terms of commitment between the states of mind expressed, and so on. These are the materials with which expressivists have to work.

---

[1] As noted in Chapter 1, I will be pretending that 'murder is wrong' is a paradigm case of a basic atomic normative sentence that is a candidate to receive an expressivist treatment. For each substantive expressivist theory, the basic sentences differ. For example, for Gibbard (1990), the problems discussed in this chapter are best raised with respect to 'rational', rather than 'wrong'; for Gibbard (2003) they are best raised with respect to 'the thing to do'; and for Horgan and Timmons (2006), they are best raised with respect to 'ought'.

A uniform account of inconsistency, then, would seem to require doing the same for ordinary descriptive sentences. (Notice, again, the expressivist commitment to surprising and strong views about ordinary descriptive language—this time for logic!) On this view, 'grass is green' and 'grass is not green' are inconsistent not because they have inconsistent propositions for their contents. Or at least, not directly. On this view, 'grass is green' and 'grass is not green' are inconsistent because there is a kind of 'inconsistency' involved with the mental states expressed by each. Which mental states are these? Well, 'grass is green' expresses the belief that grass is green, and 'grass is not green' expresses the belief that grass is not green. But there *is* something inconsistent about having both of those beliefs (if it is even possible). It is a special kind of mistake. In general, there is some kind of requirement not to have beliefs with inconsistent contents. Having them makes the *believer* 'inconsistent', in a loaded kind of way.

Not all mental states have this feature—that having them toward inconsistent contents makes the agent 'inconsistent' in such a loaded way. For example, there is nothing inconsistent about wondering whether p and wondering whether $\neg p$—in fact, there would be something weird about wondering the first *without* wondering the second. Supposing is also not subject to this constraint, and neither, plausibly, is desiring. But believing is. Beliefs can be inconsistent in a way that goes over and above the inconsistency of their contents. They can be inconsistent in the sense that it is *inconsistent of you* to have both beliefs. This is what Allan Gibbard (2003) calls 'disagreement'. In Gibbard's sense, beliefs with inconsistent contents 'disagree' with one another, because someone who has one belief *disagrees* with someone who has the other belief, and having both would involve disagreeing with yourself. Disagreeing with yourself, in Gibbard's sense, is what I mean by personal inconsistency. It is the kind of inconsistency that is instantiated by someone who has contradictory beliefs, but not by someone who is supposing contradictory things, or wondering contradictory things.

Given the facts that each descriptive sentence expresses a belief, that the belief expressed by a descriptive sentence has the same propositional content as the sentence does, and that beliefs are inconsistent just in case their contents are, it is easy to see how to switch the order of explanation for the inconsistency of sentences. Instead of explaining the inconsistency of sentences in terms of the inconsistency of their contents, expressivists can give an account that will be formally adequate, according to which descriptive sentences are inconsistent just in case the states of mind they express are. You may not find this account attractive—you may think that it gets things the wrong way around. But there is no formal problem with the proposal, considered only for beliefs. The idea behind all expressivist attempts to explain the inconsistency of 'murder is wrong' and 'murder is not wrong' is to try to generalize this approach to sentences that express noncognitive attitudes.

Unfortunately, we already know that not just any old kind of mental state is subject to the kinds of inconsistency that beliefs are. In particular, supposing and wondering do not seem to be subject to the requisite kinds of inconsistency. Their *contents* can be inconsistent, but that does not mean that there is anything inconsistent about *having* the attitude toward inconsistent contents. So expressivists need to establish that there can be noncognitive attitudes that are subject to the required kind of inconsistency, and this is a substantial explanatory burden.

3.2 INCONSISTENCY-TRANSMITTING ATTITUDES

Fortunately, there is at least one good model for expressivists to focus on. Intention, it seems, is subject to the required kinds of inconsistency. It is inconsistent of someone to intend to do inconsistent things. If you are intending to do inconsistent things, that reflects badly on you in the same kind of way that believing inconsistent things reflects badly on you, and in which it does *not* reflect badly on you to suppose inconsistent things. Moreover, on the face of it, intention is a noncognitive, or desire-like, attitude. That is, it is essentially tied to motivation and practical deliberation in a way that belief is not. So it provides a good model for expressivists' attempts to explain how the noncognitive attitudes expressed by normative sentences could be inconsistent in the ways that would enable them to explain why 'murder is wrong' and 'murder is not wrong' are inconsistent. For precisely this reason, intention has always been a good model for expressivists, beginning with Stevenson's (1937) first attempts to argue that there can be disagreement in attitude. Allan Gibbard's 2003 book, *Thinking How to Live*, takes intention as such a serious model that his primary claim is to construct an expressivist language to express *intentions—plans*, as he calls them. If he can get expressivism to work for intentions, Gibbard thinks, then that would show that expressivism can be made to work.

So a good idea for expressivists is to take the inconsistency of intention as a model for explaining the inconsistency between the mental state expressed by 'murder is wrong' and that expressed by 'murder is not wrong'. But unfortunately, there is a large obstacle to this strategy. And this is that many philosophers have argued that the only reason why intending inconsistent things makes you inconsistent is that intention *involves belief.* Inconsistency in intention, these philosophers have argued, reduces to inconsistency in belief.[2] Michael Bratman (1993, forthcoming a, forthcoming b) calls this view *cognitivism about instrumental reason.*[3] If cognitivism about instrumental reason is correct, then there are no good models for expressivists to appeal to, of noncognitive states that can be inconsistent in the way that beliefs can be inconsistent. So that would be a blow to the optimism of expressivists that they will be able to explain why the mental states expressed by 'murder is wrong' and by 'murder is not wrong' are inconsistent, even though they are not beliefs. If cognitivism about instrumental reason is correct, then it will not be at all obvious that there is any kind of inconsistency between mental states that does not reduce to the inconsistency between beliefs.

Fortunately for expressivists, Michael Bratman (1993, forthcoming a, forthcoming b) has offered what look like powerful arguments that cognitivism about instrumental reason is very unpromising. Bratman argues that there are several different kinds of norms governing intentions, including not only the consistency requirement, but also the requirement of means-end coherence, to intend what you believe to be the necessary means to your intended end, and a requirement of agglomeration—to intend *A&B*, if you both intend *A* and intend *B*. And he argues that cognitivists about instrumental reason have a very hard time accounting for all three of these norms in the full range of cases to which they apply. In particular, he argues, the norms of consistency and means-end coherence apply in a wider range of cases than those in which an intention-like state plausibly involves belief. I am going to assume, so as to give expressivists their best-case scenario, that Bratman's arguments are successful, and the inconsistency of having intentions with inconsistent contents does not reduce to the inconsistency

---

[2] Views in this family have been advocated by, for example, Harman (1976, 1986), Velleman (1989), Wallace (2001), Broome (forthcoming), and Setiya (2007).

[3] Notice that 'cognitivism' in 'cognitivism about instrumental reason' does not mean the same thing as 'cognitivism' as opposed to 'noncognitivism', the umbrella category that expressivism falls under.

of having beliefs with inconsistent contents. But this is a difficult issue for expressivists.[4]

I will assume, since this is required for expressivists' best-case scenario, since I find it plausible, and since I wish to focus on the issues for expressivism in the philosophy of language, rather than those in the philosophy of mind, that Bratman and Gibbard are right about intention, and cognitivism about instrumental reason is mistaken. I will assume that intention is subject to a basic, noncognitive kind of inconsistency, the kind of inconsistency on which expressivists ought to hope to be able to model their account of the inconsistency between the mental state expressed by 'murder is wrong' and that expressed by 'murder is not wrong'. Everyone, I will assume along with Gibbard, needs to be able to explain why intending inconsistent contents makes you inconsistent, as well as why believing inconsistent contents makes you inconsistent. Everyone needs to be able to explain, as Gibbard says, why intentions and beliefs can *disagree* with each other in the right kinds of way. The hopes for expressivists to explain what is inconsistent about thinking that murder is wrong and thinking that murder is not wrong, lie in the hope that whatever this explanation is, it will also apply to the noncognitive attitudes appealed to by expressivists.

But I want to draw just a simple observation about *in what cases* beliefs are inconsistent with each other, and in what cases intentions are inconsistent with each other. Beliefs are inconsistent with each other when their *contents* are inconsistent. Similarly, intentions are inconsistent with each other when their contents are inconsistent. The *sense* in which they are inconsistent is not merely *that* their contents are inconsistent—for supposings and wonderings can have contents that are inconsistent, but there is nothing inconsistent about engaging in two such supposings or two such wonderings. As Gibbard would put it, someone who supposes that p does not *disagree* with someone who supposes that $\neg p$. But the *cases in which* beliefs and intentions are inconsistent are precisely those cases in which their contents are inconsistent. So I will say that belief and intention are *inconsistency-transmitting attitudes*:

inconsistency-transmitting An attitude A is *inconsistency-transmitting* just in case two instances of A are inconsistent just in case their contents are inconsistent.

---

[4] See Schroeder (forthcoming b), chapter 3, for further discussion of this issue in the context of expressivism.

All of the paradigm cases of inconsistency between mental states are cases of bearing the same attitude toward inconsistent contents. It is *this* kind of inconsistency between mental states that everyone needs to be able to explain. Everyone needs to be able to explain why belief and intention are inconsistency-transmitting attitudes, while supposing, wondering, and hoping are not. So if expressivists can explain the inconsistency between 'murder is wrong' and 'murder is not wrong' by appeal to the hypothesis that the attitude expressed by 'murder is wrong' is inconsistency-transmitting, then they will have explained it by appeal to the kind of thing that everyone needs to be able to explain. An explanation which appeals only to such materials is *respectable*, in the sense that it appeals to the kind of assumption that it is respectable for expressivists to hope to be able to explain.

How would such an explanation go? Well, let us stipulate that the attitude expressed by 'murder is wrong' is to be called *disapproval of murder*. Suppose that it turns out that disapproval of murder is, like belief and intention, an inconsistency-transmitting attitude. Everyone, after all, needs to understand inconsistency-transmitting attitudes. Well, then it would turn out that the states DISAPPROVAL(murdering) and DISAPPROVAL(not murdering) would be inconsistent states (I'm going to use small caps to denote psychological states). This would be explained by the fact that disapproval is an inconsistency-transmitting attitude, and murdering and not murdering are inconsistent contents. And finally, this would yield an expressivist explanation of why the sentences which express these two mental states are inconsistent. This would follow from the account that two sentences are inconsistent just in case the mental states that they express are.

3.3 THE NEGATION PROBLEM

Unfortunately, however, as Nicholas Unwin (1999, 2001) has pointed out forcefully, this does not yield expressivists an explanation of why atomic normative sentences are inconsistent with their negations. This is because the sentence that expresses disapproval of not murdering is 'not murdering is wrong'. But the negation of 'murdering is wrong' is 'murdering is not wrong'.

In fact, Unwin argues, the problem is a deep one. There are three places to insert a negation in 'Jon thinks that murdering is wrong', all of which receive distinct semantic interpretations:

w   Jon thinks that murdering is wrong.
n1   Jon does not think that murdering is wrong.
n2   Jon thinks that murdering is not wrong.
n3   Jon thinks that not murdering is wrong.

Sentence n1 denies Jon a positive view about the wrongness of murdering, n2 attributes to Jon a negative view about the wrongness of murdering, and n3 attributes to Jon a positive view about the wrongness of not murdering. According to n2, he thinks that murdering is permissible, whereas according to n3 he thinks that it is obligatory. Conflating any two of these three would be a disaster.

Yet that is precisely the danger for expressivists. For according to expressivism, thinking that murdering is wrong is being in the mental state expressed by 'murdering is wrong'. That is, it is disapproving of murdering. But there are simply not enough places to insert a negation in 'Jon disapproves of murdering':

w*   Jon disapproves of murdering.
n1* Jon does not disapprove of murdering.
n2* ???
n3* Jon disapproves of not murdering.

There is simply one place not enough for the negations to go around. There is no way to account for the meaning of n2 by applying 'not' somewhere to the meaning of w. And that makes it look very much like expressivists are not going to be able to offer a satisfactory explanation of why 'murder is wrong' and 'murder is not wrong' are inconsistent.

The problem is this. If the inconsistency of 'murdering is wrong' and 'murdering is not wrong' is to be explained, then these two sentences must express inconsistent states of mind. And so if the inconsistency between these two states of mind is to be explained in terms of the inconsistency-transmittingness of some attitude, they must be the same attitude toward inconsistent contents. So since 'murdering is wrong' expresses a state of disapproval of murdering, it follows that 'murdering is not wrong' must also express a state of disapproval. It must be disapproval of X, for some value of X that is inconsistent with murdering. But what could X be?

It could not be *not murdering*, because if 'wrong' sentences work compositionally, and 'murdering is wrong' expresses disapproval of murdering and 'stealing is wrong' expresses disapproval of stealing, then 'not murdering is wrong' must express disapproval of not murdering.

But as Unwin pointed out, 'murdering is not wrong' should not turn out to express the same state of mind as 'not murdering is wrong'. So what else could X be? The answer is that it *couldn't* be anything else, and the proof of that is easy. Some actions are permissible without being obligatory—i.e., it is permissible both to do them and to not do them. So 'not murdering is not wrong' ('not murdering is permissible') is consistent with 'murdering is not wrong', but inconsistent with 'not murdering is wrong' ('murdering is obligatory'). So 'not murdering is not wrong' must express a state of mind that is *consistent* with the state of mind expressed by 'murdering is not wrong', but *inconsistent* with the state of mind expressed by 'not murdering is wrong'. Now, if 'murdering is wrong', 'murdering is not wrong', and 'not murdering is wrong' all express states of disapproval, then presumably 'not murdering is not wrong' must express a state of disapproval, too. But since we are assuming disapproval to be inconsistency-transmitting, it follows that 'not murdering is not wrong' must express disapproval of something that is consistent with X but inconsistent with *not murdering*.

So for all of this to work, X must be assigned a value that is inconsistent with *murdering*, but does not entail *not murdering*. But there is no such X. Every X that is inconsistent with *murdering* entails *not murdering*. So it follows that 'murdering is not wrong' cannot express disapproval of anything at all, if things are going to turn out alright. It must express another state. But if so, then its inconsistency with 'murdering is wrong' cannot be explained by the assumption that disapproval is inconsistency-transmitting! That is, it cannot be explained by appeal to the kind of assumption that it is respectable for expressivists to make.

We can put the problem another way. Let us say, stipulatively, that 'murder is not wrong' expresses an attitude called 'tolerance' toward murder, just as 'murder is wrong' expresses an attitude called 'disapproval' toward murder. Unwin's observation, together with the preceding argument, shows us that tolerance can't be defined out of disapproval and negation, but that is something that we should have known anyway. After all, it is an old observation that 'permissible', 'impermissible', 'obligatory', and 'unobligatory' can all be interdefined using negation. But the negations have to appear in *two* places, both 'inside' and 'outside' the term we are using to define the others. For example, 'permissible' is 'not obligatory not'. So given that we understand 'external' negation, we only need one of those four in order to define the others. But the problem is that the question of what mental states are expressed by sentences containing an 'external' (sentential) negation is precisely what we have not yet answered.

The whole point of solving the embedding problem for the case of negation, recall, is to say what mental state is expressed by the negation of normative sentences. So in order to do that, we need at least one attitude from the {'permissible','unobligatory'} pair *and* at least one from the {'impermissible','obligatory'} pair, both of which we take as primitive, in order to define sentential negation. Blackburn's (1988) account used the attitudes he called 'tolerance' and 'hooraying', corresponding to 'permissible' and 'obligatory'. (His earlier (1984) discussion wrongly focused on 'booing' and 'hooraying', which corresponded to 'impermissible' and 'obligatory', falling directly into the trap mentioned in the first paragraph of this section.) I'm focusing on disapproval and tolerance, corresponding to 'impermissible' and 'permissible'. It doesn't matter, really, which we choose, but the point is that we need one from each pair in order to be able to define negation.

Let me be clear that we *can* do things this way. It is not that expressivists have no answer as to what n2 means. The answer is that it means that Jon tolerates murdering. But once we do things in this way, it should be very clear that we have left completely unexplained and apparently inexplicable why 'murder is wrong' and 'murder is not wrong' are inconsistent.

Suppose, for example, that someone tells you that when she uses the word 'not' or the prefix 'im-' immediately before 'permissible', they are not to be understood as meaning what 'not' normally does. Instead, she says, she believes in distinct, unanalyzable, and non-interdefinable properties of permissibility and impermissibility. And then suppose that she tells you that she also believes that it is impossible—*logically* impossible—for something to be both permissible and impermissible. Finally, she tells you that what makes 'murder is permissible' and 'murder is not permissible' logically inconsistent is that 'murder is not permissible' just means 'murder is impermissible', which is logically inconsistent with 'murder is permissible'. Similarly, she insists, what makes 'murder is impermissible' and 'murder is not impermissible' logically inconsistent is that 'murder is not impermissible' just means 'murder is permissible', which is logically inconsistent with 'murder is impermissible'.

Surely she leaves something to be explained! Obviously, her view will be a bad view about permissibility and impermissibiliy unless it turns out that 'permissible' and 'impermissible' are inconsistent. But that does not mean that she is entitled to assume it, in order to explain why 'murder is permissible' and 'murder is not permissible' are inconsistent! On the contrary, her view seems to have written out of existence everything that could be used to explain why permissibility and impermissibility are incompatible. Expressivists are in the same position with respect to disapproval and tolerance. The negation problem shows that they can't simply be interdefined, which leads to the conclusion that they are distinct and unanalyzable attitudes. But if they are, then why on earth is it inconsistent to hold them toward the same thing?

One more observation is requisite in order to draw out exactly how difficult this problem is for expressivists, and to understand how inadequate existing answers are. The observation is to compare just how different this kind of inconsistency would be, between disapproval of murder and tolerance of murder, from the familiar kinds of inconsistency for which expressivists have good models elsewhere. All of the other good models of inconsistency between mental states arose in the case of inconsistency-transmitting attitudes. They were all cases of the same attitude toward inconsistent contents. Call this *A*-type inconsistency. *A*-type inconsistency is relatively easy to explain, because to explain it all that you need is a general fact about an attitude type (that it is inconsistency-transmitting) and an easy claim about their contents (that they are inconsistent).[5] But tolerance of murder and disapproval of murder are two *distinct* and apparently *logically unrelated* attitudes toward the *same* content. Call this *B*-type inconsistency. *A*-type inconsistency is something that we should all recognize and be familiar with. It happens with beliefs, for example. But *B*-type inconsistency is not something that expressivists can take for granted, because there are no good examples of it. Assuming that disapproval and tolerance of murder are inconsistent is taking for granted everything that expressivists need to explain.

Keep in mind that the whole problem so far arises simply from the case of negations of atomic normative sentences! But things only get harder—and rapidly so—when we start considering other kinds of complex normative sentences. If an atomic sentence like 'murder is

---

[5] In saying that it is 'relatively easy' to explain *A*-type inconsistency, I do not mean to imply that it is easy to explain it. I am not certain that anyone has given a satisfactory explanation of the *A*-type inconsistency either of intention or of belief, though some have certainly tried. See especially Velleman (2001), Bratman (forthcoming b).

wrong' expresses disapproval of something, it is not clear exactly what mental state should be expressed by 'murder is wrong and stealing is wrong', but by the same reasoning as for negation, we can't define it out of disapproval, for we again get three distinct ways of inserting a conjunction:

&1   Jon thinks that murdering is wrong and Jon thinks that stealing is wrong.
&2   Jon thinks that murdering is wrong and stealing is wrong.
&3   Jon thinks that murdering and stealing is wrong.

Since belief does not agglomerate across conjunction (you don't believe the conjunction of everything that you believe), we shouldn't collapse &1 and &2. And clearly both are distinct from &3. So the attitude expressed by 'murdering is wrong and stealing is wrong' will turn out to be distinct from disapproval as well. And once it is, it's obvious that the attitude expressed by its negation can't turn out to be just an ordinary state of tolerance, either.

If that doesn't seem like too many attitude-kinds yet, then try taking the conjunction of 'murder is wrong' with 'murder is not wrong'. And then try negating that. It's a good exercise to see just how quickly we end up needing to posit an infinite list of distinct kinds of attitude to go along with disapproval and tolerance—for every pair of which we will have to postulate primitive inconsistency relations. And that's just for one normative predicate, 'wrong'. Whereas for all descriptive predicates put together (and there are a lot of them), there is only one basic attitude: belief. If the view on which every complex construction yields a distinct attitude sounds simply too incredible to you to be worth going on, it's worth noting not only that this is essentially a commitment of all existing expressivist views, but that it has recently been defended explicitly in print.

3.4 HORGAN AND TIMMONS

The culprits are Terry Horgan and Mark Timmons (2006), who offer an 'expressivist logic', which they claim shows how to solve the embedding problem.[6] They postulate that there is a basic noncognitive attitude,

---

[6] See also Horgan and Timmons (2000), which offers an earlier version of the same view.

which they call 'ought-commitment'. There is also a basic cognitive attitude, which they call 'is-commitment' and other expressivists would simply call 'belief' (Horgan and Timmons make a big deal out of the fact that they get to call noncognitive attitudes 'beliefs', too, so they resist this characterization).

The details aren't crucial, but in Horgan and Timmons's official regimented language, they have 'non-sentential formulas', which are like sentences from ordinary predicate logic and represent the contents of mental states, and then they have 'sentential-formula-forming operators', which correspond to types of mental state. For example, the basic sentential-formula-forming operators are I[ ] and O[ ] , which represent is-commitment and ought-commitment. The 'sentences' of Horgan and Timmons's regimented expressivist language result from applying sentential-formula-forming operators to non-sentential formulas. We can think of them like descriptive names for the mental states that the sentences express; each sentence has exactly one sentential-formula-forming operator taking widest scope, which corresponds to the kind of attitude expressed by the sentence. The subsentential formulas filled in to its gaps tell us the content of that state. For example, if 'Ws' is a subsentential formula meaning that snow is white (think 'W'='white', 's'='snow'), then 'I[Ws]' is a sentence. It expresses is-commitment to snow being white (the belief that snow is white). 'O[Ws]' is also a sentence. It expresses ought-commitment to snow being white.

The way that Horgan and Timmons deal with complex sentences of all kinds is simple. Starting with negation, they tell us that for any sentential-formula-forming operator Ω, there is a distinct sentential-formula-forming operator, $\neg\Omega$. Since each sentential-formula-forming operator corresponds to a kind of mental state, starting with I[ ] corresponding to is-commitment and O[ ] corresponding to ought-commitment, all of this is just a complicated way of saying that whenever you negate a sentence, it expresses a different kind of attitude than the sentence that you negated. They give corresponding stories about conjunction, disjunction, the material conditional and biconditional, and the unary existential and universal quantifiers. Every time you take one or more sentences and make a more complex sentence, according to Horgan and Timmons, the complex sentence expresses a new and distinct kind of mental state.

Horgan and Timmons call these 'logically complex commitment states', and define them in terms of their inferential role. That is, what they tell us about the state corresponding to $\neg$O[ ], is that bearing it to some content is inconsistent with bearing O[ ] toward that content. So in essence Horgan and Timmons's view amounts to the hypothesis that there is an unfathomably huge hierarchy of distinct kinds of mental state, together with unsupported confidence that these mental states have the right inconsistency relations with one another. Of course, if their view is *true*, then these states must have the right inconsistency properties, because it is inconsistent to think that murder is wrong and to think that murder is not wrong. But that is just to say that this is a constraint of adequacy on their view, not to say that they are able to explain it. Cognitivists, on the other hand, have the easiest of times explaining why these thoughts are inconsistent. They are inconsistent because they are beliefs toward inconsistent contents, and belief is inconsistency-transmitting.

Horgan and Timmons say that the states that they postulate are 'logically complex', but that isn't really right. What is complex is Horgan and Timmons's syntax for designating these states. Each state must also play a certain role that can be specified in terms of other, simpler, states. For example, the state corresponding to ¬O[ ] must be inconsistent with the state corresponding to O[ ] when borne to the same content. That role is complex, and corresponds to the complexity in the syntax. But Horgan and Timmons give us no reason other than sheer optimism to believe that there really is a distinct state, ¬O[ ], which has these inferential properties. So there is really nothing different between their view and the one that posits both disapproval and tolerance and takes as unexplained their *B*-type inconsistency, except that Horgan and Timmons rightly go on to draw the inevitable conclusion that you have to do this over and over again, for every other complex construction. Their 'logic' constitutes an elegant list of the things that an expressivist view needs to explain, not an explanation of them.

3.5 GIBBARD AND DREIER

Unlike Horgan and Timmons, Gibbard (2003) appreciates that there is something here for expressivists to explain, rather than simply to stipulate. But Gibbard's best explanation fares even worse than Horgan and Timmons's. Even though Gibbard helps himself to *B*-type inconsistency as a primitive, his account still fails to distinguish n2 from n3.

To understand Gibbard's account, we have to understand two key ideas. The first idea is that of disagreement. Disagreement, for Gibbard, is just inconsistency between mental states. The belief that p and the belief that $\neg p$ are in disagreement, and so, hopefully, will be the states that are expressed by 'murder is wrong' and by 'murder is not wrong'. Gibbard takes disagreement as primitive, and as we'll see in a moment, disagreement so conceived includes *B*-type inconsistency. So by taking it as primitive, he is essentially helping himself to the very thing that I argued in section 3.2 that expressivists need to explain. Gibbard claims that everyone has to explain disagreement between mental states, because beliefs and intentions can disagree with one another. But, as we saw in section 3.2, this is wrong. Everyone needs to be able to explain *A*-type inconsistency. But *B*-type inconsistency is not something that everyone needs to be able to explain. Helping himself to *B*-type inconsistency is helping himself to everything.

Once we have such a notion of disagreement on board, the simplest answer to give to the question of what mental state is expressed by 'murder is not wrong' is that it is the weakest state that disagrees with disapproval of murder. Or equivalently, that it is the weakest state such that when you are in it, you disagree with every possible agent who disapproves of murder. Gibbard says *almost* this, but thins down the class of agents to those who are what he calls *hyperdecided*. He imagines agents who have a view about every possible question, practical or theoretical, and calls them *hyperplanners*. And he imagines that any given psychological state can be represented by the set of hyperplanners that you don't disagree with, just by being in it. So, for example, we represent disapproval of murder by the set of hyperplanners who you don't disagree with simply by disapproving of murder.

Then Gibbard introduces negation in the following way: he says that if the state expressed by 'murder is wrong' corresponds to some set of hyperplanners, then the state expressed by 'murder is not wrong' corresponds to the complement set of hyperplanners. This is elegant, because it allows him, at least for the 'truth-functional' connectives (and he never gets any further than these), to give what looks like the same account of each connective no matter what it is applied to. Whereas we saw with Horgan and Timmons's account, every time you apply negation to a more complex attitude you get a new and distinct kind of mental state. So there is something nice about Gibbard's account. But if we unpack it, what it is really saying is merely that 'murder is not wrong' must express a mental state that is inconsistent with all and only the hyperdecided mental states that 'murder is wrong' is not inconsistent with. And again, that looks more like a list of the criteria that we hope the attitude expressed by 'murder is not wrong' will satisfy, in lieu of a concrete story about which mental state this actually is, and why it turns out to be inconsistent with the right other mental states.

But even so, Gibbard *still* has a problem. His problem arises because he assumes that hyperplanners are always decided either to do A or to not do A, for any action A. So a hyperplanner never thinks that murdering is not the thing to do, without thinking that not murdering is the thing to do. They are never neutral between any options. This means that the set of hyperplanners with whom you disagree when you think that murdering is not wrong is the same as the set of hyperplanners with whom you disagree when you think that not murdering is wrong. And so despite helping himself to everything that it looks like expressivists need to explain, Gibbard's account still fails the test of the negation problem. It still fails to distinguish n2 from n3.

Dreier (2006), however, shows how to fix this final major problem for Gibbard's account. What Dreier proposes is to take as primitive a distinction between *indifference* and *undecidedness*. Hyperplanners, Dreier suggests, can be indifferent, even though they can't be undecided. Indifference is not a matter of having failed to make up your mind about what to do (which hyperplanners never fail to do, by definition). It is a matter of having made up your mind that it doesn't matter.

If hyperplanners can be indifferent without being undecided, Dreier argues, then permissibility without obligation, for hyperplanners, corresponds to indifference among the highest-ranked options. By allowing for hyperplanners who think that murdering is not wrong (who rank it as *one* of their top options) without thinking that not murdering is wrong (because they are indifferent between murdering and not murdering, ranking both as top options), Dreier allows for a difference in which hyperplanners you can disagree with if you think that murdering is not wrong, compared to if you think that not murdering is wrong. So Gibbard's account would go through as before, without conflating n2 with n3.

The problem that Dreier himself notes is that it may turn out that the distinction between indifference and indecision that he needs to appeal to is, like B-type inconsistency, something that expressivists need to *explain*, rather than something to which they have a right to appeal. But ignore that. Even if this distinction is one that makes perfect sense on expressivist grounds, this solution still helps itself to everything that expressivists really need to explain, because following Gibbard's account, it helps itself to *B*-type inconsistency.

To see why, suppose that you think that murdering is wrong. This state is represented by the set of hyperplanners that it does not disagree with. Intuitively, this should be the set of hyperplanners who think that murdering is wrong. But given Dreier's picture, there are three relevant sets of hyperplanners. There are those who think that murdering is wrong, those who think that not murdering is wrong, and those who are indifferent between murdering and not murdering. In order for the set of hyperplanners to correctly represent your state, its members must disagree with the hyperplanners who are indifferent as well as those who think not murdering is wrong. But that means that this disagreement can't be mere *A*-type inconsistency. It has to include the *B*-type inconsistency that holds between disapproval of and tolerance of murder.[7]

I think that none of these looks remotely satisfactory as an expressivist explanation of why 'murder is wrong' and 'murder is not wrong' are inconsistent. None answers the basic question of what makes disapproval and tolerance of murder inconsistent with one another. Each posits *that* there are such mental states that are inconsistent with one another, but none explains *why*. Moreover, it is important to observe that even if expressivists did explain why disapproval and tolerance of the same thing are inconsistent with one another,[8] the problem does not stop, there. The argument of section 3.3 leads to the conclusion that *every* structure a complex sentence might have will require its own unique attitude-kind, and for every pair of those attitudes, expressivists would need to provide a similar explanation of why they turn out to be inconsistent in just the right cases. And that was just sticking to one normative predicate, 'wrong'. So even if *B*-type inconsistencies can sometimes be explained, it is *extremely* unpromising to commit to a view with such an enormous explanatory burden to discharge. In contrast, recall that all descriptive inconsistency can be explained by a single assumption about belief—that it is inconsistency-transmitting.

---

[7] It's also worth noting that Gibbard can't accept Dreier's friendly fix, since he needs the assumption that hyperplanners can't be indifferent in order for his argument that normative terms pick out natural properties to go through. This argument and its consequences are one of the main contributions of Gibbard (2003).

[8] Blackburn (1988) may be interpreted as attempting to provide an explanation of *B*-type inconsistency for the case of atomic normative sentences and their negations, though if this is right, I don't think his explanation is satisfactory. See Hale (1993) and van Roojen (1996) for discussion.

Fortunately for expressivists, it is possible to give a rather elegant solution to the negation problem that explains everything that we want to explain, appeals only to expressivist-respectable materials, and generalizes to solve other and bigger problems for expressivism. I'll show how to construct this account in Chapter 4.

4

Its solution

4.1 THE BASIC EXPRESSIVIST MANEUVER

In order to see our way past the problem about negation, we need to have a diagnosis of what assumption made by expressivists is driving the most difficult features of the problem. Fortunately, expressivists have a ready-made strategy for performing such a diagnosis. It is the Basic Expressivist Maneuver, which we observed in section 2.1, in the expressivists' response to the modal and disagreement problems for speaker subjectivism, and again in section 2.2, in the expressivists' response to the original embedding problem as posed by Geach and Searle. The idea is, when confronted with a problem, to try to reconstruct it for ordinary descriptive language. Since there is obviously no such problem for ordinary descriptive language, it must have *some* solution, and the Maneuver helps us either to diagnose what that solution is, or simply to pass the explanatory burden off onto everyone else, who share it anyway.

In our case, the relevant assumption made by expressivists is that to each normative predicate, including 'wrong', there corresponds a distinct and unstructured attitude—for example, disapproval—such that atomic sentences ascribing that predicate express that attitude toward the subject of the sentence. This is not what we think about ordinary descriptive language! We don't suppose that every predicate corresponds to a distinct cognitive attitude. Rather, they all correspond to belief, and what each predicate does is to contribute something toward the *content* of that belief. But suppose that we did think that each descriptive predicate corresponded to its own attitude. In particular, suppose that we thought that 'green' was used to express the unanalyzable *believes-green* attitude, so that 'grass is green' expressed BELIEVES-GREEN(grass).

Then we would have a problem. For 'Jon thinks that grass is green' allows for two places in which 'not' can be inserted, yielding:

> **g**   Jon thinks that grass is green.
> **n1**   Jon does not think that grass is green.
> **n2**   Jon thinks that grass is not green.

But there is only one place to insert a negation in 'Jon believes-green grass':

> **g***   Jon believes-green grass.
> **n1***   Jon does not believe-green grass.
> **n2***   ???

So if we had this view, we would have trouble giving a constructive answer to what attitude is expressed by 'grass is not green'—the answer to how to interpret n2. It can't be the *believes-green* attitude borne toward anything, so what is it?

In answer, we might suppose that there is a distinct and also unanalyzable attitude, which we might call the *believes-not-green* attitude, and which we might assume to magically have the following property: that bearing the *believes-green* attitude and the *believes-not-green* attitude toward the same thing is always inconsistent. But of course, having assumed that these attitudes are both logically primitive, distinct, and unanalyzable, we would have no explanation of why this was so.

All of this is patently ridiculous. Thinking that grass is green and thinking that it is not green are not *sui generis* attitudes toward grass which are inexplicably inconsistent. They are both *beliefs* about grass, but with different *contents*. One is the belief that it is green, and the other is the belief that it is not green. It is because they have these contents, which are inconsistent, and because they are both cases of belief, which is an inconsistency-transmitting attitude, that they are inconsistent.

An adequate expressivist solution to the negation problem needs to take the same form. It needs to reject the assumption that led to the problem—the assumption that to each normative predicate corresponds a distinct attitude, such that atomic sentences ascribing that predicate express that attitude toward the subject of the sentence. It is this assumption that left insufficient structure for expressivists to have a constructive account of negation, as the believes-green example demonstrates. The ordinary descriptive predicate 'green' avoids this problem because the attitude that it expresses *factors* into a more general attitude, belief, and a property that is contributed by the predicate. Expressivists need to be able to say the same thing about the attitudes corresponding to normative predicates.

4.2 THE SOLUTION

Of course, expressivists can't say that the more general attitude is *belief*, in the case of normative sentences. It is part of their view that normative sentences do not express beliefs. So they will have to say that it is some kind of very general *non*cognitive attitude. Let's give it a name, and call it *being for*. The solution is to say, just as all descriptive predicates correspond to belief plus some property that is contributed by the predicate, that all normative predicates correspond to being for plus some relation that is contributed by the predicate. For each predicate, F, there is a relation, R_F, so that 'F(a)' expresses FOR(bearing R_F to a).[1]

So, for example, to borrow a proposal from Gibbard (1990), we might say that 'wrong' corresponds to *being for blaming for*, so that 'murder is wrong' expresses FOR(blaming for murder).[2] Similarly, we might say that 'better than' corresponds to *being for preferring*, so that 'a is better than b' expresses FOR(preferring a to b). Structurally, for the solution to work, it doesn't matter which account we give for each predicate, although obviously the overall plausibility of the resulting view will turn on it. But I'll retain these two accounts, of 'wrong' and 'better than', just to have something to work with.[3]

Now we can go back to Unwin's framing of the negation problem, and see that this account yields sufficient structure to offer a constructive account of the meaning of negated sentences:

---

[1] In what follows, I treat being for as an attitude that takes properties, rather than propositions, and I express these properties informally by using gerunds. Nothing in this chapter or the next two turns on this, but I work with this idea because I find it most natural, and because it allows me to make the most sense of the account of belief that I give in the later chapters. An account on which the basic noncognitive attitude took propositional contents would in all relevant respects be able to take advantage of the same response to the negation problem that I am giving here.

[2] Again, I am using small caps to denote mental states. So 'FOR(α)' is not a sentence, but a term, denoting the mental state of being for α.

[3] A common objection at this point is that this is the wrong analysis of 'wrong', and that a better analysis might be 'being for disapproving of' (in the colloquial, rather than our stipulative, sense of 'disapproval'). I'm sure that's right; nevertheless, as nothing I say in what follows turns on which analysis we choose, I'm going to stick with these, just to fix examples. If no alternatives can do better for expressivists, then so much the worse for expressivism. Another common objection at this point is that one can think that murder is wrong but also want or intend to not blame for murder (say, because people who live in glass houses shouldn't throw stones). That, I think, is not an objection, provided that being for is a distinct state from wanting or intending (or whatever other attitude gets mentioned in the objection).

w	Jon is for blaming for murdering.
n1	Jon is not for blaming for murdering.
n2	Jon is for not blaming for murdering.
n3	Jon is for blaming for not murdering.

There is no need, on this view, to posit a new attitude, *tolerance*, and to simply assume that it has the right properties. For the account leaves enough structure to offer a positive, constructive account of sentential negation: the sentential 'not' gets interpreted as falling in the new place that our structured account makes available.

A second way of seeing the virtue of this account, however, is to see what it does tell us about tolerance. 'Tolerance', recall, was our stipulative name for the attitude toward murder expressed by 'murder is not wrong'. We can see from n2, above, that this attitude is being for not blaming for murder. Likewise, recall that 'disapproval' was our stipulative name for the attitude toward murder expressed by 'murder is wrong'. But the account says that this is being for blaming for murder. Since on this view, both tolerance and disapproval of murder turn out to be complex, structured attitudes, it turns out that their inconsistency is no longer a case of brute, *B*-type inconsistency after all. It turns out to be a case of *A*-type inconsistency in our new attitude: being for. So the account reduces the *B*-type inconsistency to which all other expressivist accounts have to appeal but of which they have no systematic explanation, to *A*-type inconsistency, which as I pointed out in section 3.2, everyone needs to be able to explain.[4]

This means that the only further assumption required in order for us to have an adequate explanation of why 'murder is wrong' and 'murder is not wrong' are inconsistent, is that being for is an inconsistency-transmitting attitude. I'm not going to try and explain this, here, and it remains an explanatory burden in the philosophy of mind for expressivist accounts like this one. But the main point is that it is the kind of assumption that it is respectable for expressivists to make. Unlike the assumption of brute *B*-type inconsistency, for which there are no good models, the assumption that being for is inconsistency-transmitting is simply the assumption that it is has a property that is familiar from other sorts of mental state, including both belief and intention. Since everyone needs an account of why belief and intention have this property, it is

---

[4] As a consequence, as we'll see in Chapter 5, it allows us to reduce the logical features of our normative object-language to the logical features of the descriptive metalanguage in which we can state the contents of the states of being for.

reasonable for expressivists to hope that they will be able to defend such an explanation of why being for has it, too. Because it is reasonable for expressivists to be optimistic about this, I will assume that some expressivist explanation of why being for is inconsistency-transmitting will be forthcoming. My purpose in assuming it to be so is precisely that it is the kind of thing it is respectable to hope can be explained—I simply have nothing to add here, to its explanation.

A third way of seeing the advantage of this account is to recall that in Chapter 3, we seemed to have an argument that disapproval and tolerance were logically unrelated attitudes. After all, we needed to take both as primitive in defining sentential negation, and so we couldn't use sentential negation in order to interdefine them. This is what led to the assumption that they are logically unrelated, and hence to the view among current expressivists that their inconsistency must be taken as primitive and inexplicable. But the fact that they are not interdefinable does not really show that they must be logically unrelated—for they could really be both defined in terms of some third thing. And this is, in fact, what the account we've discovered does. It defines both disapproval and tolerance in terms of a third attitude—being for. So even though they are not interdefinable, they are still logically related. And that is why there is no puzzle about how logically unrelated attitudes could be inconsistent with one another, on this view. (This is, in fact, the thought that originally led me to this solution.)

Finally, this account yields a perfectly general constructive account of the meaning of 'not'. For any sentence 'A' expressing the attitude, FOR(α), '$\sim$A' expresses the attitude, FOR($\neg\alpha$).[5] Where does the 'not' go? It goes in the extra place that is created by the extra structure in our account, as in **n2**, above. And so the same will go for the negation of every sentence. So long as every normative sentence, atomic or not, expresses a state of being for something, we know how to negate it.

Just to reiterate what we've just accomplished: when we apply the Basic Expressivist Maneuver, it lets us see what created the problem about negation. It was created by the view that each normative predicate corresponds to an unanalyzable attitude, such that atomic sentences ascribing that predicate express that attitude toward the subject of the sentence. If we thought the same thing about ordinary descriptive

---

[5] I am going to distinguish, for clarity, between object-language and metalanguage connectives. I'll use the rounded connectives for the object-language, and pointed ones for the metalanguage ('$\sim$', '&', '$^\circ$', and '$\supset$', as opposed to '$\neg$', '$\wedge$', '$\vee$', and '>').

predicates, we would have the same problem. So the only promising way to solve the problem is to reject this assumption, and allow that the attitudes corresponding to normative predicates have a similar structure to the attitudes corresponding to descriptive predicates: that they factor into a general attitude, and a contribution made by that predicate. Predicates correspond to contents, not to attitudes.

The resulting account appears to work structurally perfectly on all counts. It adds the right kind of additional structure to disapproval, it eliminates the problem of positing brute *B*-type inconsistency by reducing *B*-type inconsistency to *A*-type inconsistency, and it allows for a constructive compositional account of the semantics of 'not'. I've given the general attitude a name, calling it 'being for', and I've thrown out two examples of how the account could work for simple normative predicates: 'wrong' and 'better than'. But the strategy is perfectly general. There is no other way of solving the negation problem, because Unwin's argument shows that only an account on which normative attitudes have structure can offer a constructive account of the attitude expressed by 'murder is not wrong'.

This isn't just *a* way of making progress on the negation problem, for expressivists. It is *the* expressivist solution to the negation problem. If the problem arises from a lack of structure, there can be only one solution: to add structure. That is the solution that I am suggesting (the further details I have added are only for the sake of illustrating how such a view would work). *Ipso facto*, the solution I am offering is the only way forward for expressivists. The only alternative is to posit, along with Horgan and Timmons, an infinite hierarchy of distinct and logically unrelated attitudes and to postulate that they miraculously bear the right inconsistency relations to one another. Views like theirs and Gibbard's don't tell us what 'not' means. They tell us what elaborate hypothesis has to be true, in order for expressivism to be true, but they don't do anything at all to make this hypothesis credible.

4.3 DOES THE PROBLEM COME BACK?

One worry that you might have with this account is that it only puts off the problems that we need to address. For now that we have the attitude of *being for*, one might think, all that we need is an indicative sentence expressing that attitude, in order to raise the problem all over again. Suppose that there is such a construction, or that we introduced one—that in order to express being for α, what you say is, 'α is fowr'. Since this is an indicative sentence of English, we can negate it, yielding 'α is not fowr'. But now we need to know how to understand what *this* means. And that would require, the natural thought goes, solving the negation problem all over again, this time for 'fowr' instead of for 'wrong'. So, the thought goes, if the attitude of being for is expressed by any indicative sentence of English, then we've only put off the problem, not solved it.

To see whether this reasoning is right, we will have to look back, and remind ourselves about why there was a negation problem for 'wrong' in the first place. The problem lay in the fact that the following two sentences do not mean the same thing:

1   murdering is not wrong.
2   not murdering is wrong.

The problem was that it would be relatively easy to explain why 'not murdering is wrong' is inconsistent with 'murdering is wrong', but that wouldn't suffice to explain why 'murdering is not wrong' is, because that sentence does not, plausibly, express the same mental state as 'not murdering is wrong' (nor a stronger one). The negation problem is that there is a further task, over and above explaining what sentence 2 means, of explaining what sentence 1 means.

So how would things work with 'fowr'? Would there still be a further problem of explaining sentential negation? Well, I don't think so. Compare the following sentences:

3   blaming for murder is not fowr.
4   not blaming for murder is fowr.

By our stipulation as to the meaning of 'fowr', sentence 4 expresses FOR(not blaming for murder). So does that leave us with a problem about how to explain the meaning of sentence 3? No—because 'blaming for murder is fowr' expresses a state of being for something, and our account of negation tells us which state will be expressed by the negations of sentences that express states of being for something. Since sentence 3 is the negation of 'blaming for murder is fowr', which expresses FOR(blaming for murder), it follows from our account that sentence 3 expresses FOR(not blaming for murder). So there is no further problem to explain—the account of what sentence 3 means drops directly out of the account.

You might think that this is *itself* a problem. For this answer is just the result that sentences 3 and 4 turn out to mean the very same thing—to express the very same state of mind. But that is precisely what we wanted to avoid in the case of 'wrong'! So shouldn't it be a bad result here, too? Again, I'm inclined to think not. Since 'wrong' is a term in ordinary English, we understand what it means, and are in a position to evaluate whether it should turn out that there will be a difference between the states of mind expressed by sentences 1 and 2. But 'fowr' is not a term of English. In fact, it is not even obvious that it *could* be a term of English. So it is not at all obvious why we should have any intuitions about whether 3 and 4 should turn out to express different states of mind, if 'fowr' were indeed introduced.

The equivalence of sentences of the form of 3 and 4 is, of course, very unusual. But again, it turns out that this is something that our semantic framework has the resources to explain. Recall that ordinary descriptive predicates do not, in general, correspond to distinct attitudes; rather, they correspond to the same attitude toward some property ascribed to the subject of the sentence. Similarly, I said, normative predicates should not be taken to each correspond to its own unanalyzable attitude, either. The predicate 'fowr' is a very unusual predicate, because it does precisely this.

The closest thing to a descriptive predicate appearing to do the same thing might be 'true'. On the redundancy view of truth, 'that grass is green is true' expresses the belief that grass is green—there is no further property of the subject of the predicate that is contributed by 'true'. But it is not at all strange, given the redundancy view, to equate the following two sentences:

     5   that grass is green is not true.
     6   that grass is not green is true.

So similarly, it seems to me, we should not find the equation of 3 and 4 to be problematic, if 'fowr' were actually successfully introduced into English. So the negation problem does not arise all over again, and so it is fair game to appeal to the state of being for in order to do the work that we have. Doing so genuinely reduces the hard problem for the negation problem—*B*-type inconsistency—to the relatively easy problem of accounting for *A*-type inconsistency.

In Chapter 5, I will continue my argument in favor of this conclusion by showing how this account can easily be generalized to yield accounts of the other truth-functional connectives, and how it yields an obvious and straightforward account of not just inconsistency, but of logical inconsistency. I'll give the first explanatory expressivist account of logical inconsistency, and use this to give the first formally adequate explanatory expressivist accounts of logical entailment and of logical validity, including as a corollary what I claim is the first explanatory formally adequate expressivist account of the validity of Geach's original moral *modus ponens* argument. After tying up some further loose ends, I'll then show in Chapter 6 how to generalize all of these same features to a language with the expressive power of the predicate calculus.

5

Composition and logic

5.1 TRUTH-FUNCTIONAL CONNECTIVES

In section 4.1, I considered the analogy between the expressivist account of normative sentences that I am developing and the obvious expressivist account of descriptive sentences. On the obvious account, descriptive sentences express beliefs. If 'P' and 'Q' are descriptive sentences meaning that p and that q, respectively, then 'P' expresses the belief that p and 'Q' expresses the belief that q. From this, we can also easily see which attitudes should be expressed by complex sentences constructed out of 'P' and 'Q': 'not P' should express the belief that $\neg p$, 'P and Q' should express the belief that $p \wedge q$, 'P or Q' should express the belief that $p \vee q$, and so on. It is because of these rules that beliefs have their logical properties. Beliefs, after all, derive their logical properties from the properties of their contents. Beliefs are inconsistent with one another when their contents are inconsistent, and it is these compositional rules that guarantee that when you negate a sentence, you get a belief with the negated content.

Since expressivists want to be able to explain how normative sentences can have all of these same properties, it is natural for them to hope that they can be explained in the same way. And that is what the account of negation that I offered in Chapter 4 allows us to do. It allows us to state analogous accounts of conjunction and disjunction that are intuitively well motivated, but behave in exactly the same way with respect to the attitude of being for that the obvious rules for descriptive sentences listed in the previous paragraph behave with respect to belief.

The definitions that I give below, and will motivate in just a moment, show how to do this. In the definitions, 'A' and 'B' are schematic letters to be replaced by sentences, for now with the restriction that they are to range only over sentences constructed recursively out of sentences that express states of being for something. The letters 'α' and 'β' replace descriptive gerundive phrases like 'blaming for murder' and 'preferring a to b', and '¬', '∧', and '∨' express gerundival connectives. So, for example, if 'α' is 'kissing' and 'β' is 'telling', then 'α∧β' is 'kissing and telling', '¬α' is 'not kissing', and so on. Treating 'is for' as taking gerunds for its complement is *strictly optional*, but since it is supposed to be a practical attitude—the sort that can motivate—I think this makes the most sense. Actions, the things that you can be motivated to do, are the kinds of thing that are expressed by gerunds. I'm thinking of them as properties of agents. Finally, I will continue to use 'FOR(α)' as a term denoting the state of being for α—it is not to be construed as a sentence.

PROPOSITIONAL LOGIC

base   Atomic sentences 'A', 'B', and so on express states of being for: FOR(α), FOR(β), and so on.

not   If 'A' expresses FOR(α), then '∼A' expresses FOR(¬α).

and   If 'A' expresses FOR(α) and 'B' expresses FOR(β), then 'A&B' expresses FOR(α∧β).

or   If 'A' expresses FOR(α) and 'B' expresses FOR(β), then 'A°B' expresses FOR(α∨β).

The intuitive idea here is simple. The attitude expressed by 'murder is wrong and stealing is wrong' should be the attitude that someone has who thinks that murder is wrong and stealing is wrong. So what should that be, if thinking that murder is wrong is being for blaming for murder and thinking that stealing is wrong is being for blaming for stealing? Intuitively, it should be the attitude of being for blaming for murder and blaming for stealing. That is what someone is for, who accepts the conjunction. And similarly for disjunction. Someone who thinks that murder is wrong or stealing is wrong is for blaming for murder or blaming for stealing.[1]

In Chapter 4, the solution that I offered to the negation problem enabled us to give a constructive compositional account of the negations of atomic normative sentences. That was an achievement, because no one else has shown how to do so. But it was still not very much. Relatively speaking, negations of atomic sentences are not very exciting. But now we can see that the account is much more powerful. It readily

---

[1] If you balk at this, be careful to distinguish whether you are balking at the treatment of conjunction or disjunction, or whether the problem derives from the treatment of 'wrong' as corresponding to being for blaming for, in the first place.

generalizes to allow us to give a constructive account of the state of mind expressed by arbitrarily complex sentences, so long as they are constructed out of the 'truth-functional' connectives. For example, take the sentence, 'if stealing is better than murdering, then it is not the case that stealing is wrong and murdering is not wrong'. This sentence expresses the state of being for (not (blaming for stealing and not blaming for murdering) or not preferring stealing to murdering), assuming the 'material' conditional to be defined in the ordinary way. And so on for any arbitrarily complex 'truth-functionally'-constructed normative sentence. The constructive account tells us what mental state it expresses, and then we can appeal to the general properties of the attitude of being for and the content of this state in particular, in order to explain its properties. This is a first, for expressivism, so it looks like progress, to me, and the progress appears not to be coincidental. It appears to come simply because we used the Basic Expressivist Maneuver to correctly diagnose what was creating the problem in the first place.

5.2 INCONSISTENCY

Among the properties that we are now able to explain are the logical properties of these states of mind. Moreover, doing so allows us to give an account of the logical properties of the sentences that express them. So let's start with inconsistency. Following the discussion in section 3.1, we say that any pair {'A','B'} of sentences is inconsistent just in case the mental states expressed by each are inconsistent. But all sentences in our toy expressivist language are normative sentences constructed out of atomic sentences that express states of being for by means of the rules listed above. So they all express states of being for. Since we are assuming that being for is an inconsistency-transmitting attitude, it follows that two such states are inconsistent just in case their contents are. So the problem of explaining why sentences in our expressivist language are inconsistent reduces to the problem of explaining why the contents of their expressed states of being for are inconsistent. So if 'A' expresses FOR(α) and 'B' expresses FOR(β), what we want is for it to turn out that α and β are inconsistent just in case 'A' and 'B' should be inconsistent.

But it turns out that our compositional rules tell us everything that we need to know about α and β in order to know whether they are inconsistent. For the compositional rules induce an isomorphism between the structure of 'A' and the structure of the content of the state of being for that it expresses. For all that each sentential connective does, is to 'move itself inside' the states of being for expressed by its components. So an arbitrary complex sentence constructed out of atomic normative sentences $A_1 \ldots A_n$, expressing the states $\text{FOR}(\alpha_1) \ldots \text{FOR}(\alpha_n)$ will express the state of being for a content that is structured out of $\alpha_1 \ldots \alpha_n$ in the same way as the original sentence is structured out of $A_1 \ldots A_n$, replacing '$\sim$' with '$\neg$', '&' with '$\wedge$', and '$^\circ$' with '$\vee$'.[2] So we will get the right logical inconsistency results for complex sentences in our normative language just in case the logic applying to the contents of states of being for has the obvious logical properties.

This would not amount to progress, if the contents of the states of being for were themselves normative. For then we would be appealing to the logic of a normative language in order to explain the logic of a normative language, and would not have gotten any further. But fortunately we know that the contents of the states of being for that are expressed by normative sentences are all descriptive. Each normative predicate 'F', we said, when ascribed to some subject, expresses the state of being for bearing some relation, R_F, to that subject. But since R_F is some descriptive relation, the states of being for that are expressed by the sentences in our language all have purely descriptive contents, and hence we can be confident that we can appeal to ordinary descriptive logic in order to understand why those contents are inconsistent when they are.

Moreover, the contents of states of being for, I've been saying, are properties, whose canonical expression (in English) is by means of gerunds. They are the kinds of thing that agents can be motivated to *do*. So all that we need, is for it to turn out that gerunds are governed by the obvious logical properties. I'll give a more rigorous treatment in Chapter 6, once we've added quantifiers to our logic, but for now the intuitive answer to this should be obvious. Kissing and telling entails kissing, and entails telling. Not kissing is inconsistent with kissing. Telling entails telling or smelling. And so on. Even though, properly speaking, gerunds express properties rather than propositions, they are still governed by the obvious logical inconsistency and entailment properties.[3] So by virtue of the isomorphism between sentences of our language and their contents, 'A' and 'B' turn out to be inconsistent when

---

[2] If this isn't immediately obvious, try proving it by induction on sentence complexity—the proof is trivial at each step.

[3] Recall, in any case, that nothing essential about my structural solution to the negation problem requires that being for be an attitude which takes a gerundival complement, rather than a sentential one.

they 'ought' to—that is, if they would, if they were governed by ordinary descriptive logic. And that is precizely the result that we wanted.

5.3 LOGIC

So far, I've only explained why 'A' and 'B' are guaranteed to be inconsistent if they would be inconsistent were they governed by ordinary propositional logic. But this is not, yet, an account of genuinely logical inconsistency. It follows from this account that if 'murder is wrong' expresses FOR(blaming for murder) and 'murder is shprong' expresses FOR(blaming for murder), then 'murder is wrong' and 'murder is not shprong' will turn out to be inconsistent. This is the right result, because if 'wrong' and 'shprong' have the same semantic interpretation, then these sentences *should* be inconsistent. But they should not turn out to be logically inconsistent, because an account of logical inconsistency should be indifferent to the actual interpretation of the non-logical terms. Logical inconsistency should be restricted to inconsistency in virtue of *form*.

It is precisely this feature of logical inconsistency for which previous expressivist accounts have typically failed to account. According to the kind of inconsistency which Gibbard has explained, for example, it turns out that 'Lake Winnebago is filled with water' and 'Lake Winnebago is not filled with H_2O' are inconsistent. But clearly this is metaphysical inconsistency rather than logical inconsistency, and is due to the interpretation of 'water' and of 'H_2O', rather than to the sentences' formal properties alone. Similarly, Michael Ridge (2006) has claimed to give a 'hybrid' expressivist account of logical validity, by appeal to the assumption that normative sentences express beliefs as well as noncognitive attitudes.[4] But Ridge's account mistakenly classifies arguments like the following as 'valid': 'Superman is a hero', 'if Clark Kent is a hero, then I'm a walrus'; 'I'm a walrus'. It fails to distinguish truth-preservingness from logical validity.[5] Finally, Horgan and Timmons (2006) expressivist 'logic' is constructed for a language in which the difference between normative and descriptive sentences is syntactically marked. But in English, normative and descriptive predicates do not

---

[4] Strictly speaking, of course, as I am using the term 'expressivist' in this book, I don't consider hybrid views like Ridge's to be versions of expressivism. See section 2.1.

[5] For a full explanation of what goes wrong with Ridge's account, see Schroeder (unpublished).

appear to be syntactically marked—whether a predicate is normative or descriptive depends on its actual interpretation. So since previous expressivist treatments of validity have failed to distinguish the inconsistency of sentences given their actual interpretation from logical inconsistency, it is important that we do so.

So 'A' and 'B' are logically inconsistent, we can say, just in case they would be inconsistent, no matter which interpretation we assigned to the atomic normative sentences of which they are composed. Interpretations for atomic normative sentences are assignments of states of being for which they express. So instead of constructing model worlds of which the sentences are true or false, what we essentially do is to construct model psychologies which involve accepting the sentences or not. 'A' and 'B' are logically inconsistent if there is no way of assigning psychological states to their basic components such that someone can consistently accept both.

Because the only assumption that I was making about inconsistency-transmitting attitudes was that bearing them simultaneously toward inconsistent contents is inconsistent, this only gives us an account of logical inconsistency for *pairs* of sentences. But we can easily generalize, and say that a set of n sentences is logically inconsistent just in case for some enumeration of those sentences, $\{'P_1', \ldots, 'P_n'\}$, $\{'P_1 \& \ldots \& P_{n-1}', 'P_n'\}$ is pairwise inconsistent, thereby reducing the more general case to the less general one. We can also give an obvious account of logical entailment, and say that a sentence 'A' entails a sentence 'B' just in case $\{'A', '\sim B'\}$ is logically inconsistent. And similarly, we can say that an argument with premises $'P_1', \ldots, 'P_n'$ and conclusion 'C' is logically valid just in case the set $\{'P_1', \ldots, 'P_n', '\sim C'\}$ is logically inconsistent.

With these definitions in tow, we can give a genuine explanation that is thoroughly expressivist-friendly of the logical validity of Geach's original *modus ponens* argument, assuming that we can treat it as involving the material conditional. Geach's argument, recall, looked like:

P1 Lying is wrong.
P2 If lying is wrong, then getting your little brother to lie is wrong.
C   Getting your little brother to lie is wrong.

By our definition of logical validity, this argument will be logically valid just in case $\{P1, P2, \sim C\}$ is logically inconsistent. But by the generalization of our account of logical inconsistency to sets larger than two, this is so just in case the set $\{P1 \& P2, \sim C\}$ is logically inconsistent.

And that will be so just in case the contents of the states of being for that are expressed by P1&P2 and by ∼C are inconsistent, no matter what interpretation we provide to the terms involved.

So to evaluate whether that is so, we have to look at what a consistent expressivist interpretation of P1, P2, and C would look like. Any interpretation must assign a state of being for to each atomic sentence involved. So without loss of generalization, P1 expresses FOR(α) and C expresses FOR(β), for arbitrary choice of α and β. Assuming the ordinary definition of the material conditional, it then follows from the rules for 'not' and 'or' that P2 expresses FOR($\beta \lor \neg\alpha$). Our rule for 'and' then tells us that P1&P2 expresses FOR($\alpha \land (\beta \lor \neg\alpha)$), and our rule for 'not' tells us that '∼C' expresses FOR($\neg\beta$).

Now, our account of logical validity says that the argument from P1 and P2 to C is logically valid just in case P1&P2 and ∼C are inconsistent under any interpretation. We are now looking at an arbitrary interpretation of P1&P2 and ∼C, so what we need to know is whether they are inconsistent. Our account of inconsistency says that they are, just in case the states of mind they express are—but since the states of mind they express are both states of being for something, and being for is inconsistency-transmitting, this follows just in case their contents are. But their contents are '$\alpha \land (\beta \lor \neg\alpha)$' and '$\neg\beta$', which are obviously inconsistent. So in this way we explain why Geach's original *modus ponens* argument is logically valid, at least in the elementary normative language that we have constructed in this chapter.

No features of this account should be in any way surprising. It works in exactly the way that the obvious expressivist account of descriptive sentences would work, except that instead of factoring into belief plus some property of the subject of the sentence, the attitudes expressed by normative sentences factor into being for plus some relation toward the subject of the sentence. I'm simply drawing out how to spell out an expressivist account that takes the analogy between normative and descriptive language seriously, and that, after all, is precisely the feature that is supposed to make expressivism promising. No surprises, here.

5.4 LOOSE ENDS—BACK TO *A*-TYPE INCONSISTENCY

So let's return, now, to the original *A*-type inconsistency between 'murdering is wrong' and 'not murdering is wrong'. When I gave my

account of disapproval in terms of being for, I passed over going back
and seeing what kind of light it shed on this case. But one objection
that one might have to my account of disapproval, is that it makes
it cease to be obvious why disapproval should be an inconsistency-
transmitting attitude, because it makes it far from obvious what is
inconsistent about disapproving of p and disapproving of $\neg p$. This is
because on my example account, 'murdering is wrong' expresses being
for blaming for murdering and 'not murdering is wrong' expresses
being for blaming for not murdering. But now it turns out that what
looked like A-type inconsistency in disapproval has turned out not to
be A-type inconsistency in being for at all. However these two states
of being for are related, they are not states of being for contents that
are the negations of one another. And so it ceases to be obvious how
we are going to capture the case of A-type inconsistency with which we
originally began.

To this I have three answers. My first answer is that it was never trivial
to show that disapproval was an inconsistency-transmitting attitude, and
this account merely draws our attention to the fact that there is something
important here to be explained. My second answer is that though I was
right to say, in Chapter 3, that capturing the inconsistency between
'murdering is wrong' and 'not murdering is wrong' *would* be easier
than capturing the inconsistency between 'murdering is wrong' and
'murdering is not wrong', provided that disapproval *were* inconsistency-
transmitting, it is far from obvious that these two sentences really *should*
turn out to be inconsistent. After all, some moral philosophers believe
in the existence of real moral dilemmas, which are supposed to be cases
in which it is wrong to do A and wrong not to do A at one and the
same time.[6] If there is a coherent view on which this is not only logically
possible, but actual, then plausibly the logic should not really yield the
result that it is impossible.

But my third answer is to show how to supplement our system
with an auxiliary assumption that will yield the result that 'murdering
is wrong' and 'not murdering is wrong' turn out to be inconsistent.
I don't know that the assumption is true, but I do think that it is
at least in the ballpark of the kind of assumption that should be

---

[6] Gibbard cites van Fraassen (1973) and Marcus (1980) as opposed to the result
that 'murdering is impermissible' and 'murdering is obligatory' should turn out to be
logically inconsistent. van Fraassen and Marcus are, as van Roojen (1996) puts it, 'no
logical slouches', so it would pay to be cautious about building this into our logic.

amenable to the sorts of folks who believe that these two sentences should turn out to be inconsistent, but would be rejectable by the folks on the other side, who believe that they should turn out to be compatible. At the very least, I think it is clear that some structurally similar account of 'wrong' can be adopted by parties on either side within which it will be possible for them to obtain the results that they prefer. In this way, my account can pass the problem off without taking a stand. Whichever the camp to which you belong, you should find the approach that I am offering amenable, provided only that you are willing to accept or to reject the required assumption, as appropriate.

In order to see what assumption we need, compare the following sentences with which we are concerned:

'murdering is wrong'	expresses	FOR(blaming for murdering)
'murdering is not wrong'	expresses	FOR(not blaming for murdering)
'not murdering is wrong'	expresses	FOR(blaming for not murdering)

Those who believe that 'not murdering is wrong' should be inconsistent with 'murdering is wrong' believe this because they believe that it entails 'murdering is not wrong'. We can capture this result, if only we can capture how the content that the first expresses being for entails the content that the second expresses being for. That is, that blaming for not murdering entails not blaming for murdering.

Now I have been proceeding on the assumption that the logic governing the gerunds that express the complements of 'being for' simply has the ordinary properties we would expect for 'not', 'and', and 'or'. In Chapter 6, I'll show how to derive its logical properties from ordinary predicate logic. But we can capture the result that blaming for not murdering logically entails not blaming for murdering, if only we are willing to supplement this with a logic of blaming which has the required property. The assumption that we would need to encapsulate in our logic of blaming would be that it is impossible to both blame for murdering and blame for not murdering. How plausible this assumption is obviously turns on how we understand what it is to blame for something. But if we could be allowed this much, then we could recast our account of inconsistency in terms of the logical inconsistency of the contents of the expressed states of being for, given ordinary predicate logic supplemented by the logic of blaming.

I don't know whether the required assumption about blaming is true or not. But strikingly, it *does* seem to be at least in the ballpark of the kind of assumption that could possibly be accepted by those who think that real moral dilemmas (situations in which you ought both to do something and to not do it) should not turn out to be possible, and the kind of assumption that would be rejected by those who think that real moral dilemmas are genuine possibilities. Those who think that real dilemmas can't be possible seem to think that you can't be to blame no matter what—that there is something incoherent about blaming someone no matter what she does. And those who think that real dilemmas are possible would reject this. They would think that there is nothing incoherent about blaming someone no matter what she does. In fact, many do say something very similar to this—that it makes sense for the agent to feel regret, or perhaps guilt, no matter what she does. In this way, we can explain the original *A*-type inconsistency in a way that should appeal to those who really think that it is a kind of inconsistency, but which relies on an assumption that would easily be rejected by those who think that there is no inconsistency in this case.

I worry a little bit that the features required of the logic of blame in order to yield the result that 'murdering is wrong' and 'not murdering is wrong' turn out to be inconsistent may be a little too strong for plausibility. But though I'm using the blaming account of 'wrong' as an illustrative example, I'm not particularly wedded to it. A different idea about 'wrong' is that 'murder is wrong' expresses being for avoiding murdering. On this account, the assumption required to yield the inconsistency is that it is impossible to both avoid murdering and avoid not murdering, which *is*, in fact, a highly plausible assumption about the logic of avoiding. So how easy it is to get 'murdering is wrong' and 'not murdering is wrong' to turn out to be inconsistent will obviously turn on which account we give of the attitude expressed by 'murdering is wrong'. And this should be no surprise; 'murdering is permissible' and 'not murdering is permissible' should not turn out to be inconsistent, so the inconsistency of 'murdering is wrong' and 'not murdering is wrong', if they really are inconsistent, clearly must turn on the meaning of 'wrong', rather than the meaning of 'not'.

So this is, again, an attractive explanatory benefit. The framework that I have offered can remain neutral on this question, offering ways for those who like either result to capture their views. Our loose ends having been covered, in Chapter 6 I'll return to the main thread, and show how to generalize the approach of this chapter to allow for a normative language with the expressive power of the predicate calculus.

6

Predicates and quantifiers

6.1 PREDICATES

The structural problem about negation was a general one. Unless the attitudes expressed by normative sentences have sufficient structure, there is simply no place in which sentential negation can operate. But it wasn't a problem simply about negation, because it also meant there was no place for conjunction to operate, for disjunction, or for conditionals. In fact, it is this place in which all interesting linguistic constructions need to work. In this chapter, I'll continue to make my case that the expressivist strategy that I'm outlining is on the only possible track, by showing that it leads immediately to a perfectly natural account of quantifiers.

To introduce the general treatment of predicates and quantifiers with precision, I'm no longer going to pretend that our object language is a fragment of English; we can translate the syntax back to a language that looks more like English once we understand how to semantically interpret the language, and why the account of logical inconsistency is formally adequate. So in general, let our normative language consist of a class of singular terms, a,b,c, and so on, variables x,y,z, and so on, and n-place predicates F,G,WRONG,BETTER, and so on.

Quantifiers, of course, require us to have a way of understanding open sentences semantically, and so to warm up for that, we are going to need a more robust understanding of the semantic contribution of predicates. I began in section 4.2 by saying what mental state 'murder is wrong' expresses, but the account yields an obvious story about what 'wrong' means, in general. And similarly for 'better'. In general:

wrong If 'a' denotes o, then 'WRONG(a)' expresses FOR(blaming for o).

better   If 'a' denotes o_1 and 'b' denotes o_2, then 'BETTER(a,b)' expresses
FOR(preferring o_1 to o_2).

Since our sentential connectives only tell us how to operate on sentences
that express states of being for something, and only yield states of being
for something, I'm going to abstract away from the state of being for,
and notice the relationship between the subject to which 'WRONG' is
ascribed, on the left, and the content of the state of being for that the
sentence expresses. The contents of states of being for, as I've been
treating them, are properties, and the content of this one is that of
blaming for o. Moreover, there is a systematic connection between the
thing said to be wrong and the property that the sentence expresses
being for.

So what the predicate 'WRONG' contributes, is a function from objects
to properties. For any object assigned to 'a' (in this case, as I'm
treating it for simplicity, the relevant category is action-types), 'WRONG'
contributes the property of blaming for that thing. And this property
is the property that the atomic sentence 'WRONG(a)' expresses being for.
Similarly, 'BETTER', which is a two-place predicate, contributes a function
from *pairs* of objects to properties—the property of preferring the first
of the pair to the second.

So far, I have been treating 'FOR' as taking gerunds for its complement.
But English gerunds are not going to be precise enough for all of our
purposes. The important thing for us is that states of being for take
as their contents properties under some description. So in order to
represent these, all that we need is some canonical way of forming
structured terms to denote these properties. English gerunds have done
fine for us so far, but they will not stand up to full generality, and are
subject to scope ambiguities that we need to avoid.

So in order to describe these properties precisely, I am going to
introduce the device of lambda-abstraction. Blaming for murder, I have
said, is a property. It is the property that Allan has, if Allan is blaming for
murder. That is, if $(\lambda z(z \text{ is blaming for murder}))(\text{Allan})$. I will be treating
'$\lambda z(z \text{ is blaming for murder})$' as a term denoting the property of blaming
for murder. So conveniently, '$\lambda z(z \text{ is blaming for } x)$' denotes a function
from values of x to properties—the properties of blaming for that value
of x. So to formalize our semantics, we will express the contribution of
predicates by employing such open lambda-abstractions. Keep in mind
that open lambda-abstractions do not denote properties. They denote
functions from objects to properties, which is how our framework

requires us to think about the semantic contribution of predicates. The following official account is formulated for full generality:

predicates   If 'F' is an *n*-place predicate, then '$F(x_1, \ldots x_n)$' is a well-formed formula, and corresponds to an $n+1$-place relation, $R_F(z, x_1, \ldots x_n)$, so that if 'a_1', . . . 'a_n' are singular terms denoting $o_1, \ldots o_n$, then '$F(a_1, \ldots a_n)$' expresses FOR$(\lambda z(R_F(z, o_1, \ldots o_n)))$. We say that $\lambda z(R_F(z, x_1, \ldots x_n))$ is the *semantic value* of '$F(x_1, \ldots x_n)$'.[1]

For simplicity, I'll reserve 'z' as a metalanguage variable to be bound by the lambda operator. The intuitive idea here is simple, and the same as before; only we now say, '$\lambda z(R_F(z, o_1, \ldots o_n))$' instead of 'bearing R_F to $o_1, \ldots o_n$'. This simply allows for greater precision.

Given the obvious constraints on well-formed formulas in our normative language, we can now re-introduce our definitions of 'not', 'and', and 'or' as connectives that can apply to open sentences. Again, here they are, formulated for full generality:

PREDICATE LOGIC CONNECTIVES

~   If 'A' is a well-formed formula whose semantic value is $\lambda z(\alpha)$, then '~A' is a well-formed formula and has semantic value $\lambda z(\neg \alpha)$.[2]

&   If 'A' is a well-formed formula whose semantic value is $\lambda z(\alpha)$, and 'B' is a well-formed formula whose semantic value is $\lambda z(\beta)$, then 'A&B' is a well-formed formula and has semantic value $\lambda z(\alpha \wedge \beta)$.

o   If 'A' is a well-formed formula whose semantic value is $\lambda z(\alpha)$, and 'B' is a well-formed formula whose semantic value is $\lambda z(\beta)$,

---

[1] A note on terminology. In Chapter 2, I argued that expressivists need to be understood as claiming that sentences—even descriptive sentences—have mental states for their primary semantic values, rather than propositions or truth-conditions. The idea was that the primary job of an expressivist semantics is to assign sentences to mental states, and for descriptive sentences, that doesn't work by first assigning them to the contents of those beliefs. But here I introduce 'semantic value' as a technical term for something other than a mental state. In Chapter 11, I'll offer a complicated twist on the question of the relationship between semantic values and propositions.

[2] In Chapters 4 and 5, I used Greek letters like 'α' and 'β' as standing in for gerunds. Here and in the following chapters, I use them as schematic letters standing for arbitrary formulas in our descriptive metalanguage. Similarly, in Chapters 4 and 5, I used capital letters like 'A' and 'B' as schematic sentence letters in the object-language; here and in what follows I generalize and use them as schematic letters standing for arbitrary formulas in our object-language.

then 'A°B' is a well-formed formula and has semantic value $\lambda z(\alpha \vee \beta)$.

⊃ If 'A' is a well-formed formula whose semantic value is $\lambda z(\alpha)$, and 'B' is a well-formed formula whose semantic value is $\lambda z(\beta)$, then 'A⊃B' is a well-formed formula and has semantic value $\lambda z(\alpha > \beta)$.

Given the definition of closed sentences (below), these definitions simply generalize our earlier definitions to apply to open sentences, and add the appropriate (interdefinable) clause for the 'material' conditional. So any sentence open in n variables, $x_1, \ldots x_n$, is to be understood semantically in the same way as a predicate with n arguments. It contributes a function from n-tuples of objects to properties, where the property is the content of the state of being for that would be expressed by the closed sentence that we would get by replacing each variable with a singular term denoting the corresponding object.

6.2 QUANTIFIERS

So, for example, in order to be able to say, 'everything is either wrong or not wrong', we are going to need to be able to abstract out the contribution of 'wrong or not wrong'. Its contribution, as noted in the previous paragraph, is *also* a function from objects to properties. For each object o, it contributes the property of blaming for o or not blaming for o. That is, $\lambda z(z$ is blaming for o or z is not blaming for o). And this is the property the sentence 'o is wrong or o is not wrong' expresses being for.

So imagine someone who thinks that everything is wrong. What is she for? Well, the obvious answer is that she is for blaming for everything. But what is this thing, blaming for everything? Well, it is a property. It is the property that Allan has when he is blaming for everything. That is, when Allan has the property, $\lambda z(\forall x(z$ is blaming for x)). So plausibly, thinking that everything is wrong is just being in the following state: FOR($\lambda z(\forall x(z$ is blaming for x))). Unsurprisingly, this is exactly the same kind of picture as we had for the sentential connectives. With each sentential connective, the move from the sentence to the attitude expressed involved 'pushing the connective inside' the state expressed. The same goes, it seems, for the quantifiers. So this yields the following account:

∀ If 'A' is a well-formed formula whose semantic value is $\lambda z(\alpha)$, then '∀x(A)' is a well-formed formula and has semantic value $\lambda z(\forall x(\alpha))$.

∃   If 'A' is a well-formed formula whose semantic value is $\lambda z(\alpha)$, then
    '∃x(A)' is a well-formed formula and has semantic value $\lambda z(\exists x(\alpha))$.

We then define closed sentences in the normal way, and say that only closed sentences express states of mind. The state of mind expressed by a closed sentence 'A' is FOR(α), where α is the semantic value of 'A'.

6.3 LOGICAL INCONSISTENCY

We are now in a position to give an explanatory account of logical inconsistency for the normative language that we have just introduced, under its expressivist interpretation. Start by defining binary inconsistency as follows: any set of two object-language sentences, {P,Q}, is inconsistent just in case it is inconsistent for anyone to accept both P and Q. Accepting a sentence is having the state of mind that the sentence expresses, so it follows that {P,Q} is inconsistent just in case it is inconsistent to be in the states of mind expressed by each. Since each sentence in our language expresses a state of being for, and we are assuming that being for is an inconsistency-transmitting attitude, the inconsistency of P and Q can therefore be explained by the inconsistency of the contents of the states of being for that they express.

But now note that our definitions induce an isomorphism between the structure of any sentence in our object-language and the content of the state of being for that it expresses. Start with any sentence in the object-language. Replace each predicate F with its corresponding relation R_F, replace each occurrence of the object-language '∼' with '¬', each occurrence of '&' with '∧', each occurrence of '∘' with '∨', and each occurrence of '⊃' with '>'. Replace each object-language singular term with a co-referential metalanguage singular term, and each object-language variable with a corresponding metalanguage variable, each occurrence of the object-language '∀' with the metalanguage '∀', and each occurrence of the object-language '∃' with the metalanguage '∃'. Then place a lambda-operator out front binding the variable z, which appeared when you replaced any predicate F with R_F. What you have before you is a lambda-abstraction which denotes the content of the state of being for expressed by the object-language sentence with which you started. By hypothesis, it involves only non-normative terms.[3]

---

[3] Again, if this seems less than obvious, prove it by induction on formula complexity—the compositional rules guarantee that the proof is trivial at each stage.

So what remains is to establish that the 'right' inconsistency relations hold for these lambda-abstractions. This is the problem of rigorously establishing that gerunds obey the right logic, which I intuitively motivated, but deferred, in section 5.2. But now we have the right tools in order to see why they do. Since only closed sentences express states of mind, we know that the formula governed by the lambda-operator is open only in z. So for each lambda-abstraction, $\lambda z(R(z))$, remove the lambda-operator, and replace the variable 'z' with an arbitrary fixed constant, 'z*'. (Intuitively, since being for a property is being for *having* that property, 'z*' designates the agent.) So long as you supply the same constant 'z*' to every sentence, we have now replaced the properties, which strictly speaking are the contents of states of being for, with closed sentences in a non-normative language employing the predicate calculus.

So we can now help ourselves to the ordinary account of logical inconsistency for predicate logic, in order to explain why these sentences are inconsistent in the right cases. That induces the right inconsistency results for the logic of properties, expressed by the lambda-abstractions that we get by substituting the variable 'z' for each appearance of 'z*' and binding z by a lambda-operator. And that, in turn, induces the right inconsistency results in our object language, by means of the isomorphism that we constructed.

So this is a general account of inconsistency, and we can generalize it in the same way to obtain an account of logical inconsistency. 'A' and 'B' are logically inconsistent if they would be inconsistent under any interpretation. We can also define inconsistency for sets of more than two sentences in the obvious way, as before, and likewise for logical entailment and logical validity. Let's apply the account, in order to illustrate how it can account for the logical validity of the following improvement on Geach's example:

> P1 Everything is wrong or better than murdering.
> P2 Defenestration is not better than murdering.
> C   Defenestration is wrong.

The sentences of our normative object-language which formulate this argument are as follows:

> P1 $\forall x(\text{WRONG}(x)^\circ\text{BETTER}(x,\text{murdering}))$
> P2 $\sim\text{BETTER}(\text{defenestration},\text{murdering})$
> C $\text{WRONG}(\text{defenestration})$

Again, by our definitions, what we need to show in order to show that the argument is logically valid, is to show that the set, {P1&P2,∼C}, would be an inconsistent set no matter what interpretation we provide of 'murdering', 'defenestration', 'WRONG', and 'BETTER'. By our actual semantics, P1 expresses FOR($\lambda z(\forall x(z$ is blaming for x or z is preferring x to murdering))), P2 expresses FOR($\lambda z(z$ is not preferring defenestration to murdering)), and C expresses FOR($\lambda z(z$ is blaming for defenestration)).

Without loss of generality, under any interpretation we can replace 'blaming for' with the arbitrary two-place relation 'R_F', 'preferring . . . to' with the arbitrary three-place relation 'R_G', 'murdering' with the arbitrary term 'm' and 'defenestration' with the arbitrary term 'd'. So under any interpretation, P1 would express a state that could be represented as FOR($\lambda z(\forall x(R_F(z,x)\lor R_G(z,x,m)))$), P2 would express a state that could be represented as FOR($\lambda z(\neg R_G(z,d,m))$), and C would express a state that could be represented as FOR($\lambda z(R_F(z,d))$). So then P1&P2 would express FOR($\lambda z(\forall x(R_F(z,x)\lor R_G(z,x,m))\land\neg R_G(z,d,m))$), and ∼C would express FOR($\lambda z(\neg R_F(z,d))$). So to see whether these are inconsistent, what we do is to see whether their contents are inconsistent, and to do that, what we do is to strip off the lambda-operators, replace z with a constant, z^*, and apply ordinary propositional logic.

This is easy to do: the content of the state of being for expressed by P1&P2 corresponds to $\forall x(R_F(z^*,x)\lor R_G(z^*,x,m))\land\neg R_G(z^*,d,m)$, and that of ∼C corresponds to $\neg R_F(z^*,d)$. By universal elimination, the first of these entails $(R_F(z^*,d)\lor R_G(z^*,d,m))\land\neg R_G(z^*,d,m)$ in ordinary predicate logic, which is equivalent to $R_F(z^*,d)\land\neg R_G(z^*,d,m)$. And this is obviously inconsistent with $\neg R_F(z^*,d)$, because its first conjunct is. So the contents of the states of being for expressed by P1&P2 and by ∼C would be inconsistent, no matter what interpretation we assigned to the nonlogical terms, and hence the argument considered is logically valid, as it should be.

6.4 TAKING STOCK

So far, what we have is an account of how to give an expressivist semantics for a purely normative language with the expressive power of the predicate calculus. For such a language, I've explained how to give a compositional semantics that tells us exactly what mental state is expressed by arbitrarily complex sentences, in a way that is constructive, unlike any other currently advocated expressivist account. Such states are all states of being for, and our semantics tells us what their content is. This is just as we would expect for a compositional expressivist semantics for descriptive sentences—we would expect them all to express beliefs, and for the semantics to allow us to pick out *which* beliefs by their contents.

For such a language, I've shown not only how to solve the pesky negation problem, but how to give a formally adequate account of logical inconsistency, and derivatively of logical entailment and logical validity. This constitutes an affirmative answer to Bob Hale's (1993) question, 'Can There Be a Logic of Attitudes?'. The answer is 'yes, at least so long as they are all, at bottom, attitudes of the same kind toward different contents'. And finally, the *only* assumption required in order to carry off this explanation, was that being for is an inconsistency-transmitting attitude: that it is inconsistent to be for α and also be for $\neg\alpha$. And this is something that expressivists needed to explain anyway, and which it is at least respectable for them to hold out optimism that they will be able to explain, since belief and intention provide good models.

So this is a powerful explanatory account. But I think it should be in no way surprising. All that I did, was to follow the playbook for the compositionality of descriptive language. As I pointed out in section 4.1, there would be a negation problem for descriptive language, too, if we assigned to each descriptive predicate its own unanalyzable attitude. So following the Basic Expressivist Maneuver, I proposed that there is no choice for expressivists but to apply the same solution to normative language. Corresponding to each normative predicate, I proposed, we should have not a unique and unanalyzable distinct noncognitive attitude, but rather simply a different case of being for. This gave us an 'extra place' in which to have a negation, so that we could have a genuinely compositional account in exactly the same way as it worked for ordinary descriptive sentences and belief.

The very same move that solved the negation problem gave us the same 'extra place' in which to locate sentential conjunction and disjunction and the quantifiers. In each case, the connectives and quantifiers 'hopped inside' the attitude of being for. But this is again not strange or unexpected—it is exactly what happens for descriptive sentences and belief. Conjunctive sentences express beliefs in conjunctions, disjunctive sentences express beliefs in disjunctions, existentially quantified sentences express beliefs in existential quantifications, and so on. The very same principles worked for us, for normative sentences.

And finally, we were able to use ordinary logic in order to explain the inconsistency of normative states of mind in *exactly the same way* as we would use ordinary logic in order to explain the inconsistency of beliefs. In each case, we need two things: first, an assumption in the philosophy of mind, to the effect that belief and being for are inconsistency-transmitting attitudes. And second, we simply needed to know what the contents of these states were. The fact that they are inconsistency-transmitting, together with their actual contents, tells us everything that we might like to know about them, in terms of their consistency with one another.

So I take it that this constitutes more than a possibility proof that expressivists can explain certain things that many had previously despaired of their explaining. I take it that it constitutes a positive argument that any viable expressivist view will have to look something very much like the account that I am offering. It will have to factor the attitudes corresponding to normative predicates into a more general attitude and a property of or relation to the subject, use that to distinguish between internal and external negation, and likewise for every other sentential connective and the quantifiers. The resulting account succeeds at what it does in precisely the way that I advertised that expressivism hopes to succeed—by insisting on the idea that normative and descriptive language work in the *same way*.

This doesn't mean that the view collapses into cognitivism, however, because the general attitude that normative sentences express is not belief. It is, instead, a noncognitive attitude. Correspondingly, though this was an optional feature of the way I proceeded, I've been treating the state of being for as having a somewhat different structure from belief. Instead of treating it as taking propositions for its objects, as if it were representing how the world is in the way that beliefs do, I've been treating it as taking properties for its objects. Properties are how I think about things that you can *do*, in the broadest sense, and so I've been thinking of being for as concerned with what you can *do*, rather than with how things *are*. Blaming for murder is something that you can do; so are avoiding murdering and preferring stealing to murdering. They are the kinds of properties that you are for, when you have normative thoughts. So normative thought, on this picture, is tied to action, in the broadest possible sense. When you are for something, I think, then other things being equal, that is what you do. So understood, it is a motivating state, and hence naturally understood as akin to desire, rather than belief.

Moreover, this initial success in carrying out the expressivists' semantic program corresponds to grounds that expressivists and their predecessors have traditionally cited for optimism that it should be possible to do such a thing. As I noted in Chapter 1, for example, Hare (1952) and Smart (1984) cite the logical behavior of complex commands as evidence that it *must* be possible to give a semantics for 'truth-functional' compounds of normative sentences, and their reasoning applies equally well to quantifications over normative sentences. After all, they point out, the two commands 'shut the door' and 'don't shut the door' are contradictory commands. And we can give conjunctive commands as well: 'shut the door and open the window' is the conjunction of 'shut the door' and 'open the window', and behaves as we would expect a conjunction to behave—it contradicts all of the commands which contradict either of its conjuncts, for example. And similar evidence goes for disjunctive commands, such as 'shut the door or open the window'. Finally, we can even give quantified commands such as 'shut every door', which also behave in the right ways—for example, by being contradicted by 'don't shut this door', for any given value of 'this door'.

In a similar vein, Gibbard (2003) has argued that the existence of negative, conjunctive, and conditional intentions is evidence that it must be possible to construct an expressivist account for normative language that can deal with constructions like negations, conjunctions, and conditionals. Moreover, we might add to Gibbard, we can also have quantified intentions, such as the intention to shut every door, which behaves in all relevant ways like a quantified intention ought—including that it conflicts with the intention to not shut *this* door, for any given door. As with Hare and Smart's evidence, Gibbard's evidence is grounds for expressivist optimism that it *must* be possible to construct an expressivist semantics for a simple normative language with these kinds of constructions, which will yield the right sort of logical properties.

The problem with Hare, Smart, and Gibbard's grounds for optimism, however, is that they don't stretch very far. Though we can conjoin imperatives, conjoining imperatives with indicatives is a tricky matter, except in very unusual cases. Similarly, though we can disjoin imperatives, disjoining imperatives with indicatives is tricky, except in very unusual cases. And conditionals with imperatival antecedents are very far from having the status of 'something that everyone needs to be able to account for, anyway'.

So while considering the case of imperative sentences seems to license optimism that if normative sentences are like imperatives, it should be possible to make sense of disjunctions of normative sentences, it does not seem to license optimism that we should be able to make sense of disjunctions of normative sentences with descriptive sentences. It is to this latter problem that we turn in the next two chapters—the project of how to construct a semantics for a language containing both normative and descriptive predicates, in which they can combine into complex sentences with both normative and descriptive parts. Consideration of the case of imperatives does not inspire optimism on this score.

PART III

DESCRIPTIVE LANGUAGE

7

Descriptive language and belief

7.1 DESCRIPTIVE LANGUAGE

The result of Chapters 4 through 6 is that things are starting to look pretty good for expressivism. At least, they are looking much better than many theorists could have suspected. The elementary language that we have constructed shows that there *could* be a purely normative expressivist language with the expressive power of the predicate calculus that had all of the right logical properties. But that is still, unfortunately, a long way off seeing how the language that we actually speak could be an expressivist language. The most glaring difference for us, at this point, between our toy normative language and natural language, is that natural languages have *both* normative *and* descriptive predicates. It turns out that this is a Big Deal. Not only do natural languages have both normative and descriptive predicates, they have one set of sentential connectives that operate on normative and descriptive sentences alike. And most importantly, the very same sentential connectives can combine normative and descriptive sentences to make complex sentences with some normative parts and some descriptive parts. And all of this is some kind of major obstacle to the view that we have developed so far.

The problem is this: we have seen how to develop parallel constructive semantic accounts of descriptive and of normative sentences. The descriptive sentences express beliefs, and the compositional rules tell us how to get from the beliefs expressed by the component sentences to the belief expressed by the complex sentence. The normative sentences, on the other hand, express states of being for, and the compositional rules tell us how to get from the states of being for expressed by the component sentences to the state of being for expressed by the complex sentence. And all of this would be really swell, if we simply spoke two parallel languages, a descriptive one and a normative one, each with its own set of sentential connectives.

But the arguments are compelling that the sentential connectives should be given a univocal interpretation, whether applied to normative sentences or to descriptive sentences. We do not have to check sentences to see whether they are well formed, having a sense of 'not' which matches whether their predicates are normative or descriptive. It is due to a *single* meaning of 'not' that all cases of {'A', 'not-A'} are inconsistent; not due to two meanings of 'not' together with rules about well formedness. And so it looks like we cannot have one set of connectives that operate on sentences which express beliefs and yield sentences which express beliefs, and a distinct set that operate on sentences which express states of being for and yield sentences which express states of being for.

You might, if you weren't thinking too far ahead, suppose that the thing to do would therefore be to abstract out a little bit, and to describe what our descriptive and our normative connectives have *in common*, and say that that is the univocal meaning of the sentential connectives. For example, the account for 'not' would look like:

not If 'A' expresses attitude K toward content α, then '∼A' expresses attitude K toward content ¬α.

This would get you a univocal treatment of the connectives for purely normative sentences and for purely descriptive sentences.[1] The same set of connectives could operate indiscriminately on sentences that express beliefs or on sentences that express states of being for, doing basically the same thing to each.

But this would be no progress at all! The hard case, once we try to give a treatment of a language involving both normative and descriptive predicates, is to have a treatment of complex sentences with both normative and descriptive parts. But this tells us nothing about what we are to do with them! Compare, for example, the sentence, 'murder is wrong or grass is green'. Its first disjunct, 'murder is wrong', expresses FOR(blaming for murder). Its second disjunct, 'grass is green', expresses BF(grass is green). But what kind of attitude should the sentence as a whole express? Belief? Or being for? We would get obviously the wrong results if we applied the same compositional rules as always

---

[1] Well, to be more careful, if different attitudes take different kinds of contents—for example, if beliefs take propositional contents and being for takes properties for its contents, then even the rule just stated does not clearly provide a univocal account, because '¬' would have to be ambiguously interpreted as propositional negation in one case and as property negation in the other. The point is not important, however, because this account doesn't work, anyway.

and simply chose one of the two! But obviously no treatment of the sentential connectives will be adequate, unless it generalizes to give the same treatment, in cases of complex sentences with both normative and descriptive parts.

So I think there is really nothing for it, but to conclude that all sentences must really express the *same kind* of attitude. The Basic Expressivist Maneuver led us to the observation that it was only because all descriptive sentences express the same kind of attitude, that it is possible to give a constructive compositional semantics for complex descriptive sentences. Similarly, it was only by treating all normative sentences as expressing the same kind of attitude that we were able to give a genuinely constructive compositional semantics for complex normative sentences. So if we want to combine normative and descriptive sentences under a uniform treatment, the only possible conclusion is that they will all have to express the same kind of attitude.

An independent argument leads to the same conclusion. In the semantics of Chapter 6, we could give a formally adequate explanatory account of the logical consistency or inconsistency of arbitrary sentences. But how did that work? First, we reduced the question of the inconsistency of sentences to the question of the inconsistency of the mental states they express. And then we reduced the question of the inconsistency of mental states to that of the inconsistency of their contents. It was only because all sentences in our language expressed the same kind of mental state, and this state was inconsistency-transmitting, that we could do so. As long as there are sentences expressing different kinds of attitudes in our language, the inconsistency between the mental states they express will have to be *B*-type inconsistency, which as I argued in Chapter 3, it is both unpromising to think that expressivists should be able to explain, and moreover will need to be explained infinitely many times over, for different pairs of attitudes. So again, what we need in order to retain the advantages of Chapter 6 is for every sentence in our language to express the same kind of attitude.

And that, I think, leaves us with two options, which for the expressivist are not really two options at all. On the one hand, we can try to generalize the semantics for descriptive sentences to apply to normative sentences. This would be to go with the view that every sentence expresses a belief. But that is just to give up on expressivism altogether. On the other hand, we could try to generalize our account of normative sentences, to apply to descriptive sentences. Since on our account, the normative sentential connectives operate only on sentences which express states of being for, and descriptive sentences express beliefs, we would only be able to do this if it turned out that beliefs *really are* states of being for.

Now this, I think, should seem like an unlikely conclusion for expressivists to draw. One of the principal motivations for expressivism in the first place was the idea that belief and desire are two very different kinds of psychological state, and belief is of the wrong kind in order to motivate. But now we are considering the view that believing is really a certain kind of being for. The proposal sounds both implausible on its face, and not at all like the kind of thing to which one would have antecedently expected expressivists to be friendly. Yet I don't see any way around it. The account that I've laid out so far does so many things that no expressivist account has been able to do, and for such obvious reasons, that I think it simply has to be the only game in town. And the whole trick to actually being able to say which mental states are expressed by complex sentences, and to being able to test their properties by appeal to the fact that the general attitude expressed is inconsistency-transmitting and then appealing to properties of its content, requires that all sentences express the same general kind of attitude. So if we're forced between a choice on which all sentences express belief-like states and one on which they all express desire-like states, there's no question which choice expressivists need to make.

One appropriate reaction at this point would be to conclude that this amounts to a *reductio* of expressivism. Belief cannot, according to this reaction, be analyzed in terms of a noncognitive attitude. Belief, after all—at least according to expressivists—has a mind-to-world direction of fit, but any noncognitive attitude worth the name must have a world-to-mind direction of fit.[2] This argument might be elaborated in a number of ways. I have some sympathy for this reaction. I agree that this is a very natural place to get off of the boat. But nevertheless, if we are going to explore the commitments of expressivism, then I think we have to see how this strategy *could* be developed. Only after we see where it leads, will we be in an adequate position to see whether it is worth getting there.

So that is what I propose to do in this chapter and in Chapters 8 through 10. In the remainder of this chapter, I'll show what sort of account of belief this approach would have to lead to. Then in Chapter 8, I'll explain how to generalize the semantics and logic of Chapter 6 in

---

[2] Compare, for example, the discussions of direction-of-fit in Anscombe (1957) and Smith (1987).

order to accommodate this account of the mental states expressed by descriptive sentences. There will be a significant problem about how complex descriptive sentences will end up being assigned the right truth-conditions, and in Chapters 9 and 10, I'll explore each of two answers to this problem. That will mostly do it for my positive suggestions on behalf of expressivism; in Chapters 11 and 12, I'll consider further directions and the sort of problems that I've left untackled, and what sort of lessons we should draw from this all.

7.2 A FIRST PASS

I've just been arguing that in order to incorporate normative and descriptive language into the same account, we are either going to have to allow that being for is really to be analyzed in terms of belief, or that belief is really to be analyzed in terms of being for. And it was obvious which of these expressivists would need to choose. So I'm going to start with a first-pass account of belief in terms of being for—an account which would really be nice for expressivists, if it were adequate. But it will turn out not to be adequate, and for precisely the same reasons that our original solution to the negation problem in Chapter 3 *was* adequate. The very same thing that allowed us to get out of the negation problem turns out to ruin the first-pass account, and this is what I call the *new* negation problem. Indeed, as we'll see in Chapter 9, like the original negation problem, the *new* negation problem is not only a problem about negation. But still, the first-pass account will put us on the right track to stating a more adequate account, and will allow for an explanation of why the resulting complications are unavoidable.

So here is my first pass: I say that believing that p is being for proceeding as if p. What we need, of course, in order to analyze believing that p as being for something, is some relation to p, so that we can construct a property out of p that is something that the believer can be for. This property is something that the believer *does* with respect to p, or at least is *for* doing with respect to p, when she believes that p. And so I call this relation *proceeding as if.* On my best gloss, to proceed as if p is to take p as settled in deciding what to do. So being for proceeding as if p is being for taking p as settled in deciding what to do. Assuming that being for has the motivational property that someone who is for α will tend to do α, other things being equal, it follows that someone who believes that p will tend to proceed as if p, other things equal. That is, it follows that she will tend to treat *p* as settled in deciding what to do. This is what believers do, so this is not, after all, a crazy thing to say about belief.

At any rate, I propose that we grant the plausibility of this proposal to expressivists, at least for the sake of argument, in order to see where it will lead. Similarly, I proposed in Chapter 3 that we grant to expressivists that the basic noncognitive attitude to which they appeal is inconsistency-transmitting, at least for the sake of argument, in order to see whether they could get their view to work with that assumption. And I proposed in Chapter 4 that we grant to expressivists the plausibility of analyses like that which says that 'wrong' expresses being for blaming for. It is true that all of these assumptions are challengeable. But that is just to say that even if expressivism is *structurally capable* of working, it may still, for all that, require a number of false assumptions in order to be *made* to work. Since I'm exploring the structural question of whether expressivism even *could* work, the appropriate strategy for us is to grant the assumptions and see where they lead.

If this analysis of belief were right, then we could immediately proceed to look at the semantic contribution of descriptive predicates. For example, since 'grass is green' should turn out to express the belief that grass is green, it follows from this analysis of belief that 'grass is green' would express being for proceeding as if grass is green (from now on, 'FOR(pai grass is green)', for short). And now it is easy to interpret the contribution of 'green' within the framework of Chapter 6. Calling something green is expressing being for proceeding as if it is green. That is, it is expressing being for bearing some relation to it. Which relation? Proceeding as if it is green. So on this view, it drops out that we can interpret descriptive predicates in the same way as we interpreted normative predicates. Just as with normative predicates, every descriptive predicate's semantic value is a function from objects to properties. In the case of 'wrong', this was the blaming-for-it function. In the case of 'green', it is the proceeding-as-if-it-is-green function. And similarly for every other descriptive predicate.

It would follow from this view, if it were correct, that we would need to make no adjustments to the semantic framework of Chapter 6. All that we would have to do would be to say, for each descriptive predicate, what its semantic contribution is. But that is easy: 'green' contributes $\lambda z(z$ is pai x is green), 'tall' contributes $\lambda z(z$ is pai x is tall), 'stranger than' contributes $\lambda z(z$ is pai x is stranger than y), and so on. Of course, we have to keep in mind that the words 'green', 'tall', and 'stranger than', which appear in the accounts of the semantic value of each predicate, should not be understood as being the *same* object-language words of which we are providing a semantics; rather, we should think of them as translations of the object-language descriptive predicates into our purely descriptive metalanguage.[3] But beyond that, there are no new complications, and all of the recursive definitions of the logical connectives and the accounts of logical inconsistency and so on go through exactly as before.

For example, 'everything is tall or stranger than something wrong' would express FOR(λz($\forall$x(z is proceeding as if x is tall $\lor$ $\exists$y(z is proceeding as if x is stranger than y $\land$ z is blaming for y)))). And so on.

7.3 THE NEW NEGATION PROBLEM

As I said, all of that would be very nice. But unfortunately, it cannot be exactly right, because we again have a problem with negation. I'm first going to explain what the problem is, before I diagnose where it comes from, and then go on to offer a suggestion about how we can get around it. The problem is that on any adequate expressivist account, it should turn out that 'grass is not green' expresses the belief that grass is not green. As we saw in Chapter 2, it is *by* expressing this belief that 'grass is not green' comes to have the propositional content (truth-conditions) that grass is not green. But it is easy to see that on the account that we have offered so far, this turns out not to be the case, as can be observed from the following table:

Table 1[4]

'grass is green'	expresses	FOR(pai grass is green)	meaning postulate
'grass is not green'	expresses	FOR(not pai grass is green)	from $\sim$
BF(grass is not green)	=	FOR(pai grass is not green)	analysis of belief

[3] One natural way to think about the contents of states of being for is as stated in a purely descriptive language of thought, and to think of the state of being for something in terms of an attitude toward the contents of sentences in this language of thought.

[4] In this table and in most of the discussion from here on, I drop the explicit lambda-abstractions, in order to make it easier to see what the important issues are. Strictly speaking, 'pai grass is green' is short for something that could more precisely be put something like 'λz(pai(z,that(G(g))))', where 'G' is a descriptive metalanguage predicate meaning 'green', 'g' is a metalanguage term denoting grass, and 'that' is a

So 'grass is not green' does not turn out to express the belief that grass is not green. In fact, under the semantics of Chapter 6, if there *were* a sentence expressing this belief, then it would not even be equivalent to 'grass is not green', unless proceeding as if grass is not green turns out to be equivalent to not proceeding as if grass is green.

Now, I haven't said very much at all about the notion of proceeding as if, yet. But still, it seems very unlikely that this could be so. It seems highly likely that someone could not take *p* as settled in deciding what to do, without thereby taking $\neg p$ as settled in deciding what to do. In fact, the problem is especially bad, because if anything, it looks like the belief that grass is not green is a state of being for a content that is *stronger* than that of the state expressed by 'grass is not green'. And this looks like a problem because it makes it look especially hard to see how the sentence could come to have the content of the belief, in that case. And so it looks like this view would be fated to assigning ordinary descriptive sentences the wrong truth-conditions, because it fails to assign them the right beliefs.

The problem, it turns out, is very general, and would result from any analysis of believing that *p* as being for some relation to *p*. Compare:

g   Jon thinks that grass is green.
gn1   Jon does not think that grass is green.
gn2   Jon thinks that grass is not green.

There are two places in which we can insert a negation in g. But the problem with our new analysis is that it yields three such places:

g*   Jon is for pai grass is green.
gn1*   Jon is not for pai grass is green.
gn2*   Jon is for not pai grass is green.
gn3*   Jon is for pai grass is not green.

The problem now is not allowing for too *few* ways of negating our original sentence; it is allowing for too *many*. We want gn2* and gn3* to both correspond to gn2, but there is no general reason to think that they are equivalent.

The problem arises for the same reasons that our solution to the negation problem worked. Just as we solved the negation problem for descriptive sentences by factoring *believing-green* into believing and

term-forming operator in the metalanguage that takes sentences and makes them into terms denoting their propositional contents. Clearly, it would be hard to see the key issue brought out by Table 1, if I wrote things out in this sort of way.

green, and solved the negation problem for normative sentences by factoring disapproval into being for and blaming, our analysis of belief in terms of being for factors belief into being for and proceeding as if. So the very same features that allowed us to get the requisite place in which to have a negation in order to solve the negation problem in the first place, create one too many places for a negation, here. And the problem is particularly pressing, because our compositional account of the meanings of the sentential connectives 'moves' them directly inside the attitude of being for—that is, directly into the new location, between being for and proceeding as if, where we don't want anything to be able to go!

Moreover, the same would go for any analysis of belief in terms of being for something. Every such analysis would have the form of saying that believing that *p* is being for bearing *some* relation R to *p*. But no matter our choice of the relation R, whether it is *proceeding as if* or something else entirely, the problem is that it would need to commute with 'not'. But it is simply very hard to see what choice of R would both do so and result in a plausible analysis of belief.

It is crucially important to emphasize here, as a lot of what happens in Chapters 8 to 10 and 12 turns on this, that this is not merely a technical problem. The problem is one of principle, and the technical issue is merely its symptom. The issue is that expressivists are committed, solely in virtue of their account of purely normative sentences, to an account of the sentential connectives that works in a certain way, and this *forces their hand*, when it comes to applying the account to ordinary descriptive sentences. The new negation problem, at its highest level of generality, is the problem that the kind of account expressivists *need* for normative language gets the wrong results about descriptive sentences.

If we are going to solve this important problem, we are going to need some way in order to cancel the effects of this extra location in which we can now place negations. In the next section, I'll show how to do so. The trick that it requires is going to complicate our semantic apparatus, but it is also going to make things more interesting. For it is not entirely unmotivated, and it yields what I think are some interesting predictions about the nature of belief.

7.4 BIFORCATED ATTITUDES

The trick to solving this problem, I say, is to conclude that believing that *p* is not a matter of being for some relation to *p*. It is being for each of *two* relations to *p*. Believing that *p* involves being for proceeding as if *p*, true. But it also involves being for not proceeding as if ¬*p*. Believing that *p* is being for *each* of these things. It is, I shall say, a *biforcated attitude*—an attitude consisting of two states of being for.[5]

I first want to point out that although this complicates things, and strengthens our account of belief, given a plausible assumption, it does not strengthen it terribly much. For on a plausible assumption about the logic of proceeding as if, it is not possible to both proceed as if *p* and simultaneously proceed as if ¬*p*. Doing so would require both treating *p* as settled in deciding what to do and treating ¬*p* as settled in deciding what to do, and it would not be crazy to assume that it is not possible to do both.[6] At any rate, this is an assumption that I propose that we grant to the expressivist, for the sake of seeing where it leads. So if we supplement the logic of the contents of being for with a simple logic of proceeding as if which has this property, then it turns out that proceeding as if *p* entails not proceeding as if ¬*p*. And so it follows that if there were a sentence expressing FOR(pai *p*) and a sentence expressing FOR(¬pai ¬*p*), the former sentence would entail the latter, on the view from Chapter 6. So in that sense, it is not strengthening our account of belief terribly much to add in the state of being for not proceeding as if ¬*p*.

The relationship between the states, FOR(pai *p*) and FOR(¬pai ¬*p*), I call *commitment*. I will say that FOR(pai *p*) *commits* to FOR(¬pai ¬*p*), on the grounds that any state of mind that is inconsistent with the latter is also inconsistent with the former. That is what I will mean by 'commitment'. It follows that for states of being for, FOR(α) commits to FOR(β) just in case α logically entails β, given ordinary predicate logic plus the logic of proceeding as if. But I will also talk about beliefs, and in general, other *biforcated attitudes*, as committing to each

[5] As Mark van Roojen has pointed out to me, the motivation for this move is not immediately obvious. Be patient; it is motivated by its fruits, which I explain in the rest of this section. I don't have a tidier way of explaining why this is the kind of move we should expect to work, that is distinct from showing *how* it *does* work. Although, compare section 5.4.

[6] This assumption is not, however, obviously true. If propositions are Millian, then Jon may quite plausibly proceed as if *p* under one guise or mode of presentation, and yet proceed as if ¬*p* under a different guise or mode of presentation of *p*. I propose to grant the assumption, however, in order to see where the view leads. Perhaps the right way to elaborate this view is to treat proceeding as if as a sentential attitude. (This would complicate the analysis of belief somewhat.)

other, and in general, one attitude commits to another just in case every mental state that is inconsistent with the latter is inconsistent with the former. Two mental states are *commitment-equivalent*, I will say, just in case each commits to the other. For the case of states of being for, commitment-equivalence reduces to equivalence of their contents.

In general, I will say, *biforcated attitudes* consist of two states of being for, a *major* and a *minor*, where the major attitude commits to the minor. I'll use asterisks (*) to designate which attitude is major just to help us keep track. In the case of biforcated attitudes, it suffices to show that one attitude commits to another, to show that the first's major attitude commits to the major attitude of the second. For example, compare:

$$\text{BF}(p \wedge q) \quad = \quad \langle \text{FOR}(\text{pai } p \wedge q)^*, \text{FOR}(\neg \text{pai } \neg(p \wedge q)) \rangle$$
$$\text{BF}(p) \quad = \quad \langle \text{FOR}(\text{pai } p)^*, \text{FOR}(\neg \text{pai } \neg p) \rangle$$

Here is an argument that believing that $p \wedge q$ commits to believing that p. Why? Well, to believe that $p \wedge q$, you have to be in its major attitude. That is, you have to be in the state, $\text{FOR}(\text{pai } p \wedge q)$. But this state commits to the state, $\text{FOR}(\text{pai } p)$, on the assumption that proceeding as if $p \wedge q$ entails proceeding as if p (we'll consider whether, in fact, to accept this assumption in Chapter 9). But by the hypothesis that this is the major attitude of believing that p, it commits to the minor attitude of believing that p. It follows from the definition of commitment that it is transitive, so it follows that someone who believes that $p \wedge q$ is committed to each of the states of being for that are involved with believing that p. So it follows that she is committed to believing that p, *tout court*. It follows as a corollary that to show that two biforcated attitudes are commitment-equivalent, it suffices to show that their major attitudes are commitment-equivalent.

So why the long run-through about biforcated attitudes, major and minor attitudes, commitment, and commitment-equivalence? It sets us up to see why analyzing belief as a biforcated attitude puts us in a position to have a response to the new negation problem. Actually, to do that, I need to make just one more assumption. Our existing account of negation does not tell us how to negate a sentence that expresses a biforcated attitude; only how to negate a sentence that expresses a state of being for. So what we need to do is to generalize it. I'll assume that the account of negation for sentences that express biforcated attitudes is to apply our old account of negation to each attitude. Given that, let's go back and compare the mental state expressed by '∼P' to the belief that ¬*p*:

Table 2

'P'	expresses	$\langle \text{FOR}(\text{pai } p)^*, \text{FOR}(\neg \text{pai } \neg p)\rangle$	meaning postulate
'∼P'	expresses	$\langle \text{FOR}(\neg \text{pai } p), \text{FOR}(\neg\neg \text{pai } \neg p)^*\rangle,$	from ∼
BF(¬*p*)	=	$\langle \text{FOR}(\text{pai } \neg p)^*, \text{FOR}(\neg \text{pai } \neg\neg p)\rangle$	analysis of belief

It still does not turn out that the state of mind expressed by '∼P' is identical to the belief that ¬*p*. But we get something close: the two states are commitment-equivalent. The major attitude of the state expressed by '∼P' is FOR(¬¬pai ¬*p*), and the major attitude of the belief that ¬*p* is FOR(pai ¬*p*). But the contents of these two states of being for are logically equivalent. So since their major attitudes are commitment-equivalent, the state expressed by '∼P' and the belief that ¬*p* are commitment-equivalent. And that's the next-best thing to getting it right. Close enough, perhaps, for shaving.

At any rate, I think that this is the best that we can do, without losing one of the other advantages that we have already won. I think it is the solution to the new negation problem that expressivists are going to need. In fact, as I'll proceed to argue in the next two sections, this account of belief has at least two very nice features which grant it at least some interest quite independently of its relation to the expressivist project. In Chapter 8, I'll show how to complete the generalization of our semantics to sentences which express biforcated attitudes and show that the new semantics still attributes the right logical properties to sentences.

7.5 INCONSISTENCY-TRANSMISSION, BELIEF, AND INTENTION

One of the attractive features of the analysis of belief in terms of the attitude of being for is that it changes the dialectical situation with respect to the assumption that being for is *inconsistency-transmitting* — the assumption that we needed, in order to get all of this started. In Chapter 3, I proposed to grant to the expressivist that whatever noncognitive attitude they need to appeal to is inconsistency-transmitting, taking belief and intention as models, and allowing expressivists optimism that a third attitude might share that feature. But we had no positive reason to think there was any such attitude.

But now we can use the assumption that being for is inconsistency-transmitting in order to explain why belief is. Given that explanation, it follows that the assumption that being for is inconsistency-transmitting has explanatory value—we can *explain* why belief is, if we assume that being for is. The explanation is simple. We want to explain why believing that p and believing that $\neg p$ is inconsistent. According to our analysis, believing that p involves being for proceeding as if p. Likewise, according to our analysis, believing that $\neg p$ involves being for proceeding as if $\neg p$. But we assumed that proceeding as if p is inconsistent with proceeding as if $\neg p$. So on the assumption that being for is inconsistency-transmitting, it is inconsistent to be in both of these states, and hence inconsistent to have both of those beliefs.

Having explained the inconsistency-transmitting character of belief in terms of that of the attitude of being for, one might hope that the same approach could be extended to intention. There is no space here to consider the options completely, but among the possibilities is that intending to do A involves or commits to being for not proceeding as if you won't do A and also involves or commits to being for doing A. The latter claim would explain the motivational character of intention in terms of the motivational properties of being for, as well as guarantee that intention is inconsistency-transmitting. Whereas the former claim would explain why intending to do A is inconsistent with believing that you will not, without requiring that it involves any positive belief that you will, or even that you might.

If we took a view like this, then perhaps that would make it legitimate to take the inconsistency-transmitting character of being for as primitive. It would be licensed by its explanatory benefits, including its explanations of the inconsistency-transmitting character of both belief and intention, even though intention does not involve belief. There is no space to pursue the matter further here, but this seems an avenue worthy of further inquiry in its own right.[7]

---

[7] Recall from Chapter 3 that according to the view Bratman calls *cognitivism about instrumental reason*, the inconsistency-transmitting character of intention can and needs to be explained by the inconsistency-transmitting character of belief. The arguments that this does not work do not generalize to show that they can't both be explained by the inconsistency-transmitting character of some third attitude. See Bratman (forthcoming a).

7.6 DISBELIEF

According to the analysis that I have just offered, believing that *p* is a biforcated attitude, consisting both of the state of being for proceeding as if *p* and of the weaker state to which it commits: being for not proceeding as if ¬*p*. I noted that the second conjunct of this analysis added no great cost, because it is a commitment of being for proceeding as if *p*, anyway. But I think we can go further, and say that this is actually an *advantage* of this account of belief. For this account gives us an easy and obvious way of making sense of a state of *disbelief* or *doubt*, which is inconsistent with belief, but weaker than belief in the negation.

Disbelieving *p*, I say, or *doubting* it, is being for not proceeding as if *p*. It is inconsistent with believing *p*, because it is inconsistent with being for proceeding as if *p*, which is the major attitude of the belief that *p*. But it is weaker than believing ¬*p*. Believing ¬*p* involves both being for proceeding as if ¬*p*, and being for not proceeding as if ¬¬*p*. It is a nice feature of this account of belief, I think, that it allows us to make sense of a state of disbelief or doubt that is weaker than believing the negation.[8]

Take the case of a paradoxical sentence, such as the strengthened liar: a sentence which says of itself that it is not true. You don't believe the strengthened liar, but you don't believe its negation, either. Yet it would be odd to say that you are merely withholding belief, as if what you need is simply further evidence. Unlike mere withholding, your situation with respect to the strengthened liar is a settled one. You've worked out what your position is going to be, and it is to disbelieve both the strengthened liar and its negation.[9] What you are for, I say, is not proceeding as if *p*, and you are *also* for not proceeding as if ¬*p*.

---

[8] It was Barry Lam who independently convinced me that we plausibly need to be able to make sense of a state of disbelief that is weaker than belief in the negation. I owe many of the ideas here to discussions with him. But all problems with their application are due to me.

[9] Without going into too much detail, it is worth noting that the view that paradoxical sentences always fail to express propositions, and hence that we don't really need an alternative propositional attitude to belief and belief in the negation, in order to have toward paradoxical propositions, is not, I think, a very plausible one. Whether a given sentence is a case of the strengthened liar may turn on entirely contingent, extra-linguistic facts. In Scott Soames's example, consider the case of the sentence, 'Every sentence written in place P is not true' (Soames 1999: 193). Sentences like this are surely meaningful, and

Disbelief also comes in handy in surprising but nonparadoxical cases. Suppose that a purple elephant wanders into your office this afternoon and starts rooting around in your CD collection looking for 'Abbey Road'. You will be in a state of disbelief. You won't, very likely, believe that there is no purple elephant in your office rooting around for 'Abbey Road'—it will surely be making too much of a mess for that belief to stick around for very long. But if you are like me, you probably won't really believe that there is a purple elephant in your office rooting around for 'Abbey Road', either—even while it is happening, it will be too hard to credit. But neither will you be merely withholding about whether there is a purple elephant in your office rooting around for 'Abbey Road'. Or so I say. (Perhaps it will depend on how long the purple elephant stays for.) I say that you will be in a state of disbelief—you will be for not proceeding as if there is a purple elephant in your office (and probably for not proceeding as if there is not one, either).

Disbelief is again useful, in the case of unreliable testimony, like that involved in strategic games. If Cindy is a reliable source and tells you that *p*, about which you previously held no view, you are likely to come to believe that *p*. If she is reliably a liar but in a position to know whether *p*, then when she tells you that *p*, it makes sense for you to go on to believe that ¬*p*. And if she is completely unreliable, then your epistemic situation has in no way improved after she tells you that *p*, and you should continue to withhold. But if she is in a position to know whether *p* and also has the aim of trying to trick you about it, then when she tells you that *p*, you should be very cautious. Your epistemic position has improved, but in a way about which you need to be very careful. She could be lying, because you know that she is trying to trick you. Yet she could be trying to trick you *by* getting you to believe that she is lying. She is doing one or the other; you simply don't know which. What you ought to do is to *disbelieve* or *doubt* what she says, until you acquire further evidence, but not to believe that it is false.

So disbelief, or doubt, is I think an intuitive concept, of which it is natural to think that we have some pre-theoretical grasp, and which we can put to some philosophical work. I think it is an advantage, rather than a cost, of the analysis of belief as a biforcated attitude that

often either true or false. But if this very sentence is the only one written in place P—a contingent fact about place P—then it is paradoxical in the way that the strengthened liar is. So there are good arguments to think that even paradoxical sentences express propositions, and there is a good question about what attitude it is appropriate to take to them.

it leads immediately to the conclusion that there is such a state. This is a positive prediction of the account. Moreover, on the assumption that all sentences express biforcated attitudes, we can generalize the concept of disbelief to a general state of *disacceptance*. Disaccepting 'A', we can say, is being in the minor attitude of the state expressed by '∼A'.

It followed immediately from my definition of disbelief that disbelieving p and believing p are inconsistent states of mind. So one thing that we might hope for from our generalized account of disacceptance is that, in general, disaccepting 'A' is inconsistent with the state expressed by 'A'. But it is easy to observe that this is so. Without loss of generality, suppose that the state expressed by 'A' is the biforcated attitude, $\langle \text{FOR}(\alpha^1)^*, \text{FOR}(\alpha^2) \rangle$. Then the state expressed by '∼A' is $\langle \text{FOR}(\neg\alpha^1), \text{FOR}(\neg\alpha^2)^* \rangle$. So disaccepting 'A' is the minor attitude of this latter state: $\text{FOR}(\neg\alpha^1)$. And this is clearly inconsistent with the major attitude of the state expressed by 'A', above. So in general, disaccepting 'A' is inconsistent with accepting 'A'. Disaccepting 'A' is also, in general, weaker than accepting '∼A', because it is only the minor attitude of the state expressed by '∼A'. So in general, disaccepting 'A' is both inconsistent with accepting 'A' and weaker than accepting '∼A'. This is in general, I think, a nice result.

I take it that I have said enough, however, to illustrate that the analysis of belief I have given has certain attractions. Though it may be surprising that expressivists of all people would go in for such a view, it is not in being committed to such an analysis, I think, that the view breaks down. In the next chapter, I'll show how to generalize the semantic framework of Chapter 6 to a framework in which all sentences express biforcated attitudes, and then begin to assess some of its merits and demerits. I'll also prove that this generalized semantic framework will still allow us to capture the right logical properties of sentences. Readers who are willing to trust me on the details of the logic should look at sections 8.1 and 8.4, but may otherwise continue to Chapter 9.

8

Biforcated attitude semantics

8.1 BIFORCATED ATTITUDE SEMANTICS

In this section, I'm going to lay out how to generalize the semantics of Chapter 6 to a language in which all sentences express biforcated attitudes, rather than simple states of being for. The details look complicated, but the ideas are simple. Saying that normative sentences like 'murder is wrong' express pairs of noncognitive attitudes, $\langle$FOR(blaming for murder)*,FOR(blaming for murder)$\rangle$, where the two states of being for are the same, changes nothing, as far as the normative part of our language goes, from saying that they express just a single state. The only thing that changes is that we have to write everything twice. So the idea is that *all* sentences, not just descriptive ones, express pairs of noncognitive attitudes. All that remains, then, is essentially to write out the compositional rules in such a way that they apply to pairs of attitudes. The only real complication is that the binary sentential connectives will have to be sensitive to which attitude is major and which is minor in the biforcated attitudes that they operate on.

So there are no real surprises in the following definitions; the main complication is that conjunction and disjunction pair the major attitudes together and pair the minor attitudes together, which is dictated by the need to make conjunction and disjunction interdefinable (the definition for '$\supset$' is fixed by those for the others, and is slightly more complicated):

predicates If 'F' is an n-place predicate, then '$F(x_1, \ldots x_n)$' is a well-formed formula, and corresponds to a pair of $n{+}1$-place relations, $\langle R^1_F(z,x_1, \ldots x_n)^*,$ $R^2_F(z,x_1, \ldots x_n)\rangle$, so that if '$a_1$', $\ldots$ 'a_n' are singular terms denoting $o_1, \ldots o_n$, then '$F(a_1, \ldots a_n)$' expresses the biforcated attitude consisting of the pair, $\langle$FOR$(\lambda z(R^1_F(z,o_1, \ldots o_n)))^*,FOR(\lambda z(R^2_F(z,o_1, \ldots o_n)))\rangle$. We say that $\langle(\lambda z(R^1_F(z,x_1, \ldots x_n))^*,\lambda z(R^2_F(z,x_1, \ldots x_n)))\rangle$ is the *semantic value* of '$F(x_1, \ldots x_n)$'.

CONNECTIVES

$\sim$ If 'A' is a well-formed formula with semantic value
        $\langle\lambda z(\alpha^1)^*,\lambda z(\alpha^2)\rangle$, then '$\sim$A' is a well-formed formula and
        has semantic value $\langle\lambda z(\neg\alpha^2)^*,\lambda z(\neg\alpha^1)\rangle$.

&   If 'A' is a well-formed formula with semantic value
        $\langle\lambda z(\alpha^1)^*,\lambda z(\alpha^2)\rangle$, and 'B' is a well-formed formula with
        semantic value $\langle\lambda z(\beta^1)^*,\lambda z(\beta^2)\rangle$, then 'A&B' is a
        well-formed formula and has semantic value
        $\langle\lambda z(\alpha^1\wedge\beta^1)^*,\lambda z(\alpha^2\wedge\beta^2)\rangle$.

$\circ$ If 'A' is a well-formed formula with semantic value
        $\langle\lambda z(\alpha^1)^*,\lambda z(\alpha^2)\rangle$, and 'B' is a well-formed formula with
        semantic value $\langle\lambda z(\beta^1)^*,\lambda z(\beta^2)\rangle$, then 'A$\circ$B' is a well-formed
        formula and has semantic value $\langle\lambda z(\alpha^1\vee\beta^1)^*,\lambda z(\alpha^2\vee\beta^2)\rangle$.

$\supset$ If 'A' is a well-formed formula with semantic value
        $\langle\lambda z(\alpha^1)^*,\lambda z(\alpha^2)\rangle$, and 'B' is a well-formed formula with
        semantic value $\langle\lambda z(\beta^1)^*,\lambda z(\beta^2)\rangle$, then 'A$\supset$B' is a
        well-formed formula and has semantic value
        $\langle\lambda z(\alpha^2>\beta^1)^*,\lambda z(\alpha^1>\beta^2)\rangle$.[1]

$\forall$ If 'A' is a well-formed formula with semantic value
        $\langle\lambda z(\alpha^1)^*,\lambda z(\alpha^2)\rangle$, then '$\forall$x(A)' is a well-formed formula and
        has semantic value $\langle\lambda z(\forall x(\alpha^1))^*,\lambda z(\forall x(\alpha^2))\rangle$.

$\exists$ If 'A' is a well-formed formula with semantic value
        $\langle\lambda z(\alpha^1)^*,\lambda z(\alpha^2)\rangle$, then '$\exists$x(A)' is a well-formed formula and
        has semantic value $\langle\lambda z(\exists x(\alpha^1))^*,\lambda z(\exists x(\alpha^2))\rangle$.

Given these definitions, we say that only closed sentences express mental
states, and that the mental state expressed by a closed sentence 'A' is the
biforcated attitude, $\langle\text{FOR}(\alpha^1)^*,\text{FOR}(\alpha^2)\rangle$, where $\langle\alpha^{1*},\alpha^2\rangle$ is the semantic
value of 'A'.

8.2 TWO COMPLICATIONS IN LOGIC FOR BIFORCATED ATTITUDE SEMANTICS

Two complications arise in biforcated attitude semantics which mean
that the elegant proof of the logical features of the language that was

---

[1] If this rule looks at all surprising, it would be a good exercise to derive it from the
rules for '$\sim$' and '$\circ$'. Another good exercise is to verify that each of these rules allow only

used in Chapters 5 and 6 no longer works. The first complication arises because '∼' and '⊃' are 'flipping' constructions in biforcated attitude semantics: one of the things they do is to 'flip' which attitude is major and which is minor. So as a result, there is no longer a neat isomorphism between the structure of object-language sentences and the structure of the contents of the attitudes that they express.

So, just to illustrate: consider the sentence, 'P&∼P'. If the semantic value of 'P' is $\langle \pi^{1*}, \pi^2 \rangle$, then the semantic value of '∼P' is $\langle \neg\pi^{2*}, \neg\pi^1 \rangle$, and so the semantic value of 'P&∼P' is $\langle \pi^1 \wedge \neg\pi^{2*}, \pi^2 \wedge \neg\pi^1 \rangle$. So the mental state expressed by 'P&∼P' consists of two states, neither of which has a content that is isomorphic to that of the sentence. One has $\pi^1 \wedge \neg\pi^2$ for its content; the other has $\pi^2 \wedge \neg\pi^1$. But though 'P&∼P' is an inconsistent sentence, neither of these contents is inconsistent in ordinary predicate logic.[2]

However, in order to accept 'P&∼P', you don't just have to have either one of these attitudes, FOR$(\pi^1 \wedge \neg\pi^2)$ or FOR$(\pi^2 \wedge \neg\pi^1)$. You have to have *both*. But if being for is an inconsistency-transmitting attitude, then it is inconsistent to be for both of these things, if their contents are inconsistent *with each other*. That is, if the conjunction of their contents is inconsistent in ordinary predicate logic. But $(\pi^1 \wedge \neg\pi^2) \wedge (\pi^2 \wedge \neg\pi^1)$ *is* logically inconsistent in ordinary predicate logic.

This leads to the following conjecture: that a sentence, 'A', is logically inconsistent just in case $\alpha^1 \wedge \alpha^2$ is inconsistent, for any compositional assignment of semantic value $\langle \alpha^{1*}, \alpha^2 \rangle$ to 'A'. Or equivalently, that 'A' is a theorem of classical logic just in case $\neg\alpha^1 \wedge \neg\alpha^2$ is inconsistent, for any compositional assignment of semantic value $\langle \alpha^{1*}, \alpha^2 \rangle$ to 'A' (since $\langle \neg\alpha^1, \neg\alpha^{2*} \rangle$ is the semantic value of ∼A). If this is true, then the theorems of classical logic are all and only the sentences that it is inconsistent to deny under any interpretation. And if it is true, then biforcated attitude semantics allows us to, in some sense, 'account for logic'. It does turn out to be true, and I'll prove it in the next section. But first, a few words about the other major complication raised by biforcated attitude semantics.

---

the construction of biforcated attitudes from biforcated attitudes—biforcated attitudes, recall, must be pairs of states of being for, where one state (the major attitude) commits to the other (the minor attitude).

[2] Though it is important to note that $\pi^1 \wedge \neg\pi^2$ must be inconsistent in predicate logic supplemented by the logic of *proceeding as if*. Recall that in a biforcated attitude, the content of the major attitude always entails the content of the minor attitude.

The second complication that comes up in biforcated attitude semantics is due to the possibility of disacceptance. In addition to accepting
'P' (being in the state it expresses) and accepting '∼P', in biforcated attitude semantics there is no inconsistency involved in disaccepting both. As
a result, it turns out to be intelligible even to disaccept theorems
of classical logic, *so long* as you also disaccept an appropriate one of
the sentences involved. We can exhibit this problem by considering
a simple case. It should turn out that '∼(P&∼P)' is a theorem. It
is, in fact, a rather important one. Moreover, we just saw (cancelling
double-negations) that it is inconsistent to deny this sentence. But there
turns out to be no inconsistency in disaccepting it, provided that you
disaccept 'P'.

To disaccept but not deny '∼(P&∼P)', recall, is to be in the minor
attitude of the state expressed by its negation, but not its major state. The
state expressed by its negation is $\langle$FOR$(\neg\neg(\pi^1 \wedge \neg\pi^2))^*$,FOR$(\neg\neg(\pi^2 \wedge \neg\pi^1)))\rangle$, and so accepting the negation commits to being for $\pi^1 \wedge \neg\pi^2 \wedge \pi^2 \wedge \neg\pi^1$, which is inconsistent. But merely having this minor attitude
only involves being for $\pi^2 \wedge \neg\pi^1$, which is not inconsistent at all.[3] In
fact, being for $\pi^2 \wedge \neg\pi^1$ is commitment-equivalent to being for $\neg\neg\pi^2$
and being for $\neg\pi^1$, which is to say that it is commitment-equivalent to
disaccepting both 'P' and '∼P'. So someone who disaccepts 'P' and '∼P'
may also disaccept '∼(P&∼P)' without inconsistency, even though it is
inconsistent to reject it. So under biforcated attitude semantics, it does
not turn out that everyone is committed to accepting the theorems of
classical logic. Though as we saw in this case, they *are* committed to
accepting the theorems, so long as they do not bear the special attitude
to any of the appropriate atoms, of disaccepting both them and their
negations.

8.3 LOGIC

Since in biforcated attitude semantics there are *three* consistent opinionated attitudes it is possible to bear toward a given sentence, let's get clear
on how to talk about these states. I'll say that *accepting* 'A' is being in the
mental state that 'A' expresses. And I'll say that *denying* 'A' is being in
the mental state that is expressed by the negation of 'A'. And third, I'll

---

[3] That is, so long as 'P' is not a purely normative sentence—see section 8.4.

say that *disacceptance full-stop* toward 'A' is the state of disaccepting both 'A' and the negation of 'A'. These three states—acceptance, denial, and disacceptance full-stop—exhaust the consistent *settled*, or *opinionated*[4] attitudes that one can have with respect to 'A'. What I'll do in the next few paragraphs, is to show how to construct the *commitment tables* for '∼' and '&', which tell us which of these three states you are committed to having toward '∼A' and toward 'A&B', given which of the three attitudes you have toward 'A' and toward 'B'.

    Start with '∼'. It is trivial to observe that accepting 'A' is commitment-equivalent to denying '∼A'. Accepting 'A' is just being in the state it expresses, after all, which without loss of generality, is $\langle \text{FOR}(\alpha^1)^*, \text{FOR}(\alpha^2) \rangle$. And denying '∼A' is just being in the state expressed by its negation, which is $\langle \text{FOR}(\neg\neg\alpha^1)^*, \text{FOR}(\neg\neg\alpha^2) \rangle$. It is trivial to observe that these are commitment-equivalent, by observing that α^1 and $\neg\neg\alpha^1$ are equivalent. Similarly, it is trivial to observe that disacceptance full-stop of 'A' is commitment-equivalent to disacceptance full-stop of '∼A'. The former consists of these two states: $\text{FOR}(\neg\alpha^1)$ (that is, disacceptance of 'A') and $\text{FOR}(\neg\neg\alpha^2)$ (that is, disacceptance of '∼A'). While the latter consists of $\text{FOR}(\neg\neg\alpha^2)$ (that is, disacceptance of '∼A') and $\text{FOR}(\neg\neg\neg\alpha^1)$ (that is, disacceptance of '∼∼A'). Again, it is trivial to observe that these states are commitment-equivalent. Finally, the commitment-equivalence of denying 'A' with accepting '∼A' follows immediately from the definitions of 'denying' and 'accepting'. This generates the following *commitment table* for '∼' (for reasons that will become clear in a moment, I've replaced 'accept' with 'T', 'deny' with 'F', and 'disaccept full-stop' with '1/2'):

A	∼A
T	F
1/2	1/2
F	T

We can read off the table what attitude you are committed to having toward '∼A' in order to avoid inconsistency, on the basis of what attitude you have toward 'A'. If you accept 'A', deny '∼A'.

---

[4] See the appendix to this chapter for elaboration.

If you disaccept 'A' full-stop, then disaccept '~A' full-stop. And if you deny 'A', then accept '~A'. Any other combination of attitudes will result in inconsistency. That is why I call it a *commitment table*. We can construct a similar table for 'A&B', and it generates the following table (see the appendix to this chapter for the complete derivation):[5]

A&B	T	½	F
T	T	½	F
½	½	½	F
F	F	F	F

If you accept both 'A' and 'B' you are committed to accepting 'A&B', if you deny either 'A' or 'B', then you are committed to denying 'A&B', and if you bear any other combination of the three attitudes of acceptance, denial, and disacceptance full-stop to 'A' and to 'B', then you are committed to disaccepting 'A&B' full-stop.

It is worth observing that the commitment tables for '~' and '&' are identical to the truth-tables for '~' and '&' in the strong Kleene three-valued logic. This does not appear to be in any way a coincidence; the strong Kleene three-valued logic is often treated as modeling the rational relations between believing something, believing its negation, and a distinct attitude of treating it as 'indeterminate' in some sense, and that is precisely what we are modeling.

In fact, the properties of the strong Kleene logic arise precisely because it is treated as bifurcated.[6] On standard interpretations of that logic, 'p is T' is interpreted as {you are told that p, $\neg$(you are told that $\neg p$)}, 'p is F' is interpreted as {you are told that $\neg p$, $\neg$(you are told that p)}, and 'p is ½' is interpreted as {$\neg$(you are told that p), $\neg$(you are told that $\neg p$)}, it is assumed that if you are told that p, then you are not told that $\neg p$,[7] and the values of the connectives, '~' and '&', are introduced by applying them to each member of the bifurcated pairs, just as in our

---

[5] I've presented this table in a slightly different format, so as to make it graphically more tractable. The rows and columns represent the attitude with respect to 'A' and to 'B', respectively, and the interior is the attitude with respect to 'A&B'.

[6] Thanks to Jeff Horty for this observation.

[7] Relaxing this assumption leads to the four-valued logic of Belnap (1977).

semantics in section 8.1. So it is easy to observe that this framework is isomorphic to ours, simply by replacing 'you are told that' with 'pai'. I've used 'T', 'F', and '½' in the commitment tables in order to make this parallel obvious.

We are now in a position to prove that a sentence is of a form that cannot be consistently rejected in biforcated-attitude semantics just in case it is a theorem of classical logic. I start by reformulating the thesis. Since commitment tables show us the conditions under which it is consistent to hold each attitude toward a sentence under biforcated attitude semantics, it follows that the sentence-forms that cannot be consistently rejected are identical to the sentence-forms which have no 'F' in their commitment tables. What commitment tables do, after all, is to tell us under what conditions it is consistent to accept a sentence, to deny it, or to disaccept it full-stop. So a sentence-form whose table has no 'F's is a sentence-form for which there are no conditions under which such a sentence can be rejected.

To illustrate: the rightmost, shaded, column of the table below is the commitment table for '~(P&~P)', and it tells us that there are *no* conditions, in the sense of views you can have toward 'P', under which it is consistent to deny it—there are only conditions under which it is consistent to accept it, and conditions under which it is consistent to disaccept it full-stop. We can read off from the table what we already proved: that disaccepting '~(P&~P)' is okay only if you disaccept 'P'.

P	~P	P&~P	~(P&~P)
T	F	F	T
½	½	½	½
F	T	F	T

So in order to prove our result, what we now need to do, is to show that all and only the commitment tables for classical theorems have no appearance of 'F'. But given that our commitment tables are recognizable as truth tables for connectives in well-understood three-valued logics, this turns out to be a familiar result about such three-valued logics. Since the values 'T' and '½' are the values which count as 'designated' in the simplest relevance logic, it is identical to the result that that logic admits all and only the classical theorems. The proof is straightforward, but I omit it here.[8]

This shows that biforcated attitude semantics can capture the theorems of ordinary propositional logic, and the result can be expanded to apply to predicate logic. But what about the relations of inconsistency and entailment, and the property of validity? We can account for those, too. 'A' classically entails 'B' just in case 'A⊃B' is a classical theorem. But we know how to capture classical theorems—they are the sentences that are inconsistent to deny under any interpretation. So if we want to capture the classical logical entailments, then we can say that 'A' logically entails 'B' just in case 'A⊃B' is of a form all instances of which are inconsistent to deny. More generally, we can say that 'A' entails 'B' just in case it is inconsistent to deny 'A⊃B'.

Intuitively, we want it to turn out that valid arguments are ones which commit someone who accepts their premises to accepting their conclusion. So let's take this as our definition of valid arguments: an argument is valid just in case anyone who accepts its premises is committed to accepting its conclusion, and logically valid just in case it is of a form all instances of which are valid. We might *hope* that it would turn out to be true that an argument is logically valid just in case the conjunction of its premises entails its conclusion. But this turns out *not* to be true given these definitions—a theorem is entailed by any set of premises, but though theorems are inconsistent to deny, there is sometimes no inconsistency in disaccepting them full-stop.

The converse, however, does turn out to be true. Valid arguments all have premises which jointly entail their conclusions. Take an arbitrary argument, from premises 'P_1', . . . 'P_n' to conclusion 'C'. 'P_1 & . . . & P_n' entails 'C', by definition, just in case it is inconsistent to deny '(P_1 & . . . & P_n)⊃C'. But to deny this is commitment-equivalent to accepting 'P_1 & . . . & P_n & ∼C'. But accepting this is commitment-equivalent to accepting each of its conjuncts, 'P_1', . . . 'P_n' and '∼C'. But if the argument is valid, then someone who accepts each of 'P_1', . . . 'P_n' is committed to accepting 'C', and *ipso facto* to not accepting '∼C', on pain of inconsistency. So if the argument is valid, then the conjunction of the premises entails the conclusion. And conversely, if the conjunction of the premises entails the conclusion, then it is inconsistent to accept each of 'P_1', . . . 'P_n' and '∼C'—which is to say that if you accept

---

[8] See, for example, Avron [1991].

some things which entail something else, then it is inconsistent for you to deny that thing.

The relationship between entailment and validity, so defined, is the relationship between classical consequence and relevance consequence. Any arbitrary set of premises entails a theorem, but the inference from those premises to the conclusion does not count as valid. Similarly, any inconsistent set of sentences entails an arbitrary sentence, but the inference from those premises to that conclusion does not count as valid. Relevant inferences, however, do come out as valid given these definitions—and they preserve commitment. If you accept 'P' and you accept 'P⊃Q', you are committed not just to not denying 'Q', but to accepting it, as is straightforward to verify.

8.4 THE NEW NEW NEGATION PROBLEM

This all sounds like relatively good news. But biforcated attitude semantics, together with the proposal that what we do in order to assign normative sentences to biforcated attitudes is simply to list the same attitude twice, generates yet *another* problem about negation. The problem becomes visible when we focus on the notion of *disacceptance*. At the end of section 7.6, recall, we introduced a general notion of disacceptance, which behaves like disbelief for all purely descriptive and complex joint descriptive-normative sentences—it is a state that is inconsistent with accepting the sentence, but weaker than accepting its negation. But now it turns out that disacceptance collapses into accepting the negation, in the case of purely normative sentences. For by our composition rules, purely normative sentences have identical major and minor attitudes, since they are constructed out of atomic sentences with identical major and minor attitudes. I call this the *new new negation problem*, because it seems to arise due to our solution to the new negation problem.

The solution to the new negation problem, recall, was to analyze belief as a biforcated attitude. And that is why we went in for biforcated attitude semantics, the semantic framework on which the semantic assertability condition of every indicative sentence in the language is that the speaker be in some biforcated attitude. But only for the case of descriptive predicates did it turn out that atomic sentences need to express states that really require this biforcation. So for the case of normative predicates, I said, we do best to simply list twice the attitudes that already do well for us. That allowed our new semantic framework to be conservative for the case of purely normative sentences, preserving all of their properties that were already captured by the old semantic framework from Chapter 6, and merely generalizing to allow for the complications involved with descriptive predicates.

Yet it is precisely the complication involved with descriptive predicates that yielded the possibility of disbelief and in general, disacceptance. It is because the minor attitude of belief is weaker than the major one, that disbelief is weaker than believing the negation. For the case of purely normative sentences, both atomic and complex, however, the minor attitude and the major attitude are *the same*. So for such sentences, there is no distinction between disacceptance and accepting the negation.

Intuitively, the problem arose because when we analyzed belief in terms of being for, it left one too many places for a negation to go, and our account of sentential negation put it in the wrong place. We fixed that by supposing that descriptive sentences express a biforcated state of mind which involves a *minor* state of being for, and chose the minor attitude in such a way that it *did* already have the negation in the 'right' place, but also a negation in the 'wrong' place. So then what happened, was that when we applied our account of negation to the minor attitude expressed by a descriptive sentence, this minor attitude was commitment-equivalent to the belief in the negation. It was a trick designed to essentially get us the equivalent of commuting 'not' with 'proceeding as if', even though they don't really commute.

One idea for a solution might be to hope that we could get around the new new negation problem, by also supplying normative sentences with a minor attitude that is weaker than the attitudes assigned to them by the semantics in Chapter 5. For example, to 'murder is wrong', we might assign being for disliking murder as well as being for blaming for murder, under the assumption (bracket the question of its plausibility) that blaming for murder entails disliking it:

'murder is wrong'	expresses	$\langle$FOR(blaming for murder)*, FOR(disliking murder)$\rangle$
'murder is not wrong'	expresses	$\langle$FOR($\neg$blaming for murder), FOR($\neg$disliking murder)*$\rangle$

What we would essentially have to do, for every normative predicate, is to come up with *two* relations, one weaker than the other. Intuitively, the stronger relation would correspond to 'proceeding as if a is wrong', and the weaker one would correspond to 'not proceeding as if a is not wrong'. Perhaps this is the way to go, but I'm not convinced that there is any reason to think that it will lead to any plausible accounts of the meaning of 'wrong' or any other normative term, and it is not trivially conservative, with respect to the properties of purely normative sentences explained by the semantics of Chapter 6.

Another possible response to the new new negation problem might be to treat it as an interesting discovery about the scope of disacceptance. Unlike the original negation problem, which turned on an obvious datum, or the new negation problem, which needed to be solved in order for ordinary descriptive sentences to get the right truth-conditions, the new new negation problem turns on an asymmetry between purely normative and at least partially descriptive sentences that is relatively subtle. So it may not be such a terrible bullet to simply bite.

In favor of this latest suggestion lies the consideration that we are still going to have to give some kind of account of what makes some states of mind *cognitive*, and others *noncognitive*. Beliefs, after all, are cognitive attitudes, but on the account of Chapter 7, they are analyzed in terms of the state of being for, which is supposed to be a noncognitive attitude. Does that mean that beliefs are really noncognitive attitudes? Well, as I worried in section 7.1, it may make them uncomfortably close to being noncognitive attitudes, given some of the traditional motivations for expressivism in the first place. But it needn't collapse the distinction, so long as we have some way of explaining why it is that belief counts as cognitive even though it is constructed out of a noncognitive attitude. The difference between biforcated attitudes that are *genuinely* biforcated, involving two distinct states of being for, and those that are only nominally biforcated, involving the same state of being for merely listed twice, may be a promising way to start to draw this distinction. And that corresponds to the distinction that gives rise to the new new negation problem.

APPENDIX TO CHAPTER 8

In this appendix, I show how to derive the commitment table for '&' (see section 8.3), as a corollary of a more general observation about how the *settled* states of acceptance, denial, and disacceptance full-stop are rationally related to the *unsettled* states of *mere disacceptance, mere disdenial,* and *withholding*.

In biforcated attitude semantics, there are really six consistent attitudes that it is possible to have with respect to any given sentence. In order to describe them, I'll say as a shorthand that if you are in the states, FOR(α) and FOR(β), then you are *for-committed* to $\{\alpha, \beta\}$. The idea is that this shorthand lets us list some of the things you are for in a concise way. So if the semantic value of 'A' is $\langle \alpha^{1*}, \alpha^2 \rangle$, then *accepting* 'A' for-commits you to $\{\alpha^1, \alpha^2\}$ and *denying* 'A' for-commits you to $\{\neg\alpha^1, \neg\alpha^2\}$. *Mere disacceptance* of 'A' for-commits you only to $\{\neg\alpha^1\}$, and *mere disdenial* of 'A' for-commits you only to $\{\alpha^2\}$. Then we can say that you *disaccept full-stop* if you are for-committed to $\{\neg\alpha^1, \alpha^2\}$, and that in *withholding*, you are for-committed to $\{\}$.

Acceptance, denial, and disacceptance full-stop are all maximal, *settled* views with respect to 'A'. Among the four of $\alpha^1, \alpha^2, \neg\alpha^1$, and $\neg\alpha^2$, it is not possible to add any others to the for-commitment sets associated with these psychological states, without leading to inconsistent for-commitments. And they are also the only consistent settled states. It is not consistent to be for-committed to $\{\neg\alpha^2, \alpha^1\}$, because on the assumption that 'A' expresses a biforcated attitude, it follows that α^1 entails α^2. Withholding, mere disacceptance, and mere disdenial, on the other hand, are *unsettled* states. Someone in these states can increase their opinionatedness with respect to 'A' without becoming inconsistent. The following diagram shows the relationships among these six states:

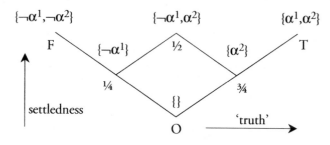

In the diagram, the states are represented by their for-commitment class, and arranged so that less settled states are at the bottom and more settled states are at the top, as indicated by the settledness arrow on the left. They are also arranged so that positive attitudes toward 'A' are on the right of the diagram, and negative attitudes toward 'A' are on the left. This is represented by the 'truth' arrow in the diagram: if you are in a state further to the right, then your attitude toward the truth of 'A' is more positive (not: 'A' is more true; hence, the scare-quotes).

For any states X and Y in the diagram, X and Y are consistent with each other just in case there is some state Z in the diagram (possibly identical to X or Y), such that there is a solely upward path (possibly a trivial one) from X to Z and from Y to Z. Otherwise, they are inconsistent.

In a natural sense, the diagram represents everything important about the rational properties of these six mental states. Not only does it tell us which states are consistent with which others and which states are more settled than which others, it also tells us how to determine which attitude is rationally required toward complex sentences, on the basis of which attitude is required toward their parts. The attitude that you are committed to having toward '∼A', for example, is the reflection of the attitude that you have toward 'A', across the vertical axis. To see why, simply observe that for '∼A', the diagram looks like this:

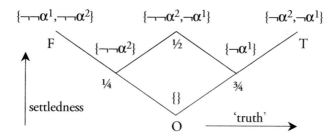

From there, all it takes is to cancel double-negations in order to obtain the reflection of the diagram for 'A'.

Similarly, the diagram already tells us what state someone is committed to being in with respect to 'A&B', on the basis of the states she is in with respect to 'A' and with respect to 'B'. It is the state that is represented by the rightmost node on the graph which is left of (in the inclusive sense in which T is left of T) the nodes that represent each of the states she is in with respect to 'A' and with respect to 'B'. In technical terms, the attitude you are committed to having toward 'A&B' is the *infimum* on the graph, with respect to the *'truth'* ordering, of the attitudes you are committed to having toward 'A' and toward 'B'.

This is easy to verify: for any choice of attitudes toward 'A' and 'B', find their for-commitment classes from the first diagram—the one for 'A'. (The for-commitment classes for 'B' are the same, except with 'β' substituted for 'α'.) Then find the infimum of those two nodes on the graph for 'A&B'; this gives the for-commitment class for that

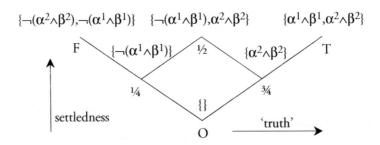

attitude toward 'A&B'. It is easy to derive the contents of this for-commitment class from those for 'A' and for 'B'. For example, suppose that you merely disaccept 'A' (value $3/4$) and merely disdeny 'B' (value $1/4$). This gives you a total for-commitment class of $\{\alpha^2, \neg\beta^1\}$. From these commitments, it is easy to derive $\{\neg(\alpha^1\wedge\beta^1)\}$. But this is the commitment-class of disdenying 'A&B'. It is not, however, possible to derive the commitment-classes for any higher node from the members of $\{\alpha^2, \neg\beta^1\}$. So in disaccepting 'A' and disdenying 'B', you are committed to disdenying 'A&B'. Since disdenial is an unsettled state, this is consistent with going on to either deny 'A&B' or to disaccept it full-stop (though you will also be committed to becoming more opinionated about either 'A' or 'B', in the process). But you are not committed to either of those merely by disaccepting 'A' and disdenying 'B'. The same goes for any other choice of nodes, as is easy to verify. The three-valued commitment table for '&' drops out as a sub-case of this observation, and the commitment tables for '∼' and '&' fix those for the other propositional connectives.

These commitment relationships constitute a generalization of the strong Kleene three-valued logic originally stated by Garcia and Moussavi (1991). Garcia and Moussavi's logic was intended to model the difference between temporary ignorance (withholding) and permanent ignorance (disacceptance full-stop), and they included the truth-values here called '$1/4$' and '$3/4$' merely because they were technically required in order to complete the logic, but had no real interpretation for them. Fitting (1991) showed how their logic was one of a wide class of generalizations on Kleene's logic, and provided an interpret-ation that took them to be ranges of credence, in a coarse-grained degree-of-credence framework, in which there are only three degrees of belief—1, $1/2$, and 0. This is really inconsistent with Garcia and Moussavi's idea that the value of $1/2$ is associated with a state of permanent or decided ignorance, rather than with a degree of belief, so it still gives us no satisfactory interpretation of '$1/4$' and '$3/4$', in their framework.

The analysis of belief as a biforcated attitude, however, provides an interpretation of these values. Each value in the six-valued logic of Garcia and Moussavi is associated with a consistent state of mind with respect to 'A', and all six states are predicted by the structural analysis of belief. So in a very real sense, I think that the biforcated attitudes analysis tells us what belief would really have to be like, if there really is a distinctive state of disbelief full-stop, that is a *settled* attitude to have, is inconsistent with belief, and is inconsistent with belief in the negation, in the same sort of way that the belief that p and the belief that $\neg p$ are inconsistent with one another.

So if there is pressure due to thinking about the appropriate attitude toward paradoxical propositions, or from some other place, to think that there is some such attitude as disbelief full-stop, in addition to mere withholding, it is not implausible that the nature of belief might be something very much like the biforcated attitudes analysis makes it out to be.

9

Assigning truth-conditions

9.1 GENERALIZING THE NEW NEGATION PROBLEM

From the beginning, I've been assuming that one of the things that expressivists will want to do is to assign truth-conditions to ordinary descriptive sentences. In Chapter 2, I made an assumption about how they would do so. I assumed that they would at least aspire to do so in the obvious way—by having them inherit those contents from the beliefs that they express. After all, the distinction between expressing and reporting is supposed to be *borrowed* from the case of descriptive sentences. If one of the data is that 'grass is green' expresses the belief that grass is green, then 'grass is green' can surely inherit its truth-conditions from those for the belief.

But one of the main lessons so far is that expressivists don't get to just stipulate that ordinary descriptive sentences express beliefs, or which beliefs they express. That needs to fall out of a general account of the semantics of complex sentences. In section 7.1, I pointed out that both the constructive nature of the semantics of Chapter 6 and its formally adequate explanatory account of logical inconsistency turn crucially on the fact that all sentences are assumed to express the same general kind of attitude. But I also argued, in Chapters 3 through 6, that there is no other promising way of attaining these advantages. The problem with other expressivist accounts, I pointed out, stems from their lack of *structure*. But if lack of structure is the problem, then there is only one solution, and that is to add structure. So the essence of my suggestions in Chapters 4 through 6 was simply to add that missing structure. And so I argued in section 7.1 that if expressivists are going to keep the idea that 'grass is green' expresses the belief that grass is green, but also acquire any of the advantages of the semantics of Chapter 6, then it will have to turn out that the belief that grass is green is a state of being for something.

This was one easy place to get off of the boat. If this is really clearly the most promising approach for expressivism, but it requires analyzing belief in terms of a noncognitive attitude, then surely expressivism is a big mistake. But in Chapter 7, I pressed onward, pointing out that the state of being for proceeding as if p, where 'proceeding as if' is understood to mean, 'taking as settled in deciding what to do', does in fact have at least some of the central features of belief. I also pointed out that if this analysis were correct, then the semantics of Chapter 6 already suffices for a language with both normative and descriptive predicates. Descriptive predicates, 'F(x)', simply have to be understood as always semantically contributing the relation of proceeding as if x is f.[1]

Since 7.2, however, our attention has been occupied with a new problem. This new problem is that though this analysis of belief allows it to turn out that 'grass is green' expresses the belief that grass is green, it does not allow it to turn out that 'grass is not green' expresses the belief that grass is not green. In fact, it expresses a quite different mental state. So this made it very unclear how 'grass is not green' would end up being assigned the right ordinary descriptive propositional content. In answer to this problem, I devised a trick. It was just a trick, but I also claimed that it made the resulting account of belief interesting for independent reasons. The trick was to instead analyze believing that p as involving *two* states of being for: being for proceeding as if p, but also being for not proceeding as if $\neg p$.

Even given this move toward biforcated attitudes, it did not turn out that the mental state expressed by 'grass is not green' was the belief that grass is not green. But the virtue of this account was illustrated in Chapter 7, where I showed that so long as we grant the assumption that proceeding as if p entails not proceeding as if $\neg p$, the state expressed by 'grass is not green' and the belief that grass is not green are what I called *commitment-equivalent*: each is inconsistent with all of the same mental states that are inconsistent with the other. I also showed, in Chapter 8, how our semantics and logic could be reconstructed within this framework. But the key idea involved giving up on the assumption that 'grass is not green' acquires its truth-conditions because it expresses the belief that grass is not green, which has those truth-conditions. We had to make do with the alternative theory that 'grass is not green'

---

[1] Wherever precision is needed, I'm following the convention of using lower-case letters as the translations of the object-language strings represented by upper-case roman letters into our descriptive metalanguage.

acquires its truth-conditions because it expresses a mental state that is *commitment-equivalent* to the belief that grass is not green, which has those truth-conditions.

That was a significant retreat—strictly speaking, as we are conceiving of things so far, biforcated attitude semantics allows us to retain the view that *atomic* descriptive sentences express beliefs, but it forces us to give up on the idea that *negations* of atomic descriptive sentences express beliefs. But I'm here to tell you that the problem is much bigger. For in biforcated attitude semantics, it does not turn out that 'A&B' expresses the belief that $a \wedge b$, that 'A°B' expresses the belief that $a \vee b$, that 'A⊃B' expresses the belief that $a > b$, that '∀x(F(x))' expresses the belief that $\forall x(f(x))$, or that '∃x(F(x))' expresses the belief that $\exists x(f(x))$, even when 'A' and 'B' are ordinary atomic descriptive sentences and 'F(x)' is an atomic descriptive formula. So for every one of these constructions, we again have a puzzle about how these descriptive sentences are going to end up with the right truth-conditions.

9.2 GLOSSING AGAIN

Things would be very bad if each linguistic construction required an extra layer of complication in our semantics that complicates things as much as it did to move from the semantics of Chapter 6 to the more complicated biforcated attitude semantics of Chapter 8! But things are not that bad. It turns out that for at least some of the constructions we are considering, we can supplement our logic of proceeding as if with new assumptions, and thereby yield the result that the states expressed by these complex descriptive sentences are commitment-equivalent to the corresponding beliefs. For example, things appear to be at least workable for '&':

Table I

'P'	expresses	$\langle \text{FOR}(\text{pai } p)^*, \text{FOR}(\neg\text{pai } \neg p) \rangle$	postulate
'Q'	expresses	$\langle \text{FOR}(\text{pai } q)^*, \text{FOR}(\neg\text{pai } \neg q) \rangle$	postulate
'P&Q'	expresses	$\langle \text{FOR}((\text{pai } p) \wedge (\text{pai } q))^*, \text{FOR}((\neg\text{pai } \neg p) \wedge (\neg\text{pai } \neg q)) \rangle$	from &
$\text{BF}(p \wedge q)$	=	$\langle \text{FOR}(\text{pai } p \wedge q)^*, \text{FOR}(\neg\text{pai } \neg(p \wedge q)) \rangle$	analysis of belief

It is easy to see from the table that the state expressed by 'P&Q' is not the belief that $p \wedge q$, given our analysis of belief in terms of being for and proceeding as if. For these two states to be commitment-equivalent, we would need two assumptions. For the state expressed by 'P&Q' to commit to the belief that $p \land q$, we would need to assume that proceeding as if p and proceeding as if q entails proceeding as if $p \land q$. And for the converse commitment, we would need to assume the converse entailment.

These are substantive assumptions, and they are rejectable, depending on how we think about the nature of proceeding as if. But they are also not crazy. We have already assumed that proceeding as if p entails not proceeding as if $\neg p$, on the grounds that to proceed as if p is to take p as settled in deciding what to do, and someone cannot take each of p and $\neg p$ as settled in deciding what to do. But it may also not be crazy to suppose that someone who takes $p \land q$ as settled in deciding what to do is *ipso facto* taking p as settled in deciding what to do. And it may also not be crazy to suppose that it takes no more to take $p \land q$ as settled in deciding what to do, than to take each of p and q as settled in deciding what to do. So if we supplement our logic of proceeding as if with these assumptions, then it turns out that the state of mind expressed by 'P&Q' is commitment-equivalent to the belief that $p \land q$, and hence we can explain how 'P&Q' comes to have the proposition that $p \land q$ as its content.

A similar move, with similar but stronger assumptions about proceeding as if, seems to work for '$\forall$'. The problem there is illustrated by the following table:

Table 2

'F(x)'	has semantic value	$\langle (\text{pai } f(x))^*, (\neg \text{pai } \neg f(x)) \rangle$	postulate
'$\forall x(F(x))$'	expresses	$\langle \text{FOR}(\forall x(\text{pai } f(x)))^*, \text{FOR}(\forall x(\neg \text{pai } \neg f(x))) \rangle$	from $\forall$
$\text{BF}(\forall x(f(x)))$ =		$\langle \text{FOR}(\text{pai } \forall x(f(x)))^*, \text{FOR}(\neg \text{pai } \neg \forall x(f(x))) \rangle$	analysis of belief

Here, in order to suppose that the state expressed by '$\forall x(F(x))$' is commitment-equivalent to the belief that $\forall x(f(x))$, we again need to make two assumptions. For the state expressed by the sentence to commit to the belief, we must assume that it is sufficient, to proceed as if everything is f, to proceed, for each thing, as if it is f. And for the converse commitment, we need to assume the converse entailment.

These entailments are both much less plausible than the ones we have discussed so far, though both may have some intuitive merit. The first assumption says that if, for every single thing, you are taking it as settled that it is f in deciding what to do, then you are taking $\forall x(f(x))$ as settled in deciding what to do. This is reasonably plausible. You may, of course, be taking $f(a)$ as settled for each value of a, but believe that there are more things that you do not know about, and so are uncertain as to whether $\forall x(f(x))$. So the assumption is highly rejectable. But it can at least be motivated as a generalization of the corresponding assumption for '&'. The second of these entailments also has plausibility. If you are taking $\forall x(f(x))$ as settled in deciding what to do, then you are plausibly *ipso facto* taking $f(a)$ as settled in deciding what to do. It is far from obvious that this is correct, either, because there may be values of a about which you have no views. If we went in for the assumption, however, we could explain this by saying that you aren't *for* proceeding as if $f(a)$, for those values of a, but you are nevertheless proceeding as if $f(a)$, for those values. In this way we would gloss the new negation problem as it arises for '$\forall$', and maintain that the mental state expressed by universally quantified descriptive sentences is commitment-equivalent to the belief in the universally quantified proposition.

This is not a brilliant success story; the assumptions that we had to make are not at all clearly correct, are all much less intuitive than the assumption that proceeding as if p entails not proceeding as if $\neg p$, from Chapter 7, and are all required, in order to achieve the required finesse. But this limited success for '&' and '$\forall$' might lead you to believe that everything is golden, and hence that buying into these required assumptions is worth the reward. After all, every construction can be defined in terms of '$\sim$', '&' and '$\forall$'. So shouldn't this be enough?

It turns out that it is not. And this is because of the way that '$\sim$' behaves—by flipping which attitudes are major, and which are minor. Disjunctions, of course, are equivalent to negations of conjunctions. And so as a result of this flipping character of '$\sim$', it is not sufficient to show that the state expressed by 'P°Q' is commitment-equivalent to the belief that $p \lor q$, to show that the major attitudes of the state expressed by 'P&Q' and of the belief that $p \land q$ are commitment-equivalent. We must also show that the *minor* attitudes of these states are commitment-equivalent. But this turns out not to plausibly be the case. The following table illustrates the problem for '°':

Table 3

| 'P' | expresses | $\langle \text{FOR}(\text{pai } p)^*, \text{FOR}(\neg \text{pai } \neg p) \rangle$ | postulate |
| 'Q' | expresses | $\langle \text{FOR}(\text{pai } q)^*, \text{FOR}(\neg \text{pai } \neg q) \rangle$ | postulate |

'P°Q'	expresses	$\langle \text{FOR}((\text{pai } p) \vee (\text{pai } q))^*, \text{FOR}((\neg \text{pai}$	from°
		$\neg p) \vee (\neg \text{pai } \neg q))\rangle$	
$\text{BF}(p \vee q)$	=	$\langle \text{FOR}(\text{pai } p \vee q)^*, \text{FOR}(\neg \text{pai } \neg(p$	analysis of
		$\vee q))\rangle$	belief

The problem is that in order for it to turn out that the state expressed by 'P°Q' is commitment-equivalent to the belief that $p \vee q$, we must assume that proceeding as if a disjunction is both necessary and sufficient for proceeding as if one of its disjuncts.

In order for the state expressed by the sentence to commit to the belief, we have to assume that proceeding as if p entails proceeding as if $p \vee q$. That does not seem to be a totally implausible assumption. It is not totally implausible that someone who takes p as settled in deciding what to do is *ipso facto* taking $p \vee q$ as settled in deciding what to do, at least in the expansive sense of 'taking as settled in deciding what to do' that is suggested by our commitment to the other assumptions about its logic. But unfortunately, it is not at all plausible that in order to take $p \vee q$ as settled in deciding what to do, you must either take p as settled in deciding what to do, or take q as settled in deciding what to do. You might be confident in the disjunction, but simply not know which disjunct is the case!

So it is not at all plausible that it will turn out that the states expressed by disjunctions under biforcated attitude semantics are commitment-equivalent to beliefs in the disjunction. And there are exactly analogous problems for '∃' and '⊃', which I'll skip, here. Though it is plausible that the state expressed by the disjunction commits to the belief, it is not at all plausible that the belief commits to the state expressed by the disjunction. So disjunctive purely descriptive sentences like 'grass is green or snow is white' turn out to be peculiarly stronger than the beliefs in their descriptive propositional contents.[2] This is positively unusual. But again, similar results hold for '∃' and for '⊃'. Existential purely descriptive sentences turn out to express states of mind that are peculiarly stronger than the belief in their descriptive propositional contents. All of this is strange and unlooked-for.

---

[2] Bob Hale (1993) argued that expressivists would be committed to something similar, based on his consideration of Blackburn (1988). Hale's argument is difficult to follow, and Gibbard (2003) claims to be able to make no sense of it. But this is, I think, the truth in the neighborhood of Hale's observation.

9.3 REVISING AGAIN

But on the other hand, at least the commitment relationships turn out to hold in the *right direction*, in order for disjunctive sentences to get assigned truth-conditions. We began in Chapter 2 by supposing that expressivists would hold that complex descriptive sentences like 'P°Q' express belief in the corresponding complex propositions, $p \vee q$, and hence that descriptive sentences inherit their propositional contents from the beliefs they express (see 'the expressivist semantic picture', in section 2.5). Then in Chapter 7, in our initial discussion of the new negation problem, it became clear that this would not do, and we moved to the revised position that complex descriptive sentences cannot express beliefs at all—but we proceeded on the assumption that they would at least express states that are *commitment-equivalent* to beliefs. So on that view, a descriptive sentence inherits its propositional content from the belief that is commitment-equivalent to the state it expresses.

But now, since this does not work for disjunctive or existentially quantified sentences, we might suppose that descriptive sentences can inherit their contents from the *strongest belief that is a commitment of* the mental states that they express. In this way, we could preserve the best of the other ideas. So long as it turns out, as it does for simple disjunctions and existential quantifications, that a complex descriptive sentence always expresses a state of mind that *commits to* the belief with the corresponding descriptive content, we can still assign complex descriptive sentences the right truth-conditions. This is simple to prove, given the assumptions in the middle column of Table 4, below, and the assumption that proceeding as if is closed under logical entailment; I do so in a brief appendix to this chapter.

9.4 WHY THIS IS ALL VERY UNSATISFACTORY

Just to recap where we are so far, the following table illustrates the assumptions that we have needed to make about the logic of proceeding as if, in order to gloss the problems arising from the new negation problem. For each connective, the table lists the assumption that we needed in order for it to turn out that the descriptive sentences involving that connective commit to the appropriate beliefs (for example, that the attitude expressed by a negated descriptive sentence commits to the belief in the negation), and the assumption that is required in order to get the converse commitment. The assumptions that I've ruled out as clearly indefensible are written in strikethrough (though the others may not be defensible, either).

Table 4

Conn-ective	Attitude expressed commits to belief	Belief commits to attitude expressed
$\sim$	pai p entails $\neg$pai $\neg p$	pai p entails $\neg$pai $\neg p$
&	(pai p)$\wedge$(pai q) entails pai $p \wedge q$	pai $p \wedge q$ entails (pai p)$\wedge$(pai q)
$\circ$	(pai p)$\vee$(pai q) entails pai $p \vee q$	~~pai $p \vee q$ entails (pai p)$\vee$(pai q)~~
$\forall$	$\forall$x(pai f(x)) entails pai $\forall$x(f(x))	pai $\forall$x(f(x)) entails $\forall$x(pai f(x))
$\exists$	$\exists$x(pai f(x)) entails pai $\exists$x(f(x))	~~pai $\exists$x(f(x)) entails $\exists$x(pai f(x))~~

In essence, what the new negation problem does is force us to accept new such assumptions for every construction we consider. If the assumptions in the middle column of the table are all *true, and* proceeding as if is closed under logical entailment, then as I indicated in the last section, every complex descriptive sentence would still express a mental state that commits to its corresponding descriptive belief, and hence we could suppose that descriptive sentences can inherit their truth-conditions from the strongest belief to which the attitude they express commits.

I say that we *could* suppose this. But this strategy looks *extremely* unpromising. Though I insisted above that the assumptions in Table 4 are not *totally* implausible, they are not, in most cases, totally plausible, either. The assumptions about the universal quantifier look particularly problematic. And things don't stop, here. Recall that the new negation problem is a problem about *every* linguistic construction. In order to preserve the result that every descriptive sentence expresses a mental state that commits to the corresponding descriptive belief, we need to make two new assumptions about the logic of proceeding as if, for every new expression increasing the expressive power of our language—one to ensure that the right result holds for that construction, and one to ensure that it holds when embedded under a negation. But if the assumptions in the table push the bounds of defensibility as things stand, they start looking much worse, as we expand and consider how to incorporate further linguistic constructions. I'll illustrate this problem in Chapter 12 by showing how implausible the required assumptions would be for accounts of 'necessarily' and of the past tense that are modeled on the accounts of '$\sim$', '&', and '$\forall$'.

The point is that there is no formal obstacle to assigning truth-conditions to complex descriptive sentences in this way. But the strategy is incredibly committing. Not only does it require very strong assumptions about the logic of proceeding as if, it requires new such assumptions for every new construction adding expressive power to our language. If this is how expressivists are going to assign truth-conditions to complex descriptive sentences, then I think it is an extremely unpromising strategy.

What pushed us to these lengths was the idea that the descriptive sentence 'P' must get its truth-conditions from the belief that *p*. Since it hasn't worked out so well, in Chapter 10, I'll explore an alternative proposal about how to assign truth-conditions to complex descriptive sentences that may be more promising, but pushes us to an even more radical view about ordinary descriptive language.

9.5 APPENDIX TO CHAPTER 9

In this appendix I prove that under biforcated attitude semantics, every descriptive sentence expresses a state that commits to the corresponding belief. I'll prove this by induction on formula complexity by proving the stronger thesis that every well-formed descriptive formula 'A' with semantic value $\langle \alpha^{1*}, \alpha^2 \rangle$ has the property that relative to every assignment of values to their unbound variables, (1) 'α^1' entails 'pai *a*', and (2) '$\neg$pai $\neg a$' entails 'α^2', where '*a*' is the translation of 'A' into our descriptive metalanguage.[3] Having proved this, it will follow as a special case that every closed descriptive sentence 'A' with semantic value $\langle \alpha^{1*}, \alpha^2 \rangle$, has the property that (1) 'α^1' entails 'pai *a*' and (2) '$\neg$pai $\neg a$' entails 'α^2'.

Since the belief that *a* is the state, $\langle \text{FOR}(\text{pai } a)^*, \text{FOR}(\neg\text{pai } \neg a) \rangle$, condition 1 implies that the state expressed by the sentence commits to the corresponding belief. Condition 2 is needed for the induction to go through smoothly, because of how '$\sim$' works. The proof requires, in addition to the assumptions in the middle column of Table 4 (above),

---

[3] Here I'm following the convention of using lower-case italics as the translations into our descriptive metalanguage of descriptive strings of our object-language represented by their corresponding capital roman letters.

the assumption that proceeding as if is closed under logical entailment. I'll assume for the sake of the induction that our language only includes as connectives '$\sim$', '&', and '$\forall$', since the other connectives can be defined in terms of these.

In the base case, we assume that 'A' is an atomic descriptive formula. It is trivial, because in biforcated attitude semantics, if 'A' is an atomic descriptive formula, then 'A' has as semantic value $\langle$pai a, ¬pai ¬$a\rangle$. Any way of assigning values to the variables open in 'A' therefore results in the corresponding descriptive belief.

The next case is '&': so suppose that 'A' and 'B' are each well-formed descriptive formulas satisfying the inductive hypothesis. That is, if 'A' has semantic value $\langle\alpha^{1*},\alpha^2\rangle$ and 'B' has semantic value $\langle\beta^{1*},\beta^2\rangle$, then relative to every assignment, 'α^1' entails 'pai a', '¬pai ¬a' entails 'α^2', 'β^1' entails 'pai b', and '¬pai ¬b' entails 'β^2'. 'A&B' expresses $\langle$FOR$(\alpha^1\wedge\beta^1)^*$,FOR$(\alpha^2\wedge\beta^2)\rangle$, so what we need to show is that relative to every assignment (1) '$\alpha^1\wedge\beta^1$' entails 'pai $a\wedge b$', and (2) '¬pai ¬$(a\wedge b)$' entails '$\alpha^2\wedge\beta^2$'. So take an arbitrary assignment S of values to unbound variables. (1) first: by the inductive hypothesis, relative to S '$\alpha^1\wedge\beta^1$' entails '(pai $a)\wedge$(pai b)'. But by the '&' assumption in the middle column of Table 4, this entails 'pai $a\wedge b$' relative to S. So (2): on the assumption that proceeding as if is closed under logical entailment, '¬pai ¬$(a\wedge b)$' entails '¬pai $(\neg a\vee\neg b)$' relative to S. Next, reasoning by contrapositive and applying the '$\diamond$' assumption from the middle column of Table 4, this entails '¬((pai ¬$a)\vee$(pai ¬b))' relative to S, which entails '(¬pai ¬$a)\wedge$(¬pai ¬b)' relative to S. Which by the inductive hypothesis entails '$\alpha^2\wedge\beta^2$' relative to S. Since our choice of S was arbitrary, this holds for every assignment.

'$\sim$': Suppose that 'A' is a well-formed descriptive formula satisfying the inductive hypothesis—that is, assuming without loss of generality that 'A' has semantic value $\langle\alpha^{1*},\alpha^2\rangle$, that relative to every assignment of values to their unbound variables, 'α^1' entails 'pai a' and '¬pai ¬a' entails 'α^2'. Since '$\sim$A' has semantic value $\langle\neg\alpha^{2*},\neg\alpha^1\rangle$, what we want to show is that for every assignment, (1) '¬α^2' entails 'pai ¬a', and (2) '¬pai ¬¬a' entails '¬α^1'. So take an arbitrary assignment S of values to their unbound variables. (1) first: reasoning by contrapositive and applying the second part of the inductive hypothesis, '¬α^2' entails '¬¬pai ¬a' relative to S and therefore entails 'pai ¬a' relative to S. So (2): assuming that proceeding as if is closed under logical entailment, '¬pai ¬¬a' entails '¬pai a' relative to S. But by contrapositive reasoning on the first part of the inductive hypothesis, this entails '¬α^1'

relative to S. Since the choice of S was arbitrary, this holds for every assignment.

Finally, '∀'. Assume that 'A' is a well-formed descriptive formula open in x and satisfying the inductive hypothesis. That is, assuming without loss of generality that 'A' has semantic value $\langle \alpha^{1*}, \alpha^2 \rangle$, that relative to every assignment of values to their unbound variables, 'α^1' entails 'pai a' and '¬pai ¬a' entails 'α^2'. '∀x(A)' has as semantic value $\langle \forall x(\alpha^1)^*, \forall x(\alpha^2) \rangle$, so what we want to show is that for every assignment of values to their unbound variables, (1) '∀x(α^1)' entails 'pai ∀x(a)', and (2) '¬pai ¬(∀x(a))' entails '∀x(α^2)'. So take an arbitrary assignment S of values to the remaining unbound variables. (1) first: by the '∀' assumption from the middle column of Table 4, '∀x(pai a)' entails 'pai ∀x(a)' relative to S. So we want to show that '∀x(α^1)' entails '∀x(pai a)' relative to S. But by the standard semantics for the universal quantifier, this is true just in case for every assignment, S*, which overlaps with S with respect to the other unbound variables but also assigns a value to x, 'α^1' entails 'pai a'. But that was entailed by the first part of the inductive hypothesis.

Similarly, (2): assuming that proceeding as if is closed under logical entailment, '¬pai ¬(∀x(a))' entails '¬pai ∃x(¬a)' relative to S. So by the '∃' assumption from the middle column of Table 4 and contrapositive reasoning, this entails '¬∃x(pai ¬a)' relative to S, and hence entails '∀x(¬pai ¬a)' relative to S. So what we want to show is that '∀x(¬pai ¬a)' entails '∀x(α^2)' relative to S. But as before, by the standard semantics for the universal quantifier, this is true just in case for every assignment, S*, which overlaps with S with respect to the other unbound variables but assigns a value to x, '¬pai ¬a' entails 'α^2'. But that was entailed by the second part of the inductive hypothesis. Since the choice of S was arbitrary, this holds for all assignments. Since there are no other ways of forming descriptive sentences (other than those definable in terms of these), that completes our proof.

10

An alternative approach

10.1 WHAT ROLE DO TRUTH-CONDITIONS PLAY?

For some time now, the problem has been how expressivists are to assign truth-conditions to ordinary descriptive sentences. I've been assuming all along that descriptive beliefs must have something to do with this, and Chapter 9 was about just how many problems are raised by trying to establish any systematic connection between the mental states expressed by complex descriptive sentences and the beliefs in the corresponding complex descriptive contents, assuming the biforcated attitude analysis of belief. As we saw, this was formally possible, but required making an indefinite string of increasingly implausible assumptions about the logic of proceeding as if. In this Chapter, I'd like to explore an alternative strategy. The strategy is to give up on first connecting complex descriptive sentences to the corresponding beliefs, and attempt to generate truth-conditions for those sentences directly from the mental states that they express, whether or not those states are beliefs, strictly speaking.

To see how to approach this question, it seems worth thinking about the *role* that truth-conditions play, for ordinary descriptive beliefs. And to consider that, I want to bring back Allison from Chapter 2. Allison, recall, is the one who believes that John Kerry is president of the United States, because she hasn't been paying very much attention since late October 2004. When you ask Allison who is president of the US and she says, 'John Kerry is president of the US', she is making a mistake, but plausibly not a linguistic one. Her mistake is about the presidency, not about English. She's mistaken in her *belief.*

It is true that Allison is also mistaken in *saying*, 'John Kerry is president of the US'. But there are two ways that such a mistake might arise. One way it could arise is if Allison says this when she does not really believe that John Kerry is president of the US. Such a case involves breaking the rules of the language, either deliberately, as in a lie, or by mistake, as might be done by someone who is not yet sure how to use the word 'president'. The other way this mistake could arise is as in the case as I actually described it: Allison makes no linguistic mistake, but is mistaken in her belief. These two sources of a mistake in her utterance lead to the following picture:

BF(Kerry is president)	is governed by rule:	be in this state only if Kerry is president	
'Kerry is president'	is governed by rule:	assert only if in state:	BF(Kerry is president)
'Kerry is president'	has truth-conditions:	that Kerry is president	

In this picture, there are two kinds of nonderivative rules, and one kind of derivative rule. First, there are nonderivative rules governing belief—to not believe that Kerry is president unless Kerry is president. Then, there are nonderivative linguistic rules governing the semantic correctness of asserting 'Kerry is president'—to not assert it unless you believe Kerry is president. And then, when you put these two kinds of rules together, you get truth-conditions for sentences, which are a sort of derivative rule governing sentence-belief combinations. On this picture, 'Kerry is president' has the truth-condition that Kerry is president, because that is the condition that must be satisfied, if the speaker is not to make a mistake either in what to believe or in what to say, given what she believes.

Given this sort of view, the reason why 'Kerry is president' gets the truth-condition that Kerry is president from the belief that Kerry is president, is not (at least, primarily) that the belief that Kerry is president is a matter of bearing the *belief* attitude toward the content, *that Kerry is president*. The reason why 'Kerry is president' gets this truth-condition from the belief that Kerry is president, on this picture, is independent of the claim that this belief is an attitude which has *that Kerry is president* as its content. It derives from the fact that it is a *mistake* to have this belief, if Kerry is not president. (Which, in turn, is probably explained by the fact that it is the belief with that content.)

This is a significant improvement. Our problem is that the mental state expressed by a complex descriptive sentence, 'P', is not an attitude toward *p*, the descriptive content of 'P'. But if this were our operating picture about how sentences get their truth-conditions, then it might allow us to assign truth-conditions to complex descriptive sentences on the basis of the mental states that they express, regardless of whether those states are beliefs—provided that those states can be mistaken in the same kind of way that beliefs can be mistaken. So the idea is to try to explain why the states expressed by arbitrarily complex descriptive sentences have *mistake conditions*. *Mistake conditions* is what I will call the conditions under which it is a mistake of the relevant kind to be in some mental state.

Start with atomic descriptive sentences. These are beliefs, but rather than taking for granted that beliefs have mistake conditions, we should try to explain, on the basis of premises about being for and about proceeding as if, why this is so. Doing so will be the best way to warm up in order to see whether the same kind of explanation can be expanded to deal with the states expressed by complex descriptive sentences.

On the original, non-biforcated analysis of belief, believing that p is being for proceeding as if p. What would explain why it is a mistake to be in this state, if p is false? Well, here is a conjecture. Assume that it would be a mistake to proceed as if p, if p is false. This is a plausible sort of assumption—proceeding as if p is taking p as settled in deciding what to do, and that will lead to bad decisions, if p is false. So next step: being for, we assumed, is a motivational state whose primary role is that someone who is for doing A will tend to do A, other things being equal. So being for proceeding as if p is the state whose primary role is to get you to proceed as if p. But if proceeding as if p is a mistake, then surely it is intelligible to suppose that being for proceeding as if p is some kind of mistake, as well. So let's assume that. It then follows that it is a mistake to believe that p if p is false—and this is something that we have explained on the basis of simpler assumptions.

The same assumptions yield the same result, if we follow the biforcated attitude analysis of belief. According to that analysis, believing that p still involves being for proceeding as if p, though it also involves being for proceeding as if $\neg p$. Since it still involves being for proceeding as if p, it will still involve a mistake whenever it is a mistake to be for proceeding as if p. So the same assumptions suffice.

Whether or not we go with the simple analysis of belief and the semantics of Chapter 6, or the biforcated attitude analysis of belief and the biforcated attitude semantics of Chapter 8, an arbitrary atomic descriptive sentence, 'P' expresses the belief that p. And so regardless of which way we go, we can explain why an arbitrary atomic descriptive sentence, 'P', expresses a mental state that it is a mistake to be in whenever p is false. So consequently, we can explain where the truth-conditions on arbitrary atomic descriptive sentences come from. In the next section, I'll show how to generalize this kind of explanation to complex descriptive sentences.

10.2 COMPLEX SENTENCES

In the last section, I was trying to be neutral as to whether, in the end, we will want to go with biforcated attitude semantics, or with the simpler semantics of Chapter 6. Why? Well, the point of the move to biforcated attitude semantics was initially to gloss the new negation problem for the case of negations. And the reason why that was an important problem, was because we were worried about how complex descriptive sentences would get assigned the right truth-conditions. But now we are exploring another strategy for how complex descriptive sentences get assigned their truth-conditions. So we should leave it at least initially open whether we really still need biforcated attitude semantics.

Nevertheless, consideration of the case of negation again shows us that the biforcated attitude approach is necessary. Consider the state expressed by the negation of an atomic descriptive sentence given the simple analysis of belief and the semantics of Chapter 6. On this view, '∼P' expresses FOR(¬pai p). So what would it take to explain why it is a mistake to be in this state whenever '∼P' is false—i.e., whenever p is true? Well, before we assumed that it is a mistake to be for something whenever it is a mistake to do that thing. So using that assumption, we could explain what we need, if only we could help ourselves to the new assumption that it is a mistake to not proceed as if p, if p is true. Before we assumed that it is a mistake to proceed as if p, if p is false. But this new assumption is stronger, and much less plausible. Assuming that p is always true or false, the new assumption entails that it is always a mistake to neither proceed as if p nor proceed as if $¬p$. But surely it is possible to take neither p nor $¬p$ as settled in deciding what to do, without making any mistake!

We don't have this problem in biforcated attitude semantics. In biforcated attitude semantics, if 'P' is an atomic descriptive sentence, then '∼P' expresses a biforcated attitude whose major attitude is FOR(¬¬ pai $¬p$). Now assuming, as we did before, that it is a mistake to proceed as if p if p is false, it follows that it is a mistake to proceed as if $¬p$ if $¬p$ is false (simply substituting '$¬p$' for 'p'). But we also assumed that if it is a mistake to do something, then it is a mistake to be for doing it. So it follows that it is a mistake to be in the state, FOR($\neg\neg$pai $\neg p$), if $\neg p$ is false. But since being in the state expressed by '$\sim$P' involves being in its major attitude, it follows that it is a mistake to be in the state expressed by '$\sim$P' if $\neg p$ is false. So this explains the mistake conditions on the states expressed by negations of atomic sentences, given biforcated attitude semantics. So we should still go with biforcated attitude semantics, after all.

In fact, we need no substantive further assumptions in order to expand this result to other constructions. Consider the case of conjunction. 'P&Q' expresses a state whose major attitude is FOR((pai p)$\wedge$(pai q)). On the assumption that it is a mistake to be for doing something if it is a mistake to do it, it is a mistake to be in this state, if it is a mistake to proceed as if p and proceed as if q. But we assumed before that it is a mistake to proceed as if p if p is false, and similarly for q. So it follows that it is a mistake to be in the state, FOR((pai p)$\wedge$(pai q)) if either p is false or q is false—i.e., if $p \wedge q$ is false. Since being in the state expressed by 'P&Q' involves being in this state, it is also a mistake to be in the state expressed by 'P&Q' if $p \wedge q$ is false.

Analogous reasoning works for disjunction. 'P°Q' expresses a state whose major attitude is FOR((pai p)$\vee$(pai q)). Given the same assumptions, it is a mistake to be in this state if it is a mistake to either proceed as if p or proceed as if q, which follows if it is a mistake to proceed as if p and a mistake to proceed as if q, which follows if p is false and q is false—i.e., if $p \vee q$ is false. So it is a mistake to be in the state expressed by 'P°Q' if $p \vee q$ is false. And the material conditional: 'P⊃Q' expresses a state whose major attitude is FOR(($\neg$pai $\neg p$)>(pai q)). So by the same assumptions, it is a mistake to be in this state if it is a mistake to be such that if you don't proceed as if $\neg p$, then you proceed as if q—i.e., to either proceed as if q or proceed as if $\neg p$. But that is a mistake if it is a mistake to proceed as if q and a mistake to proceed as if $\neg p$, i.e., if q is false and $\neg p$ is false, i.e., if $p \wedge \neg q$ or, more familiarly, $\neg(p{>}q)$. The same reasoning also works for the quantifiers, although I omit it here, in favor of a more rigorous treatment in the appendix to this chapter.

To emphasize the way that mistake conditions intuitively work, I've left a couple things out of this treatment. For one thing, I've only shown that the mistake conditions for the mental states expressed by each sentence *include* the conditions under which the content of the sentence should be false. I haven't shown that the state is only mistaken in conditions under which the content of the sentence should be false. Showing the latter turns out to require stronger assumptions. Also, strictly speaking, the arguments advanced in this section only cover the case of sentences with complexity of degree one—which are built up by one step from atomic formulas. The argument that this works equally well for descriptive sentences of arbitrary complexity needs to be formulated with significantly more abstraction. These generalizations do follow, given the appropriate assumptions, but I've reserved them, including the case of quantifiers, for the appendix to this chapter.

The important lesson of mistake conditions is this: given a relatively sparse set of assumptions—that being for doing A is a mistake if it is a mistake to do A, and that proceeding as if p is a mistake if p is false—we can explain why arbitrarily complex descriptive sentences express mental states that are mistaken whenever those sentences are false. The idea in the appendix is to employ assumptions sufficient to establish the converse, as well. So given the required assumptions, this establishes that arbitrarily complex descriptive sentences have the right truth-conditions. It does so by explaining why they express mental states with the right *mistake conditions*.

This alternative approach contrasts favorably, at least initially, with the approach investigated in Chapter 9. On that approach, to assign each sentence a truth-condition, we had to associate that sentence with the belief with that truth-conditional content. But in order to do that, we needed to make new assumptions about the logic of proceeding as if, for each and every construction that added expressive power to the language, and the plausibility of many of those assumptions was doubtful, with an open-ended list of further such assumptions to come, whenever we get around to expanding our semantics to more closely approximate the expressive powers of natural languages. This alternative strategy turns out to also need new assumptions for each construction, in order to get the converse entailment, but they are different assumptions—assumptions about mistake conditions, rather than assumptions about the logic of proceeding as if. So it looks like a reasonable alternative strategy for expressivists. I offer them both to choose from.

10.3 BELIEF ASCRIPTIONS

I've been describing the approach of this chapter as allowing that complex descriptive sentences get their truth-conditions directly from the states that they express, even though those states are not, themselves, beliefs. I've been describing it in this way, because the states expressed by complex descriptive sentences do not consist in the same attitude toward a proposition that the states expressed by atomic descriptive sentences do. The atomic descriptive sentence, 'P', expresses being for proceeding as if p and being for not proceeding as if $\neg p$. So *being for proceeding as if and for not proceeding as if not* would appear to be an attitude that one can have toward p, and if one is in the state expressed by the atomic descriptive sentence, 'P', then one has this attitude toward p. But one does not have this attitude toward $\neg p$ when one is in the state expressed by '~P', nor does one have this attitude toward $p \wedge q$ when one is in the state expressed by 'P&Q', and so on. That is why I have been saying, since Chapter 7, that they do not really express the right beliefs.

But given the approach in this chapter, we might choose to describe this same situation in another way. Instead of saying that what we have discovered is that expressivism leads to thinking that complex descriptive sentences don't really express beliefs, we could instead say that what we have discovered, is that expressivism leads to thinking that complex descriptive beliefs do not consist in bearing the same attitude toward complex descriptive contents, as simple descriptive beliefs consist in bearing toward simple descriptive contents.

But what would let us get away with this? Doesn't 'Jon believes that p' say that Jon stands in a certain relation to the proposition p? Namely, the *belief* relation? How could 'Jon believes that p' and 'Jon believes that $p \wedge q$' both be true, even though there is no attitude that Jon bears both toward p and toward $p \wedge q$?

The answer, I think, is that expressivists have independent grounds to think that things are more complicated than this. In English, we say things like 'Jon believes that murder is wrong'. If expressivists agree that 'believes that' semantically contributes a relation between Jon and the proposition picked out by the complement clause, then they can make sense of this only if they believe in such a thing as the proposition that murder is wrong. But if there is such a proposition, then it could be the semantic value of 'murder is wrong', and there would be no need to go in for expressivist semantics, in the first place. So presumably an important part of the motivation for expressivism is to avoid having to allow that there are such propositions to which Jon can stand in the *believes that* relation.

Does it follow that expressivists are committed to holding that there are no moral beliefs? Expressivism is often described in this way, as if it is all fine to say, 'Jon judges that murder is wrong' or 'Jon thinks that murder is wrong', but not fine to say, 'Jon believes that murder is wrong'. I think this is somewhat bizarre. On the face of it, 'Jon judges that murder is wrong' and 'Jon thinks that murder is wrong' both look like they, too, semantically contribute a relation between Jon and the proposition that murder is wrong. But then, it seems that expressivists have a problem. If they are to say things like, 'Jon judges that murder is wrong' or 'Jon thinks that murder is wrong', they must have some alternative semantics for these sentences, on which they do not postulate a relation between Jon and the proposition that murder is wrong. Now, either it is possible to do this, or it is not. If it is not, then this is a general problem for expressivists, about how they are to account for the semantics of complement-taking verbs—which is just one piece of the embedding problem for expressivism. But if it *is* possible for expressivists to give such a semantics, then surely they can give one for 'Jon believes that murder is wrong', too.

How would such a semantics go? Well, intuitively it should operate under the constraint that when 'P' is an ordinary descriptive sentence meaning that *p*, 'Jon believes that P' should be true just in case Jon stands in the *belief* relation to *p*. The standard idea that the *belief* relation is the semantic value of 'believes that' yields this result, true. But this result could also be yielded indirectly. For example, suppose that 'Jon believes that P' means, 'Jon is in the mental state expressed by 'P'.' Notice that if the mental state expressed by a descriptive sentence which means that *p* is always a matter of standing in the *belief* relation to *p* (which we were assuming all along would be the natural view), it follows from this account that if 'P' is a descriptive sentence meaning that *p*, 'Jon believes that P' will be true just in case Jon stands in the *belief* relation to *p*. But this would not be because the *belief* relation is the semantic value of 'believes that'. It would distinguish the metaphysics of ordinary descriptive belief from the semantics of 'believes that'.

On the other hand, if 'murder is wrong' expresses disapproval of murder, then from this account it would follow that 'Jon believes that murder is wrong' is true just in case Jon disapproves of murder. So by distinguishing the metaphysics of ordinary descriptive belief from the semantics of 'believes that', the account leaves room for it to turn out that 'Jon believes that murder is wrong' can be true, even without appealing as a theorist to any such thing as the proposition that murder is wrong, to which Jon can stand in some relation. Since 'Jon believes that murder is wrong' is something true, the expressivist can disquote, and assert outright that Jon believes that murder is wrong. But since he does, it follows that there are some moral beliefs. So expressivists can insist that there are moral beliefs, just as they can insist that there are moral thoughts and moral judgments, if only they can make some semantics like this one work.

Unfortunately, the account just given can't be exactly right, because it yields the wrong modal profile. It is also not stated within the semantic framework of expressivism itself (that was to avoid complications in order to make the idea clear). But we can fix both of these things with the following sort of account:

BEL*   If 'a' is a singular term and 'A' is a well-formed formula with semantic value $\langle \alpha^{1*}, \alpha^2 \rangle$, then 'BEL(a,'A')' is a well-formed formula and has semantic value $\langle \lambda z(z$ is pai(a is in $\langle \text{FOR}(\alpha^1)^*, \text{FOR}(\alpha^2) \rangle)))^*, \lambda z(z$ is ¬pai ¬(a is in $\langle \text{FOR}(\alpha^1)^*, \text{FOR}(\alpha^2) \rangle)))) \rangle$.

In other words, if 'A' expresses some state, S, then 'Jon believes 'A'' ('BEL(Jon,'A')') expresses the belief that Jon is in S. This incorporates the semantics of 'believes that' into the framework of biforcated attitude semantics. And it avoids the modal profile objection by being careful not to embed a description picking out which mental state Jon is in. It is, I think, broadly speaking, the sort of thing that expressivists need. If they choose not to go in for such a semantics for 'believes', they will still need it for 'thinks' and/or 'judges'.

In fact, we can do even better for the expressivist. The account I've just given treats belief as a relation between agents and sentences. And it might seem hard to do otherwise, if normative sentences don't have propositional contents. But on the other hand, under biforcated attitude semantics all sentences *are* associated with the pairs of properties that I've been calling 'semantic values'. So if we had an object-language term-forming operator, 'THAT(A)', which designates the semantic value of its argument, 'A', and a relation, jointfor(a,b), which a stands in to b just in case b is a pair of properties each of which a is for, then we could use those to define 'Jon believes that p' as follows:

THAT   If 'A' is a well-formed formula with semantic value $\langle \alpha^1, \alpha^2 \rangle$, then 'THAT(A)' is a complex singular term whose denotation is $\langle \alpha^1, \alpha^2 \rangle$.

BEL   If 'a' denotes o_1 and 'b' denotes o_2, then 'BEL(a,b)' is a well-formed formula and has semantic value $\langle \lambda z(z$ is pai (jointfor(o_1, o_2))*, $\lambda z(z$ is ¬pai ¬(jointfor(o_1, o_2)))) \rangle$.

So: If 'Jon' denotes Jon and 'P' is a closed sentence with semantic
           value S, then 'BEL(Jon,THAT(P))' has semantic value ⟨λz(z is pai
           (jointfor(Jon, S))*, λz(z is ¬pai ¬(jointfor(Jon, S)))⟩.

The foregoing account has a number of advantageous features. For
example, it allows us to explain why 'there is something Jon believes'
follows from 'Jon believes that p'. It follows in the same way that
'∃x(R(a,x))' always follows from 'R(a,b)'. Similarly, it yields an explanation of why from 'Jon believes that p' and 'Jan believes that p', it
follows, 'there is something Jon and Jan both believe—namely, that p'.
This follows in the same way that '∃x(R(a,x)&R(b,x)&(x=c))' follows
from 'R(a,c)' and 'R(b,c)'. I'll return to these kinds of advantages of this
account in Chapter 11 when we discuss truth-ascriptions.[1]

The important point—the lesson from all of this—is that once we
have this semantics in hand, we no longer need describe expressivism as
holding that there are no moral beliefs, or as holding that moral
sentences don't express beliefs. If we accepted this semantics, or one
like it, for the language that we actually speak, then using this language,
we would better describe the central thesis of expressivism as being
that moral sentences do not express states of mind that consist in
the same cognitive attitude toward propositions as ordinary descriptive
sentences do.[2]

---

[1] For simplicity, the account doesn't allow for quantifying into attitude ascriptions.
The fix requires something like the following: substitute for the two-place relation,
jointfor(a,b), a three-place relation, jointfor*(a,b,c), which holds between an agent, a pair
of functions from n-tuples of values to properties, and an n-tuple of values, just in case
the agent is jointfor the pair of properties that results from applying the pair of functions
to the n-tuple of values. This can't be exactly right as it stands, but it's the kind of way
you'd want to go, if you wanted to develop this kind of account.

[2] Compare, for example, Horgan and Timmons (2006), who make a very big deal of
the fact that they have a semantics for 'believes that' on which it can apply to normative
as well as descriptive sentences. To be fair, Horgan and Timmons do a fair bit of work
on the phenomenology of belief to support their claim that this semantics is not simply
an arbitrary semantic unification of totally different kinds of mental states. But their
semantics for 'believes that' is considerably less satisfactory than the one given here.
For example, it doesn't explain why when you believe something, it follows that there
is something that you believe. Strictly speaking, in Horgan and Timmons's view, you
may believe that Bush ought to be president, even though there is nothing that you
believe. Horgan and Timmons make clear that this is their view: 'On our account, talk
of nondescriptive content is to be understood as not really positing any such *items* as
overall contents or cognitive contents... such talk is not rightly construed as positing
some *entity* that *is* a nondescriptive cognitive content' (2006: 261). Moreover, this
is a non-accidental feature of their view, and actually extends to complex descriptive
contents, as well. Recall from section 3.4 that Horgan and Timmons hold that thinking

Similarly—and this is the bottom line for the approach to assigning truth-conditions in this chapter—if this semantics is correct, then we no longer need describe the result of biforcated attitude semantics as entailing that complex descriptive sentences don't really express beliefs. If the state, $\langle \text{FOR}(\neg\neg\text{pai} \neg p)^*, \text{FOR}(\neg\text{pai } p)\rangle$ is expressed by '$\sim$P', then we can describe it as 'the belief that $\sim$P', even though it is not a matter of bearing the same attitude toward $\neg p$ that you bear toward p when you are in the state we would describe as 'the belief that P'. And so consequently, we could say that complex descriptive sentences express complex descriptive beliefs after all; we've merely discovered something interesting about what complex descriptive beliefs are like—just as moral beliefs do not consist in the same attitude toward propositions that ordinary descriptive beliefs do, complex descriptive beliefs do not consist in this same attitude toward propositions, either.[3]

And this yields one more advantage of the mistake conditions approach to assigning truth-conditions, over the approach of Chapter 9. Recall that one feature of the approach of Chapter 9 was that it led to the surprising result that the mental states expressed by many complex purely descriptive sentences turned out to be peculiarly stronger than the beliefs in the corresponding descriptive contents. But given the mistake conditions approach and this semantics for 'BEL', we can now say that the mental states expressed by complex descriptive sentences *are* the corresponding descriptive beliefs, and hence avoid this uncomfortable result altogether.

10.4 WHERE WE STAND

In this chapter, I've made two suggestions. First, I've suggested the *mistake conditions* approach to assigning truth-conditions to descriptive sentences. On this view, truth-conditions are the product of the assertability conditions on sentences given by their expressivist semantics, with independent mistake conditions on the state of mind that is required

that grass is green and thinking that grass ought to be green are both kinds of belief, and have the same object—the proposition that grass is green. But it doesn't follow that if Jon believes that grass is green and Jan believes that grass ought to be green, that there is something Jon and Jan both believe. So 'believes that' can't, on their view, ascribe a relation to the objects that beliefs relate agents to.

[3] Again, compare the treatment of Horgan and Timmons (2006).

by those assertability conditions. If you make either kind of mistake, being in that state when it is a mistake to, or asserting the sentence when you are not licensed to, you violate the truth-conditions for the sentence. That is just what truth-conditions *are*, on this picture. And I've illustrated how to give an explanatory account of the mistake conditions on the attitudes expressed by arbitrarily complex descriptive sentences according to biforcated attitude semantics, by appeal to an alternative set of assumptions from those employed in Chapter 9.

The other suggestion I've made in this chapter is that if we like this view, we might still go on to say that complex descriptive sentences express beliefs, and inherit their truth-conditions from the beliefs they express. We could say this, I argued, if we had the right semantics for 'believes that' and related constructions to let us say it. And then I pointed out that expressivists have independent motivation to develop such an account, and took a few initial steps toward developing it. I stated, for example, a semantics for 'Jon believes 'P'', and one for 'Jon believes that p' which can predict some of its simple modal and inferential properties.

Put together, I think this is a much more promising approach than that investigated in Chapter 9. But it remains a radical idea. I argued in Chapters 3 and 4 that there is only one way for expressivists to explain inconsistency, even between atomic normative sentences and their negations, and that is to add the right kind of structure to their account. I then argued in section 7.1 that retaining the advantages of the resulting account requires analyzing belief in terms of a noncognitive attitude. And then we saw in section 7.3 and in Chapter 9 that this leads to the conclusion that complex descriptive sentences express mental states that are different in kind from the states that consist in the same attitude toward their contents, as do simple beliefs. Even if all of this works—and so far, I have been arguing that things are working out for the constructions we have considered, up to the expressive power of the predicate calculus—it is a surprising and radical conclusion about ordinary descriptive belief.

Moreover, the semantics for 'believes that' suggested in this chapter, though I think it is something that expressivists will need to go in for, anyway, raises many unanswered questions of its own. I've begun, but only begun, to consider questions like how the inference from 'Jon believes that p' and 'Jan believes that p' to 'there is something Jon and Jan both believe' is supposed to work, but this still leaves many questions open. For example, if expressivists are to make do without appealing to the proposition that murder is wrong, then what about 'Jon hopes that murder is wrong', 'Jon wonders whether murder is wrong', 'Jon is pleased that murder is wrong', 'Jon is assuming that murder is wrong', and so on, for each and every other complement-taking verb?

Providing an expressivist semantics for all of these constructions, and explaining why the resulting sentences behave in the right sorts of ways, is a much bigger and much more formidable obstacle than the stubborn negation problem that has been a stumbling block for over forty years. The strategy I've offered for 'believes that' offers a formula for how to approach these other questions—we need to find relations to play the kinds of roles that the jointfor(a,b) relation plays for 'believes'. But it still leaves an enormous commitment to be discharged.

APPENDIX TO CHAPTER 10

Here I prove that we get the right mistake conditions for arbitrarily complex descriptive sentences, again by induction on formula complexity.[4] Since they provide the full range of expressive power for our language, I'll again work only with '$\sim$', '&', and '$\forall$', and I'll make the following assumptions:

1 It is a mistake to be in the state FOR(α) just in case it is a mistake to be α.
2 It is a mistake to be in a biforcated attitude just in case it is a mistake to be in its major attitude.
3 It is a mistake to be $\lambda z(z$ is pai $p)$ just in case $\neg p$.
4 It is a mistake to be $\lambda z(Pz \wedge Qz)$ just in case either it is a mistake to be $\lambda z(Pz)$ or a mistake to be $\lambda z(Qz)$.
5 It is a mistake to be $\lambda z(\forall x(Fzx))$, just in case for some thing, x, it is a mistake to be $\lambda z(Fzx)$.
6 It is a mistake to be $\lambda z(Pz \vee Qz)$ just in case it is a mistake to be $\lambda z(Pz)$ and a mistake to be $\lambda z(Qz)$.
7 It is a mistake to be $\lambda z(\exists x(Fzx))$, just in case for each thing, x, it is a mistake to be $\lambda z(Fzx)$.

---

[4] This proof is the most complicated in this book; if you're rusty on or unfamiliar with inductions on formula complexity, it may help you to warm up with the proof in the appendix to Chapter 9.

The highly plausible, right-to-left, directions of these assumptions are the ones required to show that the states expressed by each sentence are mistaken when the sentence is false. The less plausible, left-to-right, directions of these assumptions are the ones used to establish the converse.

Treating quantifiers correctly requires establishing the requisite property for arbitrarily complex formulas. An arbitrary well-formed formula 'A' has a semantic value consisting of a major element and a minor element. Its major element is a function from n-tuples of individuals to properties, where n is the number of open variables in 'A', and is picked out by a lambda-abstraction, '$\lambda z(\alpha)$'. The function picked out by '$\lambda z(\alpha)$' might have the following property, call it 'P': that for any choice of values whatsoever, it yields a property that it is a mistake to have just in case 'a' is false, relative to the assignment of those values to its unbound variables, where 'a' is the metalanguage translation of 'A'.[5]

I am first going to prove by induction on formula complexity that arbitrarily complex purely descriptive formulas have major elements with property P. It will then follow trivially that *closed* descriptive sentences 'A', meaning that a, all express states whose major attitude is a matter of being for a property that it is a mistake to have just in case it is false that a. And from that and assumption 1, it will follow that the major attitude expressed by an arbitrary descriptive sentence 'A' meaning that a is a mistake just in case it is false that a. And so from that and assumption 2, it will follow that every descriptive sentence 'A' expresses a state of mind that it is a mistake to be in just in case it is false that a. And so that will be how we can establish truth-conditions for descriptive sentences.

The base case is atomic descriptive formulas. If 'A' is an atomic descriptive formula, its major element is '$\lambda z(z \text{ is pai } a)$'. So consider an arbitrary assignment S to the variables yielding, for example, '$\lambda z(z \text{ is pai } a^*)$'. By assumption 3, being $\lambda z(z \text{ is pai } a^*)$ is a mistake just in case $\neg a^*$. But $\neg a^*$, just in case 'a' is false relative to the assignment of values that generates 'a^*' from 'a'. But since our assignment of values was arbitrary, this holds for all assignments. But that is just property P: the property a sentence 'A' has of having a major element which, for all assignments of values, yields a property that it is a mistake to have just in case 'a' is

---

[5] Here I again follow the convention of using lower-case italics for the metalanguage translation of the object-language descriptive formula picked out by the corresponding capital roman letter.

false relative to that assignment of values, where '*a*' is the metalanguage translation of 'A'.

Next, conjunction. Assume that 'A' and 'B' are well-formed descriptive formulas with property P. We want to show that 'A&B' has property P. If 'A' has major element picked out by '$\lambda z(\alpha)$' and 'B' has major element picked out by '$\lambda z(\beta)$', then the major element of 'A&B' is picked out by '$\lambda z(\alpha \wedge \beta)$'. Now consider an arbitrary assignment S of values to the unbound variables in '$\lambda z(\alpha \wedge \beta)$', resulting in a property we might denote, '$\lambda z(\alpha^* \wedge \beta^*)$'. By assumption 4, it then follows that it is a mistake to be $\lambda z(\alpha^* \wedge \beta^*)$ just in case either it is a mistake to be $\lambda z(\alpha^*)$ or it is a mistake to be $\lambda z(\beta^*)$. The cases are identical, so take the first one. '$\lambda z(\alpha^*)$' results from an assignment of values to the unbound variables in '$\lambda z(\alpha)$', so according to the inductive hypothesis that 'A' has property P, it is a mistake to be $\lambda z(\alpha^*)$ just in case '*a*' is false, relative to that assignment to its unbound variables. So similarly, it is a mistake to be $\lambda z(\beta^*)$ just in case '*b*' is false, relative to that assignment to its unbound variables. So it is a mistake to be $\lambda z(\alpha^* \wedge \beta^*)$ just in case either '*a*' is false or '*b*' is false, relative to that assignment—i.e., just in case '*a*∧*b*' is false relative to that assignment. But that is the metalanguage translation of 'A&B', but since this holds for an arbitrary assignment, 'A&B' has property P, too.

On to the universal quantifier. Assume that 'A' is a well-formed formula open in x with property P. We want to show that '∀x(A)' has property P. If the major element of 'A' is picked out by '$\lambda z(\alpha)$', then the major element of '∀x(A)' is picked out by '$\lambda z(\forall x(\alpha))$'. So consider an arbitrary assignment S of values to the unbound variables in '$\lambda z(\forall x(\alpha))$', yielding a property that we might denote, '$\lambda z(\forall x(\alpha^*))$'. Assumption 5 tells us that being $\lambda z(\forall x(\alpha^*))$ is a mistake just in case for some value of x, being $\lambda z(\alpha^*)$ is a mistake. That is, just in case being $\lambda z(\alpha^{**})$ is a mistake, where '$\lambda z(\alpha^{**})$' is the result of assigning the appropriate value to x in '$\lambda z(\alpha^*)$'. But then '$\lambda z(\alpha^{**})$' is really just the result of an assignment of values to '$\lambda z(\alpha)$', which by the inductive hypothesis, yields a property that it is a mistake to have just in case '*a*' is false relative to that assignment. But '*a*' is false relative to an assignment to its other unbound variables and our given assignment to x, just in case '∀x(*a*)' is false relative to that assignment to the other unbound variables. But that is the metalanguage translation of '∀x(A)', so since our assignment was arbitrary, '∀x(A)' has property P.

We're not quite almost done. I'll do negation in four separate steps, depending on whether the formula negated is atomic, or has a widest-scope negation, conjunction, or universal quantifier. First, assume that

'A' is an atomic descriptive formula with property P. We want to show that '∼A' has P. The minor element of 'A' can be picked out by '$\lambda z(\neg(z$ is pai $\neg a))$', so the major element of '∼A' can be picked out by '$\lambda z(\neg\neg(z$ is pai $\neg a))$'. So consider an arbitrary assignment of values S to the unbound variables in this, which we might write as '$\lambda z(\neg\neg(z$ is pai $\neg a^*))$', or equivalently, '$\lambda z(z$ is pai $\neg a^*)$'. It then follows from assumption 3 that it is a mistake to have this property just in case $\neg\neg a^*$—i.e., just in case '$\neg a$' is false relative to that assignment to its unbound variables. But that is the metalanguage translation of '∼A', so since that holds for an arbitrary assignment, '∼A' has P.

Now assume that 'A' is a descriptive formula with property P, in order to show that '∼∼A' has P. If the major element of 'A' is picked out by '$\lambda z(\alpha)$', then the major element of '∼∼A' is picked out by '$\lambda z(\neg\neg\alpha)$'. An arbitrary assignment of values S to the unbound variables in '$\lambda z(\neg\neg\alpha)$' will yield a property that is equivalent to that given by the same assignment of values to the unbound variables in '$\lambda z(\alpha)$', and so presumably mistaken under the same conditions. And by the inductive hypothesis, it is a mistake to be $\lambda z(\alpha)$ just in case 'a' is false relative to that assignment of values to its unbound variables, i.e., just in case '$\neg\neg a$' is false relative to that assignment. But that is the metalanguage translation of '∼∼A', so since our assignment was arbitrary, '∼∼A' has property P.

Assume both 'A' and 'B' are formulas with property P, to show that '∼(A&B)' has property P. Since conjunction is associative, I will assume that neither 'A' nor 'B' has the form, 'C&D', and take what goes for '∼(A&B)' to go, without loss of generality, for '∼(A&B&...&N)'. From the inductive hypothesis, the assumption that neither 'A' nor 'B' is itself a conjunction, and the other cases of this proof, it follows that '∼A' and '∼B' have property P as well—and it is this assumption that we will need in the proof. Now assuming that the minor element of 'A' can be picked out by '$\lambda z(\alpha)$' and the minor element of 'B' can be picked out by '$\lambda z(\beta)$', the major element of '∼(A&B)' can be picked out by '$\lambda z(\neg(\alpha\wedge\beta))$'. So consider an arbitrary assignment S of values to its unbound variables, which we might write as, '$\lambda z(\neg(\alpha^*\wedge\beta^*))$'. Assuming that necessarily equivalent properties are mistaken under the same conditions, it follows that it is a mistake to be $\lambda z(\neg(\alpha^*\wedge\beta^*))$ just in case it is a mistake to be $\lambda z(\neg\alpha^*\vee\neg\beta^*)$, and hence it follows by assumption 6 that it is both a mistake to be $\lambda z(\neg\alpha^*)$ and a mistake to be $\lambda z(\neg\beta^*)$. But then by assumption that '∼A' and '∼B' have property P, it is a mistake to be $\lambda z(\neg\alpha^*)$ just in case '$\neg a$' is false relative to that assignment, and it is a mistake to be $\lambda z(\neg\beta^*)$ just in case '$\neg b$' is false relative to that assignment. So putting this together, it is a mistake to be $\lambda z(\neg(\alpha^*\wedge\beta^*))$ just in case '$\neg a$' and '$\neg b$' are both false relative to that assignment—i.e., just in case '$\neg(a\wedge b)$' is. But that is the metalanguage translation of '$\sim$(A&B)', so since the assignment was arbitrary, '$\sim$(A&B)' has property P.

Finally, assume that 'A' is a descriptive formula with property P. We want to show that '$\sim\forall x(A)$' has P. I'll assume without loss of generality that 'A' does not itself have a universal quantifier taking widest scope; as in the last paragraph, the same reasoning applies if it does. Similarly, as in the last paragraph, it follows from the assumption that 'A' does not have a widest-scope universal quantifier, the inductive hypothesis, and the other steps of this proof that '$\sim$A' has property P, and this is the assumption that we will need for the proof. If the minor element of 'A' can be picked out by '$\lambda z(\alpha)$', then the major element of '$\sim\forall x(A)$' can be picked out by '$\lambda z(\neg\forall x(\alpha))$'. Consider an arbitrary assignment S of values to its unbound variables, yielding a property we might denote by '$\lambda z(\neg\forall x(\alpha^*))$'. Assuming that necessarily equivalent properties are mistaken under the same conditions, it is a mistake to be $\lambda z(\neg\forall x(\alpha^*))$ just in case it is a mistake to be $\lambda z(\exists x(\neg\alpha^*))$, and hence by assumption 7, just in case for every assignment to x, it is a mistake to be $\lambda z(\neg\alpha^*)$. But since '$\sim$A' has property P, it is a mistake to be $\lambda z(\neg\alpha^*)$ for every assignment to x just in case '$\neg a$' is false relative to that assignment and to S. But '$\neg a$' is false relative to S and every assignment to x just in case '$\neg\forall x(a)$' is false relative to S. But that is the metalanguage translation of '$\sim\forall x(A)$', so since this assignment was arbitrary, '$\sim\forall x(A)$' has property P.

This completes the proof. Every descriptive formula is either atomic, or constructed from atomic descriptive formulas by conjunction, universal quantification, or negation applied to an atomic formula, applied to a negation, applied to a conjunction, or applied to a universal quantification. So every descriptive formula has property P. That means that an arbitrary closed descriptive sentence 'A' expresses a biforcated state whose major attitude has a content that it is a mistake to have just in case 'A' is false. (We can drop the 'relative to an assignment', since no more variables are unbound.) And so from assumptions 1 and 2, it is a mistake to be in that biforcated attitude just in case 'A' is false.

That means that these assumptions explain the right mistake conditions for biforcated attitudes in order to assign the right truth-conditions to arbitrary descriptive sentences. It is not clear whether all of these assumptions are plausible, and I haven't considered whether it is possible to reconstruct the proof with restricted versions of assumptions 4 through 7. In general, the direction of each assumption that is less plausible is the direction required in order for it to turn out that the state expressed by 'A' is mistaken only if 'A' is false. So it may very plausibly turn out that given plausible assumptions, sentences will end up with truth-conditions that are too restrictive. Nevertheless, I believe that the proposal in this chapter is the best that it is going to be possible to do, for expressivism.

PART IV

EXTENSIONS

11

Nondescriptivist semantics

11.1 THE ATTRACTIONS OF THIS SEMANTIC PROGRAM

The semantic program that comes out of the preceding chapters has, I think, some general attractions as a framework within which to develop a nondescriptivist semantics. For any domain about which philosophers seek to give some account, there are philosophers who advocate a 'nondescriptive' approach—the proposal that the language in that area of discourse does not really purport to describe how things are. The idea is that if the language in that domain doesn't really purport to describe how things are, then we don't really have to understand what it is for them to be that way. The pressure toward nondescriptivism in any given area is often fed by ontological parsimony or naturalistic scruples, together with a healthy skepticism about the viability of any reductive account of the domain in question.

But in various domains, different further considerations come to bear. For example, one pressure toward a nondescriptive account of moral discourse has traditionally been the motivational argument, which is obviously peculiar to the case of normative discourse. As another example, resourceful arguments have been offered by Adams (1965), Gibbard (1981), and Edgington (1995) for the conclusion that natural-language indicative conditionals cannot have truth-conditions, and their arguments are peculiar to the case of conditionals. However motivated, however, nondescriptivist accounts try to tell us what is going on *instead* of description, ordinary truth-conditions, ordinary assertion, or ordinary expression of belief.

Expressivism, I think, is a good model for nondescriptivist accounts to aspire to, because it gives a nondescriptivist account not only of some area of *language*, but also of the corresponding area of *thought*. It is not enough, after all, if you want to avoid metaphysical commitment or truth-conditions or having to say what the area of discourse is *about*, to say that something other than ordinary description is going on in the *language*. You also have to tell us what is going on with corresponding *thoughts*. If understanding those thoughts requires an account of what they are about or what makes them true, then we are no better off for avoiding such questions, than we would have been if we had to say what the *sentences* were about or what made them true.

So an important nice feature of the general form of the expressivist account, as a nondescriptivist account, is that it gives us an account both of the language in some domain and of the corresponding thought, and the account that it gives of these is rolled up into one, yielding an account of how they are related. The expressivist strategy is to explain the language in some domain *by* explaining the thought in that domain. And that strategy can be applied to any philosophical domain about which we might be tempted to give some nondescriptivist account.

Not only does the expressivist strategy yield an account both of the language and of the thought in some domain, moreover, it does so in a way that makes relatively promising the hope that we will be able to explain why the language in that domain behaves in all relevant ways like ordinary descriptive discourse does. For just as normative sentences can function in all of the same ways that ordinary descriptive sentences can, so, it seems, can sentences about fictional characters, about the past and future, about numbers, about aesthetic qualities, about truth, and so on. So if we think that the language in those domains works importantly differently than ordinary descriptive language works, then that seems to leave something big and important for us to explain.[1] On the expressivist strategy, however, we go nondescriptivist about all of those domains by taking their language to work in the *same* way as ordinary descriptive language, but explaining the difference in terms of the kind of *thoughts* that they express.

For reasons that I don't claim to understand, theorists who want to give a nondescriptivist account of some domain sometimes seem to think that they don't owe us any particular story about how the language in that domain is able to combine in the ways that it does into complex sentences, including sentences that combine with other kinds

---

[1] See Lycan (2001: ch 4) for a leveling of the embedding problems against non-truth-conditional accounts of conditionals, von Fintel and Gillies (forthcoming a) for a discussion of the embedding problem for certain accounts of epistemic modals, and Geach (1960) for similar objections to nondescriptivist accounts of truth and voluntariness.

of language. Nondescriptivists sometimes suggest that all that we need
to know is that the sentences of that domain have the syntactic structure
of ordinary indicative sentences, and so can syntactically embed in
truth-ascriptions and under negation, conjunction, disjunction, and so
on. After all, they say, once you know that 'murder is wrong' means
that murder is wrong, all that you have to know, in order to know what
'murder is not wrong' means, is that it means that murder is not wrong.
So the only important obstacle, they suggest, is to say what is meant by
the atomic sentences in the domain. Complex sentences, they suggest,
all come for free.[2]

But unfortunately, this idea is seriously problematic. For it is easy
to stipulate that a sentence can syntactically embed in truth-ascriptions
and under negation, conjunction, and the other connectives, but such
stipulations do not always generate meaningful complex sentences. In
an important paper, James Dreier (1996) makes this point forcefully
with the example of a new term 'hiyo'. To understand the term 'hiyo',
Dreier tells us, we do not need to know what it describes. We do need, of
course, to understand what falls under its extension, but understanding
that turns out not to require knowing what it describes. To fall under
the extension of 'hiyo', of course, is to be hiyo. And to understand
which things are hiyo, all that you need is to understand how to use the
term. So it follows that to understand what falls under its extension, all
that you need, is to understand how to use it. So Dreier tells us how
to use it.

You use the term 'hiyo', according to Dreier, to accost. You utter the
sentence, 'Bob is hiyo', in order to attract Bob's attention. You use it
in something like the way that you might use the sentence, 'hey, Bob!',
except that since 'hey, Bob!' does not embed in the right ways, it can't
really be an accurate translation. This is because it does not turn out that:
'Bob is hiyo' means that hey Bob! This doesn't make any sense, so the
two sentences are not synonymous. Still, you use 'Bob is hiyo' in order
to accost Bob, much as you would use 'hey, Bob!'. Moreover, Dreier's
introduction of the terms tells us how to use it in many other sentences.
You use the sentence 'Dave is hiyo' to accost Dave, the sentence 'Frank
is hiyo' to accost Frank, and the sentence 'Hal is hiyo' to accost Hal.

Now that we know how to use the word 'hiyo' and understand
sentences involving it, we are done, right? Since it is syntactically an
indicative sentence and hence apt for ascriptions of truth ('Bob is hiyo'

---

[2] Compare Stoljar (1993), Price (1994), and Horwich (1993).

is true just in case Bob is hiyo), we can use it to construct complex sentences like 'Bob is not hiyo' and 'if Bob is hiyo, then Dave is hiyo' and 'Everyone is either hiyo or funny-looking and someone is, if hiyo, then tall'. After all, 'Bob is not hiyo' just means that Bob is not hiyo, and 'Everyone is either hiyo or funny-looking and someone is, if hiyo, then tall' just means that everyone is either hiyo or funny-looking, and someone is, if hiyo, then tall. But on the contrary, it is not at all clear that we understand what these sentences mean. And it is far from clear what it could possibly be to have the corresponding *thoughts*—to think that everyone is either hiyo or funny-looking and someone is, if hiyo, then tall. The mere facts that we understand the atomic sentences involved and that our syntax allows for such constructions do not by themselves guarantee any semantic interpretation to such complex sentences.

It is easy to come up with an indefinite supply of such examples. The first lesson to learn from them is that there is more to explaining why our language works in the way that it does, than stipulating it to have certain syntactic properties. The second lesson to learn is that not just any old thing that we can do will be something we can do with an indicative sentence that will embed in the right ways and yield complex sentences that make sense. Expressivists' concerns about the embedding problem are rooted in the attempt to try and understand why ordinary descriptive language is able to behave in the ways that it does, and build a model on which both normative and descriptive language behave in that same way. The efforts of Blackburn and Gibbard to confront the embedding problem have all along been the effort to explain why normative sentences are not like 'hiyo', and their basic idea has all along been to explain why normative sentences are not like 'hiyo' on the same model as the ordinary descriptivist will use to explain why 'green' is not like 'hiyo'.

So this is a model that any nondescriptivist theorist should aspire to. Any nondescriptive account needs an explanation of why, if their account is correct, the sentences in the area of discourse for which they are giving an account are not like 'Bob is hiyo'. And any such nondescriptivist should see, I think, the appeal of looking to the model of what ordinary descriptive theorists would say, in order to model their explanation on that. To do so is to buy into the expressivist strategy.[3]

---

[3] It should be noted, however, that not every domain will face the same obstacles. It may not be obvious, for example, that natural language conditionals or epistemic modals can be embedded arbitrarily. See Edgington (1995) and Kölbel (2000) for discussion.

So it would be interesting to observe whether the semantic framework developed here on behalf of expressivism can be generalized in any natural way in order to accommodate nondescriptivist views in other domains. Indeed, I think that it generalizes in a pretty obvious way. In the remainder of this chapter, I'll show how to think about this generalization, and apply the ideas of this framework to nondescriptivist accounts of the indicative conditional and of truth, building in part on one of the ideas from Chapter 10 about attitude ascriptions.

11.2 GENERALIZING

Thinking that grass is green, according to descriptivists about 'green', is believing that grass is green. But this is, according to the analysis of Chapter 7, a matter of being for proceeding as if grass is green and being for not proceeding as if grass is not green. So thinking that grass is green is being for proceeding as if grass is green and being for not proceeding as if grass is not green. Thinking that murder is wrong, according to descriptivists about morality, is believing that murder is wrong. So it is being for proceeding as if murder is wrong and being for not proceeding as if murder is not wrong.

Is this latter claim something with which expressivists must disagree? I don't think so. According to the account developed here, thinking that murder is wrong is being for blaming for murder. But that does not mean that it is not also correct to describe someone who thinks that murder is wrong as being for proceeding as if murder is wrong and for not proceeding as if murder is not wrong. Whether that is so turns on what it is to proceed as if murder is wrong, and to proceed as if it is not wrong.

To proceed as if murder is wrong, we can now say, *just is* to blame for murder. The way that you go about proceeding as if murder is wrong is to blame for murder. Likewise, to proceed as if murder is not wrong is just to not blame for murder. If our expressivist view accepts this hypothesis, then it can agree with the claim that descriptivists would make (assuming our analysis of belief):

wrong   thinking that murder is wrong is being for proceeding as if murder is wrong and for not proceeding as if murder is not wrong.

It will just go on to deny that this is the end of the story; being for these two things, it will say, is just being for blaming for murder, since proceeding as if murder is wrong and not proceeding as if murder is not wrong are both the same thing: blaming for murder.

In general, then, we can think of our semantic framework as one characterizable in English by the following general schema:

schema 'P' expresses the state of being for proceeding as if P and being for not proceeding as if not-P.

The schema, we may suppose, is one that anyone could accept who went in for our general semantic framework. But then anyone could pick and choose which sentences, 'P', qualify as ordinary descriptive sentences, on the grounds that it is possible to understand what it would be for it to be the case that P, and which require instead a further analysis of what it would be to proceed as if P and to not proceed as if not-P. On this picture, the basic expressivist idea is an idea about what it is to proceed as if murder is wrong.

11.3 CONDITIONALS

So conceived, the very same ideas can be applied to any other area of discourse, simply by asking what it is to proceed as if P, where 'P' is taken from that area of discourse. So, for example, we can give a nondescriptivist account of indicative conditionals within this framework. To do so, all that we need to do, is to answer the question of what it is to proceed as if A→B (where 'A→B' is an ordinary indicative conditional sentence). So what is it, so to proceed? Well, a natural view is that conditionals are for inference. So to proceed as if A→B is to infer B from A. To proceed as if ∼(A→B) is to not infer B from A. And this yields the simple view that thinking that A→B is being for inferring B from A (twice over).[4] What is it to infer B from A? Well, it is to move into the state expressed by 'B' when in the state expressed by 'A'. On this view, given our semantic framework, there is no puzzle about why conditionals can embed in more complex sentences, including within other conditionals. We have a single uniform story for all of this—it is the same one that did the work for normative sentences.

---

[4] On this account, indicative conditional sentences, like purely normative sentences, would collapse the distinction between disacceptance and accepting the negation. See section 8.4.

I'm not certain that we should really find this view very satisfying. For one thing, it is not exactly clear why, on this view, 'A→B' turns out to entail 'A⊃B'. Of course, there are complications about whether this entailment does hold in general.[5] But it is not altogether satisfying to say that we may have to know more about being for in order to explain why we would get any such inference. So perhaps a better account would combine this one with the material conditional, and say that thinking that A→B is being in the state: ⟨FOR((pai A>B) and inferring B from A)*,FOR((¬pai ¬(A>B)) and inferring B from A)⟩.[6]

This account would explain the validity of *modus ponens*, allow that the indicative conditional is stronger than the material conditional, and insist that the way in which it is stronger cannot be captured by any kind of truth-conditions—it is non-descriptively stronger. On this account, it is possible to consistently accept 'A⊃B' and deny 'A→B', so long as you are for not inferring B from A. Not surprisingly, the conditions under which this makes sense include those in which you accept 'A⊃B' only because you accept '∼A'. Finally, the account does all this in a way that allows us to immediately understand what thoughts are expressed by complex sentences involving the indicative conditional, and why all inferences involving it are valid in the requisite ways. So it has many of the features that one might hope for out of a nondescriptivist account of the indicative conditional.

11.4 TRUTH

Another good example—and one with important applications for core ideas about expressivism—is that of truth. So suppose that we are uncomfortable about there being anything deep that we could say about what it is for it to be the case that 'P' is true. Then we would want to have a nondescriptivist account of truth. And we now have a recipe for doing so. To do so, all that we have to do, is to fill in an answer to the question, 'what is it to proceed as if 'P' is true?'

On the simplest answer to this question, proceeding as if 'P' is true is proceeding as if P, and proceeding as if 'P' is not true is proceeding as if

---

[5] See Lycan (2001: ch 3).

[6] Stating this account precisely would require solving some technical problems about how to allow quantification into conditionals, given that our intuitive notion of 'inferring from' seems to only work for closed sentences.

not-P. So on this view, to think that 'P' is true is to be for proceeding as if P and for not proceeding as if not-P. That is, it is the same thing as thinking that P. This is the redundancy theory of truth.

The redundancy account of truth is subject to some straightforward objections, of course. One problem with the redundancy account of truth is that it is not clear that it is necessary to have the concept of truth in order to have any thoughts at all, but according to the redundancy account, if you think that P, for any value of 'P', you think that 'P' is true. So if you have any thoughts at all, you have thoughts about truth. And the same objection generalizes; in any given case, even if the inference to "P' is true' from 'P' is a trivial one, it is still an inference—it is possible to think 'P' without thinking "P' is true'. And most importantly, if you don't know that 'P' is a sentence which means that P, then you can think that P without thinking that 'P' is true, or think that 'P' is true without thinking that P.

So the strict redundancy account of truth is not be the best way to go. But it is also possible, however, to get natural minimalist but non-redundant accounts of truth out of our framework. To do so, we merely need to give a different answer to the question of what it is to proceed as if 'P' is true. Here is an alternative answer: to proceed as if 'P' is true is to be in the mental state expressed by 'P', and to proceed as if 'P' is not true is to be in the mental state expressed by '∼P'. So on this account, thinking that 'P' is true is being for being in the mental state expressed by 'P' and for not being in the mental state expressed by '∼P'.

This yields an account of truth on which thinking that 'P' is true does not collapse into thinking that P. But it is still a minimalist account; there is still a direct connection between thinking that P and thinking that 'P' is true. Thinking that 'P' is true involves being for thinking that P. On this view, you may think that 'P' is true without thinking that P—for example, if you don't know what 'P' means. And you may also think that P without thinking that 'P' is true—either if you don't know what 'P' means or if you are not for being in the state that you are in. But there is still a natural and simple connection between the two states. Of course, the problem with *this* account is still a serious one: it no longer explains why '∼P' and "P' is true' are inconsistent sentences.

A third account does, I think, considerably better. It starts with the idea that we need ultimately to be able to give an account not just of ascriptions of truth to *sentences*, but of claims of the form, 'it is true that *p*'.

Moreover, an account of truth will have to generalize to deal with sentences like 'what he said is true' and 'everything Jon believes is true'. Inspired by the treatment of 'Jon believes that p' in section 10.3, we can treat 'TRUE' as a predicate which can take arguments that may be given by 'THAT(P)' terms, which in section 10.3 we treated as being ordered pairs of properties. Recall:

THAT   If 'A' is a well-formed formula with semantic value $\langle \alpha^1, \alpha^2 \rangle$, then 'THAT(A)' is a complex singular term whose denotation is $\langle \alpha^1, \alpha^2 \rangle$.

Now, if 'true' is a predicate applying to pairs that are semantic values of sentences, then proceeding as if THAT(P) is true must be a matter of being in some relation to this pair. So what relation could it be? Well, the following is the simplest thing it could be. Let '$I^{major}(x,y)$' pick out the relation that x stands in to y when y is a pair of properties and x instantiates the stronger member of y. And similarly, let '$I^{minor}(x,y)$' pick out the relation that x stands in to y when y is a pair of properties and x instantiates the weaker member of y. Finally, let 'neg(p)' denote the pair of properties that are the negations of the properties in a pair of properties, p. We can then define 'TRUE' and 'FALSE' in the following way:[7]

TRUE   If 'a' denotes o, then 'TRUE(a)' has semantic value
$\langle \lambda z(I^{major}(z,o)), \lambda z(I^{minor}(z,o)) \rangle$.[8]

FALSE   If 'a' denotes o, then 'FALSE(a)' has semantic value
$\langle \lambda z(I^{major}(z,neg(o))), \lambda z(I^{minor}(z,neg(o))) \rangle$.[9]

So: If 'P' is a closed sentence with semantic value $\langle \pi^1, \pi^2 \rangle$, then 'TRUE(THAT(P))' is a well-formed formula and has semantic value
$\langle \lambda z(I^{major}(z,\langle \pi^1, \pi^2,\rangle)), \lambda z (I^{minor}(z,\langle \pi^1, \pi^2 \rangle)) \rangle$.

Since π^1 is the stronger of $\langle \pi^1, \pi^2 \rangle$, being π^1 and being $\lambda z(I^{major}(z,\langle \pi^1, \pi^2 \rangle))$ are equivalent. And that means that on this view, 'P' and

---

[7] Here I define 'FALSE(THAT(P))' to mean 'TRUE(THAT($\sim$P))'. Notice that a further virtue of this third account over the two previous accounts is that unlike the others, it does not identify 'p is false' with both '$\neg p$ is true' and with 'p is not true'.

[8] Exercise: check to verify that the sentences formed in this way express biforcated attitudes whenever o is a pair of properties one of which is stronger than the other. This account correctly predicts that the sentence results in a category mistake in any other case.

[9] Again, verify that this results in biforcated attitudes in the appropriate cases.

'TRUE(P)' are equivalent. But since π^1 is not identical to $\lambda z(I^{major}(z,\langle\pi^1,\pi^2\rangle))$, 'P' and 'TRUE(P)' have different semantic values, and hence it is possible to think that p without thinking that it is true that p. So this account solves the major problems noted for each of the prior accounts.

A further virtue of this account is that it deals successfully with sentences like 'everything Jon believes is true'. This sentence would get represented as '$\forall x(\text{BEL}(Jon,x)\supset\text{TRUE}(x))$', and its semantics and logical properties follow straightforwardly.

11.5 A DIGRESSION ON 'PROPOSITIONS'

Another virtue of this account, is that along with the account of 'believes that' in Chapter 10, it allows us to explain why from 'Jon believes that p' and 'it is true that p' it follows that Jon believes something true. In fact, we can expand, and offer an account of indirect discourse reports modeled on the account of 'believes that'. To do so, let 'utt(a,b)' pick out the relation that a stands in to b when a has assertively uttered a sentence whose semantic value is b.

SAID   If 'a' denotes o_1 and 'b' denotes o_2, then 'SAID(a,b)'
        is a well-formed formula and has semantic value
        $\langle\lambda z(z \text{ is pai } (utt(o_1,o_2))),\lambda z(z \text{ is } \neg pai \ \neg(utt(o_1,o_2)))\rangle$.

So: If 'Jon' denotes Jon and 'P' is a closed sentence with
        semantic value S, then 'SAID(Jon,THAT(P))' has
        semantic value $\langle\lambda z(z \text{ is pai } (utt(Jon,S))),\lambda z(z \text{ is } \neg pai \ \neg(utt(Jon,S)))\rangle$.

Like the account of belief in Chapter 10, this is a uniform account of 'said that' which applies equally well to normative as to descriptive sentences.

Having endorsed these accounts of 'BEL', 'TRUE', and 'SAID', the expressivist can now say that Jon believes that murder is wrong, that it is true that murder is wrong, and that Jan said that murder is wrong. Moreover, the expressivist can agree that it then follows that there is something that Jon believes, Jan has said, and which is true—namely, that murder is wrong. But philosophers have a name for the things which are the objects of attitudes like belief, which are the objects of assertion, and which are the bearers of truth and falsity: they are called *propositions*. So an expressivist who accepts a semantics like this one will insist that she really does believe in moral propositions, such as the proposition that murder is wrong. She simply has a funny view about what propositions are like, and of the nature of their constituents.

Of course, an expressivist who says this will have to coin another word for the kinds of thing that we have been calling 'propositions' all along, which are the objects of the attitudes expressed by atomic descriptive sentences, as ordinarily understood, and which have their truth-conditions intrinsically. Still, this seems like the kind of thing expressivists have hoped to be able to say, and these sorts of semantic views explain why they would get to be able to say it. There is far more to be said about this topic, but we need to return to the main thread.

11.6 WHY TRUTH IS IMPORTANT FOR EXPRESSIVISTS

The reason I've spent so much time over the account of truth is that expressivists *need* some kind of minimalist account of truth. This is not always acknowledged—as recently as 1990, Allan Gibbard characterized his view as being that normative sentences are not really true or false. But if I correctly characterized the main advantages of expressivism over speaker subjectivism in Chapter 2, then expressivists are committed to at least a minimalist account of 'false'. Recall that the deep disagreement problem for speaker subjectivism was that according to speaker subjectivism it turns out that different speakers can at best disagree with each other by negating what they say, but can't disagree by attributing falsity to what each other say. On the contrary, it is a prediction of speaker subjectivism that when two speakers disagree, they both speak truly. Yet if Sally can deny what Phil says, then on the face of it, she should be able to say that it is false. That was the deep disagreement problem.

It turns out not to be enough to solve the deep disagreement problem just to say that whatever solves it for 'grass is green' will solve it for 'murder is wrong'. For to solve the problem, expressivists need to be able to say that 'it is false that murder is wrong' is typically co-assertable with 'murder is not wrong'. So they need an account of 'false'. Expressivists can think about this problem in the same way as they think about all complex contexts. What they need to do, is to give an account of the meaning of complex sentences that involve the word 'false' as a function of the meanings of their component sentences. And this account needs to be perfectly general—it needs to apply to descriptive sentences as well as normative sentences, and it needs to apply to all normative sentences—'wrong' sentences, 'better' sentences, 'unjust' sentences, and so on. And 'it is false that P' and '~P' must turn out to be equivalent. The account given of 'false' in section 11.4 satisfies these needs.

Another reason why expressivists need an account of 'true' is that it is not enough, to capture the validity of an argument, to show that it is inconsistent to accept the premises and deny the conclusion. Valid arguments, we normally think, are arguments with the feature that if their premises are true, then their conclusion must be true. Expressivists can't agree with this, however, if they deny that normative sentences can be true or false. So they need an account of 'true' on which it can apply to a normative sentence.

Consider just one argument form: *modus ponens*. To say that *modus ponens* is valid is to say, for every argument of the form, 'P','P⊃Q';'Q', that if its premises are true, then its conclusion is, also. So consider the sentence, '(TRUE(THAT(P))&TRUE(THAT(P⊃Q)))⊃TRUE(THAT(Q))'. One thing expressivists might hope for, from a minimalist account of how 'TRUE' works, is that it would explain why it is inconsistent to deny this sentence, and hence that it is a theorem—the idea being that this would be an explanation, for the case of this argument, of the phenomenon that if its premises are true, then its conclusion must be so as well.

Denying this sentence, after all, would be commitment-equivalent to accepting 'TRUE(THAT(P))&TRUE(THAT(P⊃Q))&~TRUE(THAT(Q))'. But anyone who accepted this sentence would be committed to accepting each of its conjuncts. So she would be committed to accepting 'TRUE(THAT(P))' and 'TRUE(THAT(P⊃Q))'. But given the account of 'TRUE' from section 11.4, this means that she would be committed to accepting 'P' and 'P⊃Q'. But since the inference from 'P' and 'P⊃Q' to 'Q' is valid in biforcated-attitude semantics, this means that she would be committed to accepting 'Q'. And so, given the account of 'true' from section 11.4, she would be committed to accepting 'TRUE(THAT(Q))'. But that is inconsistent with her commitment to accepting '~TRUE(THAT(Q))'. Consequently, this shows that it is inconsistent to deny '(TRUE(THAT(P))&TRUE(THAT(P⊃Q)))⊃ TRUE(THAT(Q))', which means that it is a theorem. This demonstrates that the equivalence of 'TRUE(THAT(P))' with 'P' is just what the doctor ordered for expressivists. It is sufficient to get from the expressivist-friendly characterizations of validity with which we began, to the standard characterization of validity in terms of preservation of truth.

In summary, the indicative conditional and truth are merely two examples of how the semantic framework of biforcated attitude semantics can be generalized. It seems to me to be the right kind of thing that should be wanted by nondescriptivists, in general, in order to be able to genuinely explain why complex sentences work in the ways that they do, so it looks like if it we could be happy with it, then it could have many applications all across philosophy. And the fortunate thing is that the resulting accounts can be intuitive and have some very attractive features. But the unfortunate thing is that I don't believe that we can be happy with biforcated attitude semantics. I'll explain why not in Chapter 12, after rehearsing how it is that we've gotten to where we are.

12

The limits and costs of expressivism

12.1 HOW WE GOT HERE

In this book, we've been exploring how expressivists are to solve some of their simplest problems. Three problems, in particular, have occupied our attention. The first problem was to give an explanatory account of why 'murder is wrong' and 'murder is not wrong' are inconsistent. The second problem was to be able to give a unified semantics for the binary sentential connectives, on which they can take either normative or descriptive sentences. And the third problem was to explain how complex descriptive sentences end up with the right ordinary descriptive propositional contents or truth-conditions.

In Chapters 3 and 4, I argued that there is only one way for expressivists to approach the first of these problems. Belief and intention, I argued, provide good models of mental states that are inconsistent with one another. But they are only inconsistent with one another when they are cases of the same attitude toward inconsistent contents—*A*-type inconsistency. So a respectable expressivist account of the inconsistency between 'murder is wrong' and 'murder is not wrong' should explain this by appeal to *A*-type inconsistency in a single noncognitive attitude. But this is impossible, it turns out, if the attitudes expressed by atomic normative sentences are understood as unstructured attitudes toward the subjects of those sentences. The reason why all other present expressivist views resort to appealing to *B*-type inconsistency, is that they assume that the basic noncognitive attitudes correspond to predicates, in this way.

The Basic Expressivist Maneuver showed that the only way forward is to give up on the idea that predicates correspond to attitudes. But that didn't mean giving up on expressivism, so long as the semantic contribution of predicates factors into, *inter alia*, a general noncognitive attitude. In fact, we saw that the extra structure that this move introduces is precisely what is needed in order to state a constructive compositional semantics for a simple normative language, in which we could for the very first time give formally adequate explanatory expressivist accounts of logical inconsistency, logical entailment, and logical validity. The fact that we were able to do all of these things by appeal only to the assumption that being for has the same sorts of very general properties that belief does—that it is inconsistency-transmitting—was *very strong* evidence that we were on the right track, so far as expressivism goes. For, as I argued, no prior expressivist account has been able to do any of these things.

Assuming that was right, that placed us under substantial constraints, in trying to offer a unified semantics for the connectives. For our constructive semantics only worked for sentences that all express the same very general sort of noncognitive attitude. And moreover, the only reason why we were able to give adequate accounts of inconsistency and hence of logic, was that all of the sentences in our language expressed the same kind of state. But if normative sentences are to express noncognitive attitudes and not beliefs, it follows if that there is some kind of attitude that all sentences express, it must be a noncognitive one.

And this observation placed us under a further constraint, in trying to assign the right truth-conditions to complex descriptive sentences. For those sentences have to be formed from the same connectives that work on normative sentences—but since believing *p* is not just bearing a noncognitive attitude toward *p*, any satisfactory account of the states expressed by descriptive sentences was going to have to introduce *extra* structure—more than we needed. This was what I called the *new negation problem*. The extra structure meant that the very same rules needed for the connectives to work for normative sentences, did the wrong sorts of things for complex descriptive sentences.

It wasn't that we couldn't do logic, or various other sorts of things, in a language that met these constraints. The chief challenge, however, was to defend the way that complex descriptive sentences were treated. I offered two proposals, both of which required the semantic apparatus of biforcated attitude semantics. On the first proposal, it was argued that complex descriptive sentences commit to the beliefs with the appropriate descriptive content for that sentence. This view required some very strong assumptions about the logic of proceeding as if. And on the second proposal, it was argued that descriptive sentences can inherit their truth-conditions directly from the states that they express, so long as those states have the right *mistake conditions*. This view also required some strong assumptions, this time about what makes for a *mistake*, in the relevant sense.

12.2 WHAT WAS NEEDED

Biforcated attitude semantics, and the shenanigans of Chapters 9 and 10 in order to assign truth-conditions to descriptive sentences, may look like complicated and ugly. But the choice-points we encountered to get this far were few. My argument, to this point, is that in order to defend expressivism, you must defend a view that looks broadly like the one that I have been developing. And to this point, my argument has been that everything can work out more or less okay, provided that we are willing to buy into the requisite assumptions. Of course, those assumptions are not cheap. Let me review what they are.

First, you must choose a basic, very general, noncognitive attitude. It need not be a positive attitude—though your semantics will be ugly to write out, if you choose a negative one. And it need not take properties for its contents, as I have been imagining *being for* to do—it could take propositions, instead. But whatever sort of contents it takes, it must have the property that it is always and only inconsistent to hold it to inconsistent contents. Moreover, though I have been ignoring this, plausibly it will need to have another important feature of belief—that for any content, there is some kind of (hard to articulate) pressure to adopt the attitude either toward that content or toward its negation.[1] This is because inconsistency transmission is only enough to show that there would be a mistake involved in accepting the negation of the conclusion of an argument whose premises you accept—it isn't enough to show that you need actually accept the conclusion. Having defended the view that your basic noncognitive attitude has these two properties, you are out of the blocks.

Next, you need to defend analyses of specific normative predicates within the resulting analytical framework. If your basic noncognitive

---

[1] It is hard to articulate exactly what this sort of pressure amounts to, because it is hard to articulate what the analogous property is, for beliefs. Clearly, you are in no way lacking merely because you have no view, positive or negative, about any of a wide range of propositions you have never considered or would ever need to consider. It is certainly not the case that you are rationally obliged to draw *all* of the logical consequences of your beliefs, for example. Nevertheless, if you are confronted with a clear and simple logical argument with premises that you believe, you are under pressure to actually draw the conclusion. You cannot rest happy, simply as long as you don't actually deny the conclusion. Whatever feature of belief makes this so, the basic noncognitive attitude appealed to by an expressivist view—being for, in my version—must have that feature, too.

attitude, like *being for*, takes properties, then each *n*-place normative predicate needs to be associated with an *n+1*-place descriptive relation. On the other hand, if your basic noncognitive attitude takes propositions, then each *n*-place normative predicate needs to be associated with an *n*-place descriptive relation. I threw out the example view that 'murder is wrong' expresses FOR(blaming for murder). Many find that unintuitive, holding that you can think that murder is wrong without being moved to blame for it, if you also think that those who live in glass houses shouldn't throw stones (choose an example other than murder to make this more compelling). The point is: if you want to defend an expressivist view, it is not enough that there is a *structure* that can *possibly* work—you need to defend the assumptions that are require to *make* it work. Once you have defenses of analyses in this style of all of your favorite normative predicates, you are off and running—until you get to Chapter 7.

In order to incorporate descriptive language, you will need to provide an analysis of the states expressed by atomic descriptive sentences in terms of your general noncognitive attitude. If your general noncognitive attitude, like being for, takes properties for its contents, you will need some relation to propositions. If, on the other hand, it takes propositions, then you will need some property of propositions. It will need to be plausible that having your general noncognitive attitude toward *p* having that property (or toward that relation to *p*) just is believing that *p*. I find it very puzzling how to do this under the assumption that the general noncognitive attitude takes propositions. Moreover, whatever story you defend on this count, it must turn out that necessarily, if *p* has this property, then ¬*p* does not have it. (Or that if you bear this relation to *p*, then you don't bear it to ¬*p*.) This last assumption is required in order to get the solution to the new negation problem offered by biforcated attitude semantics up and running.

With those assumptions in hand, you are pretty much golden through the end of Chapter 8. You can provide a semantics for a language with both normative and descriptive predicates and the expressive power of the predicate calculus, in which you can give explanatory accounts of the logical properties of sentences. You will, of course, also need a solution to the *new new negation problem*. You may be content to conclude that disacceptance of a purely normative sentence is not weaker than accepting the negation. But if you want to avoid that result, then you must go back, and defend alternative analyses of each and every normative predicate, according to which each contributes *two* relations, one of which is stronger than the other. Again, you must somehow make these analyses plausible, and defend them against whatever objections arise—there is no guarantee that for each normative predicate, there will be a pair of descriptive relations that will result in an intuitively plausible account.

And now you have to make a choice about how to assign truth-conditions to complex descriptive sentences. If you take the strategy of Chapter 9, then you need to make, in addition to the assumption that proceeding as if p entails not proceeding as if $\neg p$, the following assumptions, just to get as far as a language with the expressive power of the predicate calculus:

9.1 Proceeding as if is closed under logical entailment.
9.2 (pai p)$\wedge$(pai q) entails pai $p \wedge q$
9.3 (pai p)$\vee$(pai q) entails pai $p \vee q$
9.4 $\forall$x(pai F(x)) entails pai $\forall$x(F(x))
9.5 $\exists$x(pai F(x)) entails pai $\exists$x(F(x))

Of course, if your analysis appeals to a different relation than my *proceeding as if,* what you will need, is the corresponding assumptions formulated in terms of your relation.

Whereas if you elect to pursue the alternative *mistake conditions* strategy of Chapter 10, you will need assumptions of the following sort:

10.1 It is a mistake to be in the state FOR(α) just in case it is a mistake to be α.
10.2 It is a mistake to be in a biforcated attitude just in case it is a mistake to be in its major attitude.
10.3 It is a mistake to be λz(z is pai p) just in case $\neg p$.
10.4 It is a mistake to be λz(Pz$\wedge$Qz) just in case either it is a mistake to be λz(Pz) or a mistake to be λz(Qz).
10.5 It is a mistake to be λz($\forall$x(Fzx)), just in case for some thing, x, it is a mistake to be λz(Fzx).
10.6 It is a mistake to be λz(Pz$\vee$Qz) just in case it is a mistake to be λz(Pz) and a mistake to be λz(Qz).
10.7 It is a mistake to be λz($\exists$x(Fzx)), just in case for each thing, x, it is a mistake to be λz(Fzx).

Here, premises 1 to 3 are fairly plausible, and the right-to-left directions of 4 to 7 are in general fairly plausible, but the left-to-right directions of 4 to 7 are less plausible. Anyone who takes this approach will also have to explain, in much more detail than I have done, how to think about what *mistakes* are, in the relevant sense.

Either way, though it is formally possible to assign the right truth-conditions to complex descriptive sentences, this is clearly a burdensome project, and the required assumptions are not at all obviously true. But if you are going to defend an expressivist view that is able to do these kinds of things, this looks like the way that you are going to have to go. So, at any rate, I have been arguing. So these are the costs of getting this far. But can we get any further?

12.3 TENSE AND MODALS

The important feature that allowed us to get this far is *structure*. So seeing whether the approach discussed in this book can allow for an expressivist treatment of the more complicated kinds of constructions in natural languages, needs to start with the simple observation that the same problems about structure that we observed for negation, conjunction, and so on, also exist for other constructions, including tense and modals. Compare, for example:

P1   Jon thought that murdering is wrong.
P2   Jon thinks that murdering was wrong.
P3   Jon thinks that having murdered is wrong.

□1   Necessarily, Jon thinks that murdering is wrong.
□2   Jon thinks that murdering is necessarily wrong.
□3   Jon thinks that (necessarily murdering) is wrong.

Fortunately, the structure in our account gives us a place to interpret how the past tense operates, and a place to interpret how 'necessarily' operates.

Suppose, for example, that in our descriptive metalanguage, there is a past-tense operator, so that the formula, 'past(S)' is the past-tense version of 'S', true relative to some assignment just in case 'S' was true relative to that assignment at some point in the past.[2] And suppose that 'necessarily' is an operator in our descriptive metalanguage, so that 'necessarily(S)' is true relative to some assignment just in case 'S' is true relative to that assignment at every possible world. Then, following the model for our earlier accounts, we can introduce semantic rules for

---

[2] Tenses are not always treated as operators; linguists generally favor treating them as quantifiers. See King (2003) for discussion and explanation, and the appendix to this chapter for one possible implementation of this idea in biforcated attitude semantics.

object-language operators, 'PAST' and '□', which will have the same sorts of semantic properties:

PAST If 'A' is a well-formed formula with semantic value $\langle \lambda z(\alpha^1)^*,$ $\lambda z(\alpha^2) \rangle$, then 'PAST(A)' is a well-formed formula and has semantic value $\langle \lambda z(past(\alpha^1))^*, \lambda z(past(\alpha^2)) \rangle$.

□ If 'A' a well-formed formula with semantic value $\langle \lambda z(\alpha^1)^*,$ $\lambda z(\alpha^2) \rangle$, then '□(A)' is a well-formed formula and has semantic value $\langle \lambda z(necessarily(\alpha^1))^*, \lambda z(necessarily(\alpha^2)) \rangle$.

These accounts are well formed, because they apply the 'past' and 'necessarily' operators to formulas in our descriptive metalanguage.

The accounts are also exactly what we would expect, based on the observation that all of our other rules utilize the extra structure that the account creates, and work by 'moving the connectives inside' the states of being for. So the rules do exactly what the rules do for each other construction that we've introduced. Just as negations express being for pairs of negative properties, conjunctions express being for pairs of conjunctive properties, and quantifications express being for pairs of quantified properties, past-tense sentences express being for pairs of past-tense properties and 'necessary' sentences express being for pairs of necessary properties. Moreover, they result in states that are genuinely biforcated attitudes. If 'α^1' entails 'α^2', 'past(α^1)' entails 'past(α^2)', so as long as 'A' expresses a biforcated attitude, 'PAST(A)' does so, as well. Similarly, if 'α^1' entails 'α^2', 'necessarily(α^1)' entails 'necessarily(α^2)', so as long as 'A' expresses a biforcated attitude, '□(A)' does so, as well.

Finally, observe that these accounts yield the right sorts of semantic properties. For example, that 'A' follows from '□(A)' is guaranteed by the fact that 'α^1' follows from 'necessarily(α^1)'. Also, given this semantics and our account of 'TRUE' from Chapter 11, we might hope to explain why 'TRUE(THAT(PAST(A)))⊃PAST(TRUE(THAT(A)))' cannot be consistently rejected, and hence, intuitively, why if 'PAST(A)' is true, then 'A' was true. These at least seem like the ballpark of the sorts of things that we would want an expressivist account of these constructions to explain.

But these rules simply cannot be correct. To begin with, the attitudes that they attribute to people who make past-tense and modal judgments are incoherent. Being in the state, FOR(past(α)), is being for *having had* the property, α. Being for is the sort of state to motivate you, other things being equal, to acquire that property. So this state has the role of motivating you to acquire some property in the past. Surely it never in fact plays this motivational role. Similarly, being in the state,

FOR(necessarily(α)), is being for *necessarily having* the property, α. So this state has the role of motivating you to acquire some property in non-actual possible worlds. Surely it never in fact plays this motivational role.

Moreover, the assumptions that would be required in order to assign truth-conditions to descriptive sentences involving these constructions along the lines of the strategy elaborated in Chapter 9 are not remotely defensible. The required assumptions for '□' would be:[3]

1   necessarily(pai p) entails pai necessarily(p)
2   possibly(pai p) entails pai possibly(p)

Now we can quibble about whether the bizarre assumption 1 is true. But assumption 2 is clearly false, no matter what sort of relation we substituted for *proceeding as if*. What you do in distant possible worlds does not have consequences for what you are doing in the actual world. Similarly, the required assumptions for 'PAST' would be:

3   past(pai p) entails pai past(p)
4   ¬past ¬(pai p) entails pai ¬past ¬(p)

But both of these assumptions are clearly false—what you are doing now does not depend on what you did or did not do in the past, in either of these ways. So even if we thought these were plausible accounts of what it is to have past-tense or modal thoughts (which I contended they are not), we can't use the approach of Chapter 9 in order to assign truth-conditions to descriptive sentences formed in this way.

You might think that things will be better for the alternative approach to truth-conditions offered in Chapter 10. But you would be wrong. In order for that proof to go through, we would need, for the case of '□', to make the following assumptions:

5   It is a mistake to be λz(necessarily(Fz)) just in case possibly, it is a mistake to be λz(Fz).
6   It is a mistake to be λz(possibly(Fz)) just in case necessarily, it is a mistake to be λz(Fz).

The right-to-left directions of the assumptions used in the proof in Chapter 8 were compelling. But even the right-to-left directions of 5

---

[3] Here I use 'possibly' as interdefined with 'necessarily' in the obvious way. For reasons of space, I omit the proof of how to extend the proofs from Chapters 9 and 10 using these assumptions. It is easy, however, to compare these assumptions to the ones required for the other clauses, in order to see that they are exactly structurally similar, and not an arduous exercise to extend them.

and 6 are bizarre. Take, for example, the case of 6. Suppose that in any possible world, it would be a mistake to believe that $2 + 2 = 5$ (this follows from assumptions we've already made). It is a contingent fact about Jon that he does not have this belief, for there is a very distant possible world in which he has it. Does it follow that Jon is making some mistake? It needs to, if descriptive sentences containing the '$\sim \Box$' construction are to express mental states that are mistaken whenever those sentences are false. Similarly the assumptions required by the approach of Chapter 10 for 'PAST' are:

7   It is a mistake to be $\lambda z(\text{past}(Fz))$ just in case it wasn't ever in the past not a mistake to be $\lambda z(Fz)$.
8   It is a mistake to be $\lambda z(\neg\text{past}(\neg Fz))$ just in case in the past, it was a mistake to be $\lambda z(Fz)$.

These assumptions are again clearly false, even in the right-to-left direction that was unproblematic for the earlier constructions. This time take 7. Suppose that at no time in the past was it not a mistake for Jon to believe that grass is purple (this also follows from assumptions we've already made, assuming that grass never *was* purple). But suppose that for a brief time, early in third grade, his friends convinced him that grass is purple—a condition that he has long since gotten over. Does it follow that he is now making a mistake, to have had this property in the past? It has to, if descriptive sentences containing the '$\sim$PAST' construction are to express mental states that are mistaken when those sentences are false.

The points I have been focusing on over the last page or so are matters of detail. But they are important matters of detail, if expressivists are to assign truth-conditions to complex descriptive sentences *at all*. The fact that *both* strategies I've offered to expressivists break down in obvious ways at this point should not make us at all optimistic about whether it will be possible to give a satisfactory expressivist account of modals or tense.

12.4 RESTRICTED QUANTIFIERS

And things get worse. For it turns out that there are many constructions for which applying the same moves as we have been so far doesn't yield a biforcated attitude at all. And that means that there can be no place for such sentences in biforcated attitude semantics, because biforcated attitude semantics requires *all* sentences to express biforcated attitudes.

The example I'll use to illustrate is that of essentially binary quantifiers like 'most', but there are many natural language constructions which fall into this category, including adverbs of quantification like 'usually' and constructions like generics and habituals.

'Most', as in 'most bachelors are partiers', is essentially a binary or restricted quantifier. It syntactically binds a variable in each of two open sentences, one of which functions as a restriction on the range of the quantifier. It also expands the expressive power of our language beyond first-order predicate logic; there are no ways of reformulating 'most bachelors are partiers' in first-order predicate logic.[4] To see what adding a semantics for 'most' to biforcated attitude semantics would have to look like, I'll first warm up by considering the restricted universal and existential quantifiers, which don't contribute additional expressive power to our language, and hence whose semantics is fixed by the rules we already have.

In order to say, 'all bachelors are partiers' in ordinary first-order predicate logic, you have to say, '$\forall x(x$ is a bachelor$\supset x$ is a partier)'. Similarly, or not so similarly, in order to say, 'some bachelor is a partier' in first-order predicate logic, you have to say, '$\exists x(x$ is a bachelor $\&$ x is a partier)'. So these two English sentences, which appear to have the same structure, in fact have very different logical structures, if their logical structures need to be understood in terms of the constructions of standard predicate logic—one contains a conditional, and the other contains a conjunction. This is one of many reasons for which linguists have recognized the importance of restricted quantifiers. The restricted universal quantifier takes two open sentences, one of which is quantified into, but the other of which functions as a restriction on that quantifier. It doesn't allow us to say anything for which there is not an equivalent in ordinary predicate logic, but it allows us to say it in a simpler way. If we are allowed to make use of restricted quantifiers, then 'all bachelors are partiers' can be stated as '$\forall x{:}x$ is a bachelor(x is a partier)' and 'some bachelor is a partier' can be stated as '$\exists x{:}x$ is a bachelor(x is a partier)'. So if restricted quantifiers appear in the logical form of English sentences, then the logical form of these sentences is not so different from their surface structure, after all. Rather than having very different logical forms, they have very similar logical forms.[5]

---

[4] See Rescher (1962), Wiggins (1980), and Barwise and Cooper (1981) for discussion.
[5] See Pietroski (2007) for a helpful discussion of restricted quantifiers and their importance for understanding the logical form of natural language sentences.

Because '∀x:x is a bachelor(x is a partier)' needs to be equivalent to '∀x(x is a bachelor⊃x is a partier)', however, there is no mystery about how to introduce a semantics for the restricted universal quantifier into biforcated attitude semantics, and similarly for the restricted existential quantifier. The two clauses have to look like the following:[6]

∀ :() If 'A' is a well-formed formula with semantic value $\langle \lambda z(\alpha^1)^*,$ $\lambda z(\alpha^2)\rangle$ and 'B' is a well-formed formula with semantic value $\langle \lambda z(\beta^1)^*, \lambda z(\beta^2)\rangle$, then '∀x:A(B)' is a well-formed formula and has semantic value $\langle \lambda z(\forall x:\alpha^2(\beta^1))^*, \lambda z(\forall x:\alpha^1(\beta^2))\rangle$.

∃ :() If 'A' is a well-formed formula with semantic value $\langle \lambda z(\alpha^1)^*,$ $\lambda z(\alpha^2)\rangle$ and 'B' is a well-formed formula with semantic value $\langle \lambda z(\beta^1)^*, \lambda z(\beta^2)\rangle$, then '∃x:A(B)' is a well-formed formula and has semantic value $\langle \lambda z(\exists x:\alpha^1(\beta^1))^*, \lambda z(\exists x:\alpha^2(\beta^2))\rangle$.

Because these two constructions don't add any additional expressive power to our language, we don't need any new assumptions in order to accommodate them.

But 'most' *does* add additional expressive power to our language. There is no way of translating 'most bachelors are partiers' into first-order predicate logic. So how would a biforcated attitude semantics for 'most' have to work? The rules for the restricted universal and restricted existential quantifiers don't tell us exactly how the rule for 'most' would have to go, but they give the idea. 'Most' sentences would have to express biforcated attitudes, each state of which is a state of being for a content with a wide-scope 'most', whose arguments come from the semantic values of the open sentences it takes as arguments. That leaves four possible ways of filling in the picture. Since we don't need fully general versions of the rules in order to see the problem, I'll assume that 'F' and 'G' are atomic descriptive formulas open only in x. Taking 'Mostx:Fx(Gx)' to mean, 'most Fs are Gs', we have four candidates for the semantic value of 'most F's are G's':

C1 $\langle$Mostx:pai Fx(pai Gx), Mostx: ¬pai ¬Fx(¬pai ¬Gx)$\rangle$
C2 $\langle$Mostx:pai Fx(¬pai ¬Gx), Mostx: ¬pai ¬Fx(pai Gx)$\rangle$
C3 $\langle$Mostx: ¬pai ¬Fx(pai Gx), Mostx:pai Fx(¬pai ¬Gx)$\rangle$
C4 $\langle$Mostx: ¬pai ¬Fx(¬pai ¬Gx), Mostx:pai Fx(pai Gx)$\rangle$

---

[6] It is a useful exercise to check these, by writing out the translations of 'all bachelors are partiers' and 'some bachelor is a partier' using ordinary predicate logic, and applying the rules from section 8.1.

These are all four possible ways of applying the metalanguage 'most' to two pairs from the major and minor elements of the semantic values for 'F' and 'G'.

Unfortunately, none of these candidates results in a biforcated attitude, because in no case does the content of the first state of being for entail the content of the second state of being for. This was an essential part of the definition of biforcated attitudes, and we appealed to it in order to prove all of the interesting results about biforcated attitude semantics. To verify this, consider just two cases, depicted below. The first case is represented by the top row; the second by the bottom row. In each case, there are exactly four items, and the boxes represent for which Jon is proceeding as if they are F, proceeding as if they are ¬F, proceeding as if they are G, and proceeding as if they are ¬G.

F	F	F	
G	G	¬G	¬G

	F	F	¬F
G	G	¬G	¬G

The top row is a counterexample to C1 and C2 being biforcated attitudes, and the bottom row is a counterexample to C3 and C4 being biforcated attitudes. Here's why: the top row is a scenario in which, for most things such that Jon is proceeding as if they are F (namely, the first three), he is proceeding as if they are G, and for most things such that Jon is proceeding as if they are F (namely, the first three), he is not proceeding as if they are ¬G. But for the top row, it is not the case that for most things such that Jon is not proceeding as if they are ¬F (namely, everything), he is not proceeding as if they are ¬G (i.e., only for half), and similarly, it is not the case that for most things just that Jon is not proceeding as if they are ¬F (namely, everything), he is proceeding as if they are G (i.e., only for half).

Similarly for the bottom row and C3 and C4. The bottom row is a scenario in which for most things such that Jon is not proceeding as if they are ¬F (namely, the first three), he is proceeding as if they are G, and in which for most things such that Jon is not proceeding as if they are ¬F, he is not proceeding as if they are ¬G. But for only half of the things for which he is proceeding as if they are F (namely, the middle two), is he not proceeding as if they are ¬G, and for only half of the things for which he is proceeding as if they are F, is he proceeding as if they are G.

So unlike all of the other constructions that we have considered so far, 'most' does not have the property that 'pushing it inside' some pair from the semantic values of its arguments results in a biforcated attitude. But we needed the assumption that all sentences of our language express biforcated attitudes for almost everything that we've done—including the definitions of '&', '∘', '⊃', '∀:()', and '∃ :()'! It follows that there is no natural way of incorporating 'most' into this semantic framework. Yet sentences like 'most bachelors are partiers' are perfectly natural constructions in natural languages. An account that doesn't even have the right structure to allow that there *could* be a construction like 'most' is not, I think, a very promising hypothesis about the semantics of natural languages like English. Consequently, I think expressivism is a very unpromising hypothesis about the semantics of natural languages like English.

And the problem is not just about an isolated word. Natural languages are full of constructions that behave like 'most' in this way, including adverbs of quantification like 'usually' and 'often', and the same sorts of problem look very likely to arise for generics and habituals like 'tigers have stripes' and 'Jeff skis'. It is a thoroughly discouraging result to discover that the central insights which have allowed us to build a constructive expressivist semantics and to incorporate descriptive language don't even allow any coherent semantics for this wide range of important natural language constructions.

Of course, it is only within the details of the view developed here that there is such a problem. So you may think that this is a problem only for my idiosyncratic development of expressivism. But allow me to remind you that the moves required to get this far were few, and that the advantages garnered along the way were demonstrably powerful, by the modest standards set by previous elaborations of expressivism. Moreover, at each point, I argued that there was only one way forward. It may be that my argument has in some important place gone astray. But I think the important lesson remains: if the most promising way of addressing the simplest possible questions leads so directly to an account that cannot accommodate the semantics of 'most', then expressivism should not inspire our confidence.

12.5 THE MORAL

Recall that much of the initial appeal of expressivism was that since moral language and descriptive language work in the same way, there are no real puzzles for expressivism in the philosophy of language—only an explanatory project in the philosophy of mind. This is both why expressivism has seemed like the antidote to the embedding problem, and why Blackburn (1998) and Gibbard (1990, 2003) spend so much time discussing normative thought, and so very little explicitly discussing normative language. What we've seen, is that this idea is right—sort of. It is right that a view according to which normative language and descriptive language work in the same way can solve a lot of the traditional problems of noncognitivism. But the idea is also sort of wrong. None of these advantages come by taking what we know about descriptive language and applying it to normative language—they all require drawing progressively more radical conclusions about how ordinary descriptive language works. That is one of my most important morals for this book. It is not, I think, an entirely new moral, but I've done my best to make it vivid, and I think that unlike previous treatments, my observations follow from a fully general understanding of what expressivism must be like.[7]

I'll stop short of announcing that I've constructed a *reductio* of expressivism, and return to my main lesson. Expressivism centrally involves a hypothesis about the workings of natural languages like English. This hypothesis is that (1) the meaning of a sentence is the mental state that it expresses, and (2) some sentences express beliefs, but other sentences express noncognitive attitudes which are not beliefs. A certain amount of initial progress has been made in thinking about some of expressivism's problems. But many metaethicists have proceeded largely as if this kind of hypothesis about natural language semantics does not need to be tested by the same kinds of criteria as any other hypothesis about natural language semantics. Some have even taken Simon Blackburn's stipulations of the goals of his research program of 'quasi-realism' as authoritative on his success in achieving those goals.

In my view, this is intellectually irresponsible. If, as metaethicists, we really care whether expressivism is true, we need to evaluate it

---

[7] Compare, for example, Hale (1993) and Kölbel (2002).

as a hypothesis about natural language semantics. And there is a well-understood way of doing this. You construct semantic theories for fragments of English, and you test their predictions against the data. That is the sort of thing I have been trying in this book to show how to do, within the kind of framework in which an expressivist must think about these problems. The fruit of theorizing is always in the details. Proponents of expressivism need to do the kind of thing I have been doing in this book—and they need to do it better.

But the central challenge facing any attempt to formulate an expressivist semantics is simple. The hypothesis that some sentences express mental states that are not beliefs sets a *constraint* on the accounts of each kind of sentential connective that is not faced by non-expressivist semantics. For each construction, in addition to all of the challenges faced by alternative semantic theories, the expressivist needs to account for how, despite the constraint set by the way that construction needs to work for normative sentences, it still yields the right truth-conditions when applied to purely descriptive sentences. That is the problem that has occupied us for most of the last six chapters. The most unpromising feature of expressivism is that natural language semantics is hard enough *without* this constraint.

Ultimately, I think that long before we got to this point, we should have started to wonder whether the benefits of expressivism are worth the costs. But the benefits of expressivism over other sorts of views in metaethics, I think, have really been quite exaggerated. Many kinds of realist view can explain, for example, why there are systematic connections between moral judgments and moral motivation.[8] Reductive realist views are also compatible with metaphysical naturalism, and surprisingly resilient against the standard objections in the philosophical literature. I myself have defended a fairly comprehensive version of reductive realism, which I think suffers not at all at the hands of any objection I know of to reductive realism as such.[9] The sorts of costs of expressivism that I've been illustrating here, are I think good cause for us to re-evaluate whether quite subtle advantages in precisely how moral motivation is explained or just why Moore's open questions feel 'open' could possibly be worth it.

---

[8] See, for example, Smith (1994), for one sort of approach, Copp (2001), Finlay (2005), and Boisvert (forthcoming) for another, and Schroeder (2007) for a third.

[9] See in particular, Schroeder (2005a, 2005b, and 2007).

Expressivism, I hope to have shown in this book, is coherent, interesting, and potentially explanatorily powerful. But I also hope to have assembled significant cause to believe that it is false. It is certainly an extremely unpromising hypothesis about the workings of natural languages. It may be a hypothesis worth investigating further—I've certainly adopted that attitude here. But its proponents have far more work to do, before it can earn its place as the sort of hypothesis on which rational investigators can place any significant credence.

APPENDIX TO CHAPTER 12

Despite the (as I've argued) dead ends that we've reached, it's tempting to keep pursuing the development of biforcated attitude semantics, just to see where it can lead. But I expect that I've tried my readers' patience quite enough. Still, if you continue to find yourself sympathetic to expressivism after all of this, and encouraged enough by the initial progress I've made to want to explore further, in this appendix I rehearse just a few of the problems that you will need to attack, and make a few small suggestions about how it might help to attack them.

Context-sensitivity

Assuming that you accept the basic framework of biforcated attitude semantics, or some equivalent framework along the lines spelled out in section 12.2, there are still some major avenues of exploration I've left untrodden. One of the most salient features of natural language is context-sensitivity, which I've left totally untouched. In order to introduce context-sensitive elements into our toy expressivist language, you will have to go back and re-visit the fundamental picture from Chapter 2 about exactly what sort of assignment the semantics makes to a sentence, and why.

The simplest approach I can envision would be to reduce all effects of context to the effects of context on referring expressions. That approach would be maximally conservative with respect to the treatment of predicates in biforcated-attitude semantics. The idea would be to treat contexts as generating assignments to referring terms, and then to treat sentences as having the mental states that they express in the ordinary way, taking those assignments as given. This yields a picture of the role of context akin to that in King and Stanley (2005), in which individual

terms have Kaplanian characters, but there is no further need for a
sentence as a whole to have a character (Kaplan 1989).[10] Anyone who is
serious about defending expressivism will need to develop this approach
or some alternative, for context-sensitivity is one of the most dominant
and important features of natural languages. And once they do develop
it, the resulting theory should be testable by comparison with the vast
range of competing conceptions of context-sensitivity, and needs to
still allow us to make sense of how truth-conditions are assigned to
descriptive sentences.

Complement-taking verbs

Another huge topic I've barely broached is that of complement-taking
verbs. In Chapter 10, I considered how to approach the semantics of
'believes that', and in Chapter 11, I added 'it is true that' and 'said
that'. The approach I outlined provides a model for how accounts of
further cases would have to go—a formula for constructing further
accounts, such as for 'wonders whether', 'hopes that', 'is pleased that',
'is ecstatic that', 'is amused that', and so on, for the vast range of such
constructions. But this leaves wide open whether it will be possible
to construct even remotely plausible accounts for most of these cases.
Anyone who is serious about defending expressivism needs to pay very
close attention to this very large project.

Epistemic modals and conditionals

In chapter 11, I barely began to consider how biforcated attitude
semantics might be exploited to construct accounts of further, non-
normative, areas of discourse. There are, in fact, a number of such
topics in the philosophy of language that lend themselves to expressivist
treatments. For example, epistemic modals like 'might' and 'must' seem
to require supplementation by some kind of background evidence, but
it has recently been argued by several authors that examples similar to
those brought out in the disagreement problem for metaethical speaker

---

[10] In fact, there is a substantive complication, given expressivism, for any view which
does want to assign descriptive sentences to descriptive Kaplanian characters, and then
only derivatively to assign them to truth-conditions as a function of context of utterance.
This is because of the lesson from Chapter 2, that for expressivists, sentential connectives
have to be understood as operating on mental states, and because mental states don't
have characters for their contents.

subjectivism show that this background evidence cannot be supplied in any context-dependent way.[11] Although these arguments have been used to support relativism about truth, a different plausible moral modeled on the expressivists' moral for metaethical speaker subjectivism, is that they motivate an expressivist treatment, instead. On such a model, 'grass might be green' isn't about a special state of affairs—that grass might be green—but rather expresses a state of mind which leaves open whether grass is green—perhaps a positive credence in grass's being green.[12]

Epistemic modals, like other constructions such as natural-language indicative conditionals, present challenges that might provide collateral motivation for an expressivist semantics for English. If so, it will be an especially important challenge for anyone sympathetic to expressivism to sort out how to understand the mental states expressed by such sentences within a framework like that of biforcated attitude semantics, and in addition, to evaluate how these constructions interact with other constructions, such as tense.[13]

The important thing to observe about any account of epistemic modals in biforcated attitude semantics, is that it needs to be able to apply to both normative and descriptive sentences. 'it might be that *p*' can't express simply a positive degree of belief in *p*, for example (even if we knew how to analyze degrees of belief as biforcated attitudes), because '*p*' might itself be a normative sentence. One elegant approach to epistemic modals in biforcated attitude semantics would be to treat 'MIGHT(P)' as having the semantic value $\langle \pi^2, \pi^2 \rangle$, where 'P' has the semantic value $\langle \pi^1, \pi^2 \rangle$—intuitively, as 'collapsing' a biforcated attitude into its minor attitude. This treatment equates thinking that grass might be green with doubting that grass is not green, an equivalence which is not entirely unintuitive, and has the result that if we define 'MUST(P)' as performing the complementary operation of 'collapsing' a biforcated attitude into its major attitude, then 'MUST(P)' is commitment-equivalent to '∼MIGHT(∼ P)'. The account also predicts, not unintuitively, I think, that 'MUST(MIGHT(P))' is equivalent to 'MIGHT(P)' and that 'MIGHT(MUST(P))' is equivalent to 'MUST(P)'. And it explains how 'MUST(P)' and 'P' could be equally strong, even though

---

[11] See Egan, Hawthorne, and Weatherson (2003), MacFarlane (forthcoming), and Stephenson (unpublished).

[12] Compare Barker (2004).

[13] Compare the problem about the scope of tense and the epistemic modal in sentences like 'grass might have been green' raised by von Fintel and Gillies (forthcoming b).

their negations are not equally strong. This is because they differ in the strength of their minor attitudes.

This is just an example of how epistemic modals might be incorporated into biforcated attitude semantics, but immediately we can see how any approach like this will raise further problems. Most saliently, given this approach, the new new negation problem becomes particularly pressing. For any sentence 'P' whose major and minor attitudes are commitment-equivalent, 'MIGHT(P)' and 'MUST(P)' will both be equivalent to 'P'. But 'murder might be wrong' is not equivalent to 'murder must be wrong' or to 'murder is wrong'. So this sort of account would require a more complicated approach to the semantic values of normative predicates—an approach which may not yield analyses as intuitive as the ones I've been working with.

Embedding under normative predicates

Another important problem still to be taken up concerns how to handle apparent embeddings of normative terms under one another. The virtue of biforcated attitude semantics was that because the subjects of normative predicates were always themselves non-normative, we could always translate them directly into our purely descriptive metalanguage, which meant that the contents of states of being for were always purely descriptive. And that, in turn, was what let us reduce the logical properties of our normative metalanguage to the logical properties of the purely descriptive metalanguage. But take, for example, the sentence, 'acting wrongly is wrong'. If we read this sentence as ascribing the predicate 'wrong' to the action, 'acting wrongly', it would have to express the attitude (simplifying, here), FOR(blaming for acting wrongly). But that clearly won't do, because all of the advantages we gleaned so far were due to assuming that the contents of states of being for were purely descriptive.

This problem goes away, of course, if instead of being atomic, 'acting wrongly is wrong' instead is properly understood as involving a quantifier—for example, if it has the form, '∀x:ACTINGWRONGLY(x) (WRONG(x))'. But anyone seriously interested in defending the idea that expressivism might be true needs to explore to what extent putative embeddings of normative terms under one another can in fact be explained away along lines like these or in any other way, and whether biforcated attitude semantics could be adjusted in any plausible way to accommodate genuine embeddings. 'It ought to be that it ought to be that P' is another important kind of embedding which might require a different kind of treatment.[14] Because this strategy constrains the possible intelligible logical forms for English sentences, it creates the risk that the readings it requires are wrong. For example, independent semantic tests should be able to adjudicate between '$\forall x$:ACTINGWRONGLY(x)(WRONG(x))' and 'WRONG(acting wrongly)' as the correct form of 'acting wrongly is wrong', potentially refuting this approach. An adequate expressivist answer to this problem will have to be built on readings of these sentences with independent support.

Tense

In section 12.3, I argued that there are serious obstacles to any expansion of biforcated attitude semantics in order to deal with tense. The problems were simple, but they turned on a particular assumption that I made about how an account of those constructions within biforcated attitude semantics would have to work. In particular, I assumed that just as sentences with widest-scope negations express being for negative properties and sentences with widest-scope conjunctions express being for conjunctive properties, sentences with a widest-scope past tense will have to express being for past-tense properties. And then I assumed, further, that a past-tense property is one you have if, in the past, you had the un-tensed property.

These were natural assumptions, because they were the most obvious way of generalizing the framework which was used to deal with the other constructions in biforcated attitude semantics. But they aren't mandatory. The mandatory feature of any account of tense, in order to take advantage of the features of biforcated attitude semantics, is that sentences with a widest-scope past tense express being for properties with some distinctive widest-scope element—call it being *past-tense**. But an account can still yield the right structural features even if being past-tense* is not a matter, intuitively, of being past tense.

A simple application of the idea that tenses are quantifiers serves to illustrate how this would go. Recall that the proofs in Chapters 9 and 10 suffice for languages with the expressive power of the predicate calculus.

---

[14] My suggestion for treating 'that' clauses from section 10.3 might be a different way in which the problem could be resolved in this second kind of case (because it treats 'that' clauses even with normative complements as referring expressions with purely descriptive referents), but that hypothesis would have to be further explored.

In section 12.3, I assumed that the past tense increases the expressive power of a language. But if the past tense is really just an ordinary existential quantifier, under a restriction to a certain range of times, then it is natural to think that it should not, after all, really increase the expressive power of our language. And that should make us suspicious of the claim that the past tense can't be accounted for within biforcated attitude semantics.

So how would this idea about tense being a quantifier go? Well, to be fully developed, it would require a developed treatment of context-dependence in our language. But I'll gloss that, assuming that there is just one time that is present, designated by 't^*'. We will further need the assumption that predicates we previously treated as n-place are now properly treated as $n+1$-place. So, for example, 'GREEN' will be a two-place predicate, one place of which will be filled by a time. Ordinary, 'present-tense' sentences will have the time-places in each predicate filled by 't^*'. So, for example, 'GREEN(grass,t^*)' would be the intuitive translation into our expressivist language of 'grass is green'. Intuitively, it would express being for proceeding as if grass is presently green and being for not proceeding as if grass is not presently green.

Within such an adaptation of our framework, we can consider sentences like '$\exists t : t < t^*$(GREEN(grass,t))', which existentially quantify into the time place, where the restriction, '$t < t^*$', is to be understood as an abbreviation of the purely descriptive relation among times, 'PRIOR(t,t^*)', to be interpreted as we interpreted descriptive predicates in Chapter 8. In such a framework, we could introduce 'PAST(GREEN(grass,t^*))' as an abbreviation for '$\exists t : t < t^*$(GREEN(grass,t))', and take this as our treatment of the past tense. Ignoring complications that arise from the context-dependence of the referent of 't^*' and from allowing for constructions whose semantic complexity is not directly reflected in the surface structure of our object-language, this treatment of the past tense would not increase the expressive power of our language over any other language with the expressive power of the predicate calculus, a term like 't^*', and a relation like 'PRIOR'. So the proofs from either Chapter 9 or Chapter 10 would suffice, after all, to supply tensed sentences in such a language with the right truth-conditions.

So how did this happen? Ignoring minor attitudes for simplicity, in the old account 'PAST(A)' expressed FOR(past(α)), where 'A' expressed FOR(α). In the new account, 'PAST(A)' expresses 'FOR($\exists t : \text{pai}(t < t^*)(\alpha)$)'. The accounts have the same structural feature that has been the advantage of our approach all along—they work by 'moving something inside' the state of being for that does the same sort of work as the connective in the object language is supposed to do. Their difference, intuitively, is that they move different things inside it.

Generalizing this account to deal with normative predicates, however, will be complicated. We've been treating 'murder is wrong' as expressing being for blaming for murder. But in order to capture 'murder was wrong', the new account requires that we replace the two-place relation between agents and actions, *blaming for*, with some three-place relation between agents, actions, and times. But the problem is that it can't just be *blaming for murder at t^**. That would make it turn out that 'murder was wrong' expresses FOR($\lambda z(\exists t:pai(t<t^*)(z$ is blaming for murder at $t)))$, which is precisely to give it the problematic reading—it is a matter of being for *having* blamed for murder. This is incoherent—as noted in section 12.3, having blamed for murder is not the kind of thing that you can be motivated to do, other things being equal.

The solution required is probably to treat the *objects* of blame as themselves incorporating a time. On this treatment, 'murder is wrong' would express being for blaming for murders-at-t^* (present murders), rather then being for presently blaming for murders. And similarly, 'murder was wrong' would express FOR($\lambda z(\exists t:pai(t<t^*)(z$ is blaming for murder-at-$t)))$. It's easy to see that this kind of complication will wreak havoc on many possible expressivist analyses of normative predicates. For example, suppose that instead of treating 'wrong' as contributing 'blaming for', we treated it as contributing 'avoiding' (which, as noted in section 5.4, is the kind of analysis to explain why 'murdering is wrong' and 'not murdering is wrong' are inconsistent). If t is a time prior to the present, then murders-at-t aren't really the kind of thing that *can* be avoided. On the other hand, it may make perfect sense to disapprove (in the intuitive, non-stipulative sense) of past actions. In that case, this proposal about the past tense fits in perfectly well with the analysis on which 'wrong' contributes disapproval, in this intuitive sense.

So the issues in developing such an account of tense are going to be complicated, and are going to impact significantly on the plausibility of the various analyses that we might propose of normative predicates in the first place. The kind of approach outlined here constitutes a structural improvement on the one in section 12.3, but much more work would need to be done in order to make it rigorous, let alone to sort out its predictions for a wide variety of cases, particularly including the ways in which tense interacts with a wide variety of other constructions.

Modals

The foregoing observations about tense might inspire you to hope that similar moves could lead to a more promising account of 'necessarily' than the obvious one refuted in section 12.3. In principle, this is right. But a great deal of work would have to be done in order to develop the idea and to test its predictions. There are conceptual and empirical reasons why semanticists have not favored treating 'necessarily' as an object-language quantifier, and all of these will present obstacles for any such approach. Nevertheless, some such avenue of research needs to be pursued by anyone serious about defending an expressivist semantics, not only because modal constructions are a ubiquitous and important feature of natural languages, but because the very modal problem which expressivism was originally motivated in order to solve involves a modal claim—about what *would* be wrong if my attitudes were different.

Similarly, the claims of Blackburn and Gibbard to accommodate supervenience require, strictly speaking, a semantics for the modalized sentence used to state the supervenience thesis, before we can even assess them. There are good reasons to interpret Blackburn and Gibbard's discussions of the modal problem as involving the idea that counterfactuals express attitudes toward merely possible objects—such as murder-in-w—and these treatments could be constructed on the basis of an approach to modals modeled on the treatment of tense just considered.[15] The next step would be to evaluate these proposals in order to see whether they stand up to ordinary kinds of semantic data.

Binary quantifiers and adverbs of quantification

In section 12.4, I claimed that the problem with two-place quantifiers like 'most' was 'the clincher'. I really do think that it is the most serious problem we have come across so far, and the prospects are not at all encouraging. Nevertheless, if you really want to defend expressivism, the problem deserves a great deal of your attention. No semantics for English that failed to make correct predictions about these constructions would be within the realm of empirical adequacy.

I don't really see any way of attacking this problem that seems promising, to me. One initial idea worth exploring might be to employ the resources of second-order quantification—paraphrase 'most Fs are

---

[15] Compare especially Blackburn (1973, 1998), and Gibbard (2003).

Gs' by a claim about the relative cardinalities of the intersection of the set of the Fs with the set of the Gs and its complement within the set of the Fs: '$|\{x : Fx\} \cap \{x : Gx\}| {>} |\{x : Fx\} \cap \{x : {\sim}Gx\}|$'. This seems unpromising both because of its lack of continuity with the treatments of the other quantifiers, and because of its resort to object-language commitment to sets in all relevant cases. But beyond this idea, my next best guess is that in order to treat 'most' correctly, we would need a different fix to the new negation problem than the move to biforcated attitude semantics in the first place. And that seems unpromising to me, because biforcated attitude semantics was necessary for *both* ways we explored of assigning truth-conditions to complex descriptive sentences, in Chapters 9 and 10.

Further problems

This is just the beginning of the kinds of problems an expressivist semantics must confront. If you're sympathetic to expressivism, the challenge has just begun. The fortunate thing, is that I think my arguments in earlier chapters set productive constraints on the shape an expressivist semantics must take, which I think make it easier to think about the further problems that come up. I find these constraints compelling, because as I've argued, expressivists cannot otherwise get a constructive semantics or an explanation of inconsistency that appeals only to respectable assumptions, nor can they retain these advantages while allowing that descriptive sentences express beliefs. But even if you got off of the boat earlier in my argument, and think that the constraints on a view like biforcated attitude semantics are only constraints on one way of developing expressivism, you face the same challenges. Expressivism owes us a detailed semantic theory with the same kind of predictive and explanatory power as competing proposals about natural language semantics, before it deserves widespread philosophical respectability as the kind of treatment it makes sense to cut and paste into the solution of our favorite philosophical problems.

References

Adams E. W. (1965). 'A Logic of Conditionals.' *Inquiry* 8: 166–97.

Anscombe, Elizabeth (1957). *Intention*. Oxford: Basil Blackwell.

Avron, Arnon (1991). 'Natural 3-Valued Logics—Characterization and Proof Theory.' *The Journal of Symbolic Logic* 56(1): 276–94.

Ayer, A. J. (1936). *Language, Truth, and Logic*. New York: Dover.

Barker, Stephen (2002). 'Is Value Content a Component of Conventional Implicature?' *Analysis* 60(3): 268–79.

_____ (2004). *Renewing Meaning: A Speech Act Approach*. Oxford: Oxford University Press.

Barwise, Jon, and Robin Cooper (1981). 'Generalized Quantifiers and Natural Language.' *Linguistics and Philosophy* 4: 159–219.

Belnap, Jr, N. D. (1977). 'A Useful Four-Valued Logic.' In J. M. Dunn and G. Epstein (eds.), *Modern Uses of Multiple-Valued Logic*. Dordrecht: Reidel, 8–37.

Björnsson, Gunnar (2001). 'Why Emotivists Love Inconsistency.' *Philosophical Studies* 104(1): 81–108.

Blackburn, Simon (1973). 'Moral Realism.' Reprinted in Blackburn (1993), 111–29.

_____ (1984). *Spreading the Word*. Oxford: Oxford University Press.

_____ (1988). 'Attitudes and Contents.' *Ethics* 98(3): 501–17.

_____ (1993). *Essays in Quasi-Realism*. Oxford: Oxford University Press.

_____ (1998). *Ruling Passions*. Oxford: Oxford University Press.

Boisvert, Daniel (forthcoming). 'Expressive-Assertivism and "The Embedding Problem".' Forthcoming in *Pacific Philosophical Quarterly*.

Brandom, Robert (2001). *Articulating Reasons*. Cambridge, MA: Harvard University Press.

Bratman, Michael (1993). 'Cognitivism about Instrumental Reason.' Reprinted in Bratman, *Faces of Intention*. Cambridge, UK: Cambridge University Press (1999), 250–64.

_____ (forthcoming a). 'Intention, Belief, Theoretical, Practical.' Forthcoming in Jens Timmerman, John Skorupski, and Simon Robertson (eds.), *Spheres of Reason*.

_____ (forthcoming b). 'Intention, Belief, and Instrumental Rationality.' Forthcoming in David Sobel and Steven Wall (eds.), *Reasons for Action*.

Broome, John (forthcoming). 'The Unity of Reasoning?' Forthcoming in Jens Timmerman, John Skorupski, and Simon Robertson (eds.), *Spheres of Reason*.

Chrisman, Matthew (2006). PhD dissertation, 'Ethical and Epistemic Expressions: Cognition, Commitment, and Truth' University of North Carolina at Chapel Hill.

—— (2007). 'From Epistemic Contextualism to Epistemic Expressivism.' In *Philosophical Studies* 135(2): 225–54.

Copp, David (2001). 'Realist-Expressivism: A Neglected Option for Moral Realism.' *Social Philosophy and Policy* 18: 1–43.

Cuneo, Terrence (2006). 'Saying What We Mean: An Argument Against Expressivism.' *Oxford Studies in Metaethics* 1: 35–71.

Davis, Wayne (2003). *Meaning, Expression, and Thought.* Cambridge, UK: Cambridge University Press.

—— (2005). *Nondescriptive Meaning and Reference.* Oxford: Oxford University Press.

Dreier, James (1996). 'Expressivist Embeddings and Minimalist Truth.' *Philosophical Studies* 83(1): 29–51.

—— (2006). 'Negation for Expressivists: A Collection of Problems with a Suggestion for their Solution.' *Oxford Studies in Metaethics*, 1: 217–33.

Edgington, Dorothy (1995). 'On Conditionals.' *Mind* 104: 235–329.

Egan, Andy, John Hawthorne, and Brian Weatherson (2003). 'Epistemic Modals in Context.' In Gerhard Preyer and Georg Peter (eds.), *Contextualism in Philosophy: Knowledge, Meaning, and Truth.* Oxford: Oxford University Press, 131–68.

Eriksson, John (2006). *Moved by Morality: An Essay on the Practicality of Moral Thought and Talk.* PhD dissertation, Uppsala University.

Field, Hartry (2000). 'Apriority as an Evaluative Notion.' In Paul Boghossian and Christopher Peacocke (eds.), *New Essays on the A Priori.* Oxford: Oxford University Press, 117–49.

Finlay, Stephen (2005). 'Value and Implicature.' *Philosophers' Imprint* 5(4), www.philosophersimprint.org/005004/.

Fitting, Melvin (1991). 'Kleene's Logic, Generalized.' *Journal of Logic and Computation* 1: 797–810.

Garcia, Oscar, and Massoud Moussavi (1990). 'A Six-Valued Logic for Representing Incomplete Knowledge.' In G. Epstein (ed.) *Proceedings of the Twentieth International Symposium on Multiple-Valued Logic.* IEEE Computer Society Press, 110–14.

Geach, P. T. (1960). 'Ascriptivism.' *Philosophical Review* 69: 221–5.

—— (1965). 'Assertion.' *Philosophical Review* 74: 449–65.

Gibbard, Allan (1981). 'Two Recent Theories of Conditionals.' In William Harper, Robert Stalnaker, and Glenn Pearce (eds.), *Ifs.* Dordrecht: Reidel.

—— (1990). *Wise Choices, Apt Feelings.* Cambridge, MA: Harvard University Press.

—— (2003). *Thinking How to Live.* Cambridge, MA: Harvard University Press.

Hale, Bob (1993). 'Can There Be a Logic of Attitudes?' In John Haldane and Crispin Wright (eds.), *Reality, Representation, and Projection*. New York: Oxford University Press.

Hare, R. M. (1952). *The Language of Morals*. Oxford: Oxford University Press.

———(1970). 'Meaning and Speech Acts.' *The Philosophical Review* 79(1): 3–24.

Harman, Gilbert (1976). 'Practical Reasoning.' Reprinted in Harman, *Reasoning, Meaning and Mind*. Oxford: Oxford University Press (1999), 46–74.

———(1986). *Change in View*. Cambridge, MA: MIT Press.

Horgan, Terry, and Mark Timmons (2000). 'Nondescriptivist Cognitivism: Framework for a New Metaethic.' *Philosophical Papers* 29: 121–53.

———(2006). 'Cognitivist Expressivism.' In Horgan and Timmons (eds.), *Metaethics after Moore*. Oxford: Oxford University Press.

Horwich, Paul (1993). 'Gibbard's Theory of Norms.' *Philosophy and Public Affairs* 22: 67–78.

Jackson, Frank, and Philip Pettit (1998). 'A Problem for Expressivism.' *Analysis* 58(4): 239–51.

Kaplan, David (1989). 'Demonstratives.' In John Perry, Joseph Almog, and Howard Wettstein (eds.), *Themes from Kaplan*. Oxford: Oxford University Press, 481–564.

King, Jeffrey (2003). 'Tense, Modality, and Semantic Values.' *Philosophical Perspectives* 17 (language and philosophical linguistics): 195–245.

———and Jason Stanley (2005). 'Semantics, Pragmatics, and the Role of Semantic Content.' In Zoltan Szabó (ed.), *Semantics vs. Pragmatics*. Oxford: Oxford University Press, 111–64.

Kölbel, Max (2000). 'Edgington on Compounds of Conditionals.' *Mind* 109(1): 97–108.

———(2002). *Truth Without Objectivity*. New York: Routledge.

Lycan, William (2001). *Real Conditionals*. Oxford: Oxford University Press.

MacFarlane, John (forthcoming). 'Epistemic Modals Are Assessment-Sensitive.' Forthcoming in a volume on epistemic modals edited by Andy Egan and Brian Weatherson.

Marcus, Ruth Barcan (1980). 'Moral Dilemmas and Consistency.' *Journal of Philosophy* 77: 121–36.

Miller, Alexander (2003). *An Introduction to Contemporary Metaethics*. Cambridge: Polity.

Pietroski, Paul (2007). 'Logical Form.' *Stanford Encyclopedia of Philosophy*, http://plato.stanford.edu/entries/logical-form/. First published 19 October 1999; substantive revision 17 January 2007.

Price, Huw (1994). 'Semantic Deflationism and the Frege Point.' In S. L. Tsohatzidis (ed.), *Foundations of Speech Act Theory: Philosophical and Linguistic Perspectives*. London: Routledge.

Rescher, Nicholas (1962). 'Plurality Quantification.' *Journal of Symbolic Logic* 27(4): 373–4.

Ridge, Michael (2006). 'Ecumenical Expressivism: Finessing Frege.' *Ethics* 116(2): 302–36.

Schroeder, Mark (2005a). 'Realism and Reduction: The Quest for Robustness.' *Philosophers' Imprint* 5(1), www.philosophersimprint.org/005001/.

—— (2005b). 'Cudworth and Normative Explanations.' *Journal of Ethics and Social Philosophy* 1(3). www.jesp.org.

—— (2007). *Slaves of the Passions*. Oxford: Oxford University Press.

—— (2008). 'Expression for Expressivists.' *Philosophy and Phenomenological Research* 76(1): 86–116.

—— (forthcoming a). 'How Expressivists Can and Should Solve Their Problem with Negation.' Forthcoming in *Noûs*.

—— (forthcoming b). *Noncognitivism in Ethics*. Under contract with Routledge.

—— (n.d.). 'Finagling Frege.' Unpublished paper.

Schueler, G. F. (1988). 'Modus Ponens and Moral Realism.' *Ethics* 98(3): 492–500.

Searle, John (1962). 'Meaning and Speech Acts.' *Philosophical Review* 71: 423–32.

Setiya, Kieran (2007). 'Cognitivism about Instrumental Reason.' *Ethics* 117(4): 649–73.

Shah, Nishi, and David Velleman (2005). 'Doxastic Deliberation.' *The Philosophical Review* 114(4): 497–534.

Sinnott-Armstrong, Walter (2000). 'Expressivism and Embedding.' *Philosophy and Phenomenological Research* 61(3): 677–93.

Smart, J. J. C. (1984). *Ethics, Persuasion, and Truth*. London: Routledge and Kegan Paul.

Smith, Michael (1987). 'The Humean Theory of Motivation.' *Mind* 96(1): 36–61.

—— (1994). *The Moral Problem*. Oxford: Basil Blackwell.

Soames, Scott (1999). *Understanding Truth*. Oxford: Oxford University Press.

—— (2002). *Beyond Rigidity: The Unfinished Semantic Agenda of Naming and Necessity*. Oxford: Oxford University Press.

Stephenson, Tamina (unpublished). 'Judge Dependence, Epistemic Modals, and Predicates of Personal Taste.' http://semanticsarchive.net/Archive/mU20EM32/Revised-Manuscript-June-2007.pdf. Last accessed 2 December 2007.

Stevenson, C. L. (1937). 'The Emotive Meaning of Ethical Terms.' Reprinted in Stevenson (1963), 10–31.

—— (1944). *Ethics and Language*. Oxford: Oxford University Press.

—— (1963). *Facts and Values*. Westport, CT: Greenwood Press.

Stoljar, Daniel (1993). 'Emotivism and Truth Conditions.' *Philosophical Studies* 70: 81–101.

Unwin, Nicholas (1999). '*Quasi*-Realism, Negation and the Frege-Geach Problem.' *The Philosophical Quarterly* 49(196): 337–52.

—— (2001). 'Norms and Negation: A Problem for Gibbard's Logic.' *The Philosophical Quarterly* 51(202): 60–75.

van Fraassen, Bas (1973). 'Values and the Heart's Command.' *Journal of Philosophy* 70: 5–19.

van Roojen, Mark (1996). 'Expressivism and Irrationality.' *The Philosophical Review* 105(3): 311–35.

Velleman, David (1989). *Practical Reflection*. Princeton: Princeton University Press.

von Fintel, Kai, and Anthony Gillies (forthcoming a). 'An Opinionated Guide to Epistemic Modality.' Forthcoming in *Oxford Studies in Epistemology*, volume 2.

—— (forthcoming b). 'CIA Leaks.' Forthcoming in *Philosophical Review*.

Wallace, R. Jay (2001). 'Normativity, Commitment, and Instrumental Reason.' *Philosophers' Imprint* 1, no. 3.

Wiggins, David (1980). '"Most" and "All": Some Comments on a Familiar Programme and on the Logical Form of Quantified Sentences.' In M. Platts (ed.), *Reference, Truth, and Reality*. London: Routledge and Kegan Paul.

Williamson, Timothy (2000). *Knowledge and its Limits*. Oxford: Oxford University Press.

—— (2006). 'Must Do Better.' In Patrick Greenough and Michael Lynch (eds.), *Truth and Realism*. Oxford: Oxford University Press, 177–87.

Zangwill, Nick (1992). 'Moral Modus Ponens.' *Ratio* (new series) 5(2): 177–93.

Index